T0292925

Get the eBook FREE!

(PDF, ePub, Kindle, and liveBook all included)

We believe that once you buy a book from us, you should be able to read it in any format we have available. To get electronic versions of this book at no additional cost to you, purchase and then register this book at the Manning website.

Go to https://www.manning.com/freebook and follow the instructions to complete your pBook registration.

That's it!
Thanks from Manning!

Software Testing with Generative AI

MARK WINTERINGHAM

FOREWORD BY NICOLA MARTIN

MANNING
SHELTER ISLAND

For online information and ordering of this and other Manning books, please visit www.manning.com. The publisher offers discounts on this book when ordered in quantity.

For more information, please contact

> Special Sales Department
> Manning Publications Co.
> 20 Baldwin Road
> PO Box 761
> Shelter Island, NY 11964
> Email: orders@manning.com

 Manning Publications Co.
20 Baldwin Road
PO Box 761
Shelter Island, NY 11964

Development editor:	Becky Whitney
Technical editor:	Robert Walsh
Review editor:	Kishor Rit
Production editor:	Kathy Rossland
Copy editor:	Lana Todorovic-Arndt
Proofreader:	Olga Milanko
Typesetter:	Tamara Švelić Sabljić
Cover designer:	Marija Tudor

ISBN 9781633437364
Printed in the United States of America

In memory of Sam Moore

brief contents

contents

v

      generation   218

      11.1   Extending prompts with RAG   219

      11.2   Building a RAG setup   221
             Building our RAG framework   221 ▪ *Testing our RAG*
             framework   230

      11.3   Enhancing data storage for RAG   233
             Working with Vector databases   233 ▪ *Setting up a*
             vector-database-backed RAG   234 ▪ *Testing a Vector-*
             database-backed RAG framework   237 ▪ *Going forward*
             with RAG frameworks   240

12   *Fine-tuning LLMs with business domain knowledge   242*

      12.1   Exploring the fine-tuning process   243
             A map of the fine-tuning process   243 ▪ *Goal setting   243*

      12.2   Executing a fine-tuning session   245
             Preparing data for training   245 ▪ *Preprocessing and*
             setup   249 ▪ *Working with fine-tuning tools   255*
             Setting off a fine-tuning run   255 ▪ *Testing the results of a*
             fine-tune   257 ▪ *Lessons learned with fine-tuning   260*

      appendix A   Setting up and using ChatGPT   262

      appendix B   Setting up and using GitHub Copilot   266

      appendix C   Exploratory testing notes   272

                   index   275

foreword

The integration of generative AI in software testing is not just a leap forward, but a transformative journey that demands both enthusiasm and critical thinking. In 2022, the world as we know it changed forever with the launch of OpenAI's AI chatbot, ChatGPT. Soon after, Google and Microsoft introduced their own LLM tools, followed by many other companies. This brought generative AI into the public consciousness.

The shock that the growth of these tools has sent through the software engineering community has given a jolt to the heart of the tech industry and set the task of quick take-up of tools and skills. This development has been thrilling at best and challenging at worst for software engineering teams worldwide. Roles tasked with testing often feel the seismic shifts of changes in tech, and this time is no different as engineering teams attempt to juggle advanced automation adoption with the additional herculean task of integrating LLMs.

From a testing perspective, this requires that we stay informed and ready in terms of skills. Automation has now become synonymous with testing platforms using LLMs. Following a holistic approach that is human-centered and brings different approaches to testing platforms is still important, and *Software Testing with Generative AI* encourages this. It reminds us that while LLMs offer powerful support, human judgment and understanding remain at the core of effective testing.

Today, there are numerous courses that cover AI testing, but for someone trying to decide which course to take and how to implement what they have learned, this can be overwhelming. The beauty of Mark's book is that, while it takes big concepts around LLMs and explains them, it also includes worked test examples the user can put into action straightaway. It is also not just about learning every tool, but giving thought pieces around why we use them and what to consider in terms of strategy and planning for products we are trying to build and test.

This book is a detailed guide to integrating generative AI into the testing process thoughtfully and effectively. It offers practical insights and emphasizes the need for balance and critical thinking when adopting AI tools, particularly in the context of automation.

In essence, *Software Testing with Generative AI* is a must-read for anyone who wants to understand AI-assisted testing from a technical perspective. It equips readers with the reference knowledge and examples needed to approach their projects.

I am excited to see how this book will help engineers with approaches and best practices. I highly recommend it to anyone looking to stay ahead of the curve.

—NICOLA MARTIN
FOUNDER, NICOLA MARTIN COACHING & CONSULTANCY, AND CHAIR, BCS SIGiST

preface

My journey into the world of AI began back in 2017 in a hotel bar. Sitting with a friend, I expressed an interest in what the future might hold for those in quality and testing, in a world where AI was becoming increasingly prevalent. My friend shared some blog posts and beers with me, and despite the hangover the next day, I was hooked. Learning about the potential effects that AI could have on all of us, I sought to absorb as much as I could to understand better both how to test AI and use it to elevate testing. The challenge, or at least what I believed then, was that the barrier to understanding and using AI was too high for someone like me. I felt I could scratch the surface, but without the luxury of time and resources, I couldn't drill deeper.

This, however, is no longer the case. The explosion of large language models (LLMs) such as ChatGPT, Gemini, and Llama has shifted the balance of those who can use AI and benefit from it. LLMs have become widespread in software development with the introduction of code assistants, chatbots, and more. I'm writing this preface with the support of an AI assistant. This, of course, opens a range of questions. How will this affect me and my role, and what skills do I need to get the most from AI? So, when the opportunity to write this book and further explore the world of AI came about, I jumped at it.

During this book's development, I've had the opportunity not only to learn new technologies but also to appreciate that the lessons from the past can inform our future AI use. LLMs are, after all, software. Therefore, lessons we've learned from using tools in the past can be applied to AI. Throughout this book, we'll learn not only how to use LLMs to enhance and extend our testing abilities, but also to better define our relationship with them. This is necessary if we want to use AI in a way valuable to us and our teams.

Therefore, this book is for anyone interested in learning how to use AI to improve their testing craft. Whether you are a quality engineer, analyst, or software developer, in these chapters you'll explore the practical application of LLMs. You'll learn how to improve your testing abilities, enhance quality, and develop a productive mindset toward the use of LLMs. This book is by no means the final word on how AI will be used in the future, but I hope that it is a solid foundation to build on so that we can all successfully use LLMs to help us become more productive and valuable members of our teams.

I hope your journey through AI is as enjoyable as mine has been so far.

acknowledgments

When writing a book, an author can be excused for not fully appreciating the time it can take one away from others. So, I should start with the biggest and most important thanks to Steph, for her patience and support when I decided to embark on this journey for the second time. Thank you for encouraging me to continue writing, giving me the time and space to create this book, and for listening to my endless waffle about the potential of AI.

A special thank you to Nicola Martin for her kind words in the book's foreword. It's still a rare thing to find someone else who is thinking about AI, testing, and tooling the same way I do, and I'm glad our paths finally crossed.

This book stems from many different conversations about AI. I'm indebted to those who were willing to speak to me as I formulated my ideas. Thank you, Anand Bagmar, Nikolay Advoldokin, Bob Marshall, Alden Peterson, and Vesna Leonard for your time and insights. A special thanks goes to Richard Bradshaw who through our work on automation in testing helped guide me toward the principles this book has laid out in how we incorporate AI and tooling in general into testing.

I'm also grateful to Bruno Lopes at Virtuoso, Adam Carmi at Applitools, James Walker at Curiosity, and Tobias Müller and Daniela Bohli at Testreport.io, all of who gave up time from their busy schedules to talk with me and share some of their work. I wish I had more time and pages to cover the work that you are all doing to push testing tooling further.

Also, a huge thank you to Carlos Kidman who with one question turned part 3 of the book on its head. Your guidance was vital to forming the approach of educating others on fine-tuning.

Finally, thanks to everyone at Manning for bringing this book into the world. Special thanks to Brian Sawyer for kick-starting the idea for this book and changing my trajectory in testing, Becky Whitney for support and direction throughout the writing process, and Robert Walsh for technical support as each chapter was produced. Robert, the owner of Excalibur Solutions, Inc., and the founder of the Excalibur Solutions STEM Academy, is a former mathematics teacher who has also worked as a hardware technician, an IT director, a trainer, a programmer, a software tester, a technical writer, and a business owner. Additionally, he has presented his work at numerous software development and testing conferences and has had multiple articles published on these subjects.

I'm also grateful for all the feedback from all the book reviewers: Abhay Dutt Paroha, Anandaganesh Balakrishnan, Andres Sacco, Andy Wiesendanger, Ankit Virmani, Anto Aravinth, Beth Marshall, Brian Beagle, Daniel Knott, Esref Durna, Greg Grimes, Greg MacLean, Gregorio Piccoli, Henrik Gering, Javid Asgarov, John Donoghue, Julien Pohie, Karol Skorek, Laurence Giglio, Marco Massenzio, Marlin King, Marvin Schwarze, Mikael Byström, Mirsad Vojnikovic, Piotr Wicherski, Riccardo Marotti, Ron Hübler, Samuel Lawrence, Simeon Leyzerzon, Simon Verhoeven, Sumit Bhattacharyya, Theo Despoudis, and Zac Corbett. Your feedback was instrumental in molding this book into what it is now.

about this book

Software Testing with Generative AI was written to help you exploit LLMs to elevate and enhance your testing. This is done by focusing on three key principles of successful use of LLMs in testing: mindset, technique, and context. We'll explore each in depth, starting with mindset, before learning and employing prompt engineering techniques, and finishing with an exploration of why context matters with LLMs and how to embed it into our interactions with them.

Who should read this book

We are all responsible for quality and testing as part of a team, and this book follows that mindset closely. Whether you are a developer or an automator focusing on test automation, a quality engineer focusing on continuous testing, or a more traditional tester, this book explores a range of testing activities and how LLMs can help support them. However, to get the most of this book, some necessary skills are required.

If you are looking to learn how LLMs can support test automation, then it is assumed you are familiar with it. This means you should have at least basic experience with TDD and intermediate experience with unit, integration, and end-to-end test automation, as well as using integrated development environments. The code examples in this book are written in Java, so you will need to be confident in reading and writing Java. (We'll talk more about code choice and examples shortly.)

Beyond test automation, I have assumed that readers have basic experience in exploratory testing and intermediate knowledge of data management and related data structures such as SQL, JSON, and XML. Finally, every effort has been made to find tools that make the more advanced topics in part 3 of this book accessible to anyone, regardless of technical ability. However, to use these tools, a basic understanding of YAML formatting and command line tools is necessary.

How this book is organized: A road map

This book is split into three distinct parts to cover what I believe are the three core attributes needed for success with LLMs: mindset, technique, and context. We'll explore this model of thinking more in chapter 1, but here is a summary of each part and their chapters to give you a sense of what we'll cover.

Part 1: Mindset—Establishing a positive relationship with LLMs

- *Chapter 1*—Establishes how LLMs can be of use in testing and what we need to obtain value from them.
- *Chapter 2*—Dives into the inner workings of LLMs and introduces the concept of prompt engineering, which will become an essential tool in part 2.
- *Chapter 3*—Concluding the mindset portion of the book, this chapter explores the relationship between AI, automation, and testing, arguing why a clear understanding of the capabilities of each is essential for successful LLM use.

Part 2: Technique—Task identification and prompt engineering in testing

- *Chapter 4*—This chapter demonstrates how activities such as test-driven design when combined with LLM-backed Copilot tools can help improve code quality and speed up work.
- *Chapter 5*—This chapter looks into how LLMs act as a tool to enhance and extend our test-planning capabilities, and the risks and traps to avoid over-trusting LLMs in this process.
- *Chapter 6*—Here we delve into different recipes and approaches for creating test data with LLMs, whether it's for test automation purposes or general testing use.
- *Chapter 7*—Looking at more high-level test automation activities such as end-to-end automation, this chapter explains how LLMs are best used for solving specific tasks in automation, rather than attempting to rely on LLMs for the complete automation process.
- *Chapter 8*—Next, we focus on how we can apply LLMs to exploratory testing activities by identifying subtasks that LLMs can help with inside a wider exploratory testing session.
- *Chapter 9*—Finally, we conclude this part by exploring how we can take our prompting techniques to the next level by utilizing LLM functions to create testing assistants.

Part 3: Context—Customizing LLMs for testing contexts

- *Chapter 10*—We open the final part of the book by exploring why context is key to maximizing the value of an LLM's response, as well as getting acquainted with more advanced techniques that can help with adding context.
- *Chapter 11*—This chapter helps us learn how retrieval-augmented generation (RAG) works and its value by building our own RAG frameworks.

- *Chapter 12*—We finish the book by examining the process of fine-tuning models and how it can help us embed context into the models we use to support our testing.

Depending on your background and interest, you might want to pick and choose specific chapters in parts 2 and 3. Perhaps you are a developer looking to learn more about how LLMs can help with production code and test automation. Or you are in a role that relies on more human-based testing activities, and you want to learn more about how LLMs can help with planning and manual testing activities. Regardless of your goals, it is recommended you read part 1 in full to appreciate the mindset that underpins parts 2 and 3. The activities throughout the book are devised to further help your learning and are optional but encouraged.

About the code

Throughout this book, we will explore examples of both LLM prompts (instructions we send to an LLM) and code that we can implement. Although every effort has been made to select tools that are free to use, tools such as GitHub Copilot (after a 30-day trial) and the Runpod cloud platform will incur a fee. There are also specific details to keep in mind for both types of examples.

PROMPTS

All example prompts sent to an LLM and responses returned are formatted in a proportional font like this to separate it from ordinary text. Each example of a prompt has been crafted to demonstrate different techniques and tactics; however, as LLMs are indeterministic systems, **the contents of the responses returned to you will differ** from the ones mentioned. Therefore, please keep in mind that your experience will vary from those shared within these pages depending on which type of LLM you use and its current version.

CODE

This book contains many examples of source code, formatted in a `fixed-width font` `like this` to separate it from ordinary text. Sometimes, code is also **in bold** to highlight code that has changed from previous steps in the chapter, such as when a new feature adds new code to an existing line of code.

In many cases, the original source code has been reformatted; we've added line breaks and reworked indentation to accommodate the available page space in the book. In rare cases, even this was not enough, and listings include line-continuation markers (➥). Additionally, comments in the source code have often been removed from the listings when the code is described in the text. Code annotations accompany many of the listings, highlighting important concepts.

You can get executable snippets of code from the liveBook (online) version of this book at https://livebook.manning.com/book/software-testing-with-generative -ai. All supporting code and prompt examples can also be referenced, downloaded and copied from the supporting repository at https://github.com/mwinteringham/ ai-assisted-testing/. The complete code for the examples in the book is also available for download from the Manning website at https://www.manning.com/books/ software-testing-with-generative-ai.

liveBook discussion forum

Purchase of *Software Testing with Generative AI* includes free access to liveBook, Manning's online reading platform. Using liveBook's exclusive discussion features, you can attach comments to the book globally or to specific sections or paragraphs. It's a snap to make notes for yourself, ask and answer technical questions, and receive help from the author and other users. To access the forum, go to https://livebook.manning .com/book/software-testing-with-generative-ai/discussion. You can also learn more about Manning's forums and the rules of conduct at https://livebook.manning.com/ discussion.

Manning's commitment to our readers is to provide a venue where a meaningful dialogue between individual readers and between readers and the author can take place. It is not a commitment to any specific amount of participation on the part of the author, whose contribution to the forum remains voluntary (and unpaid). We suggest you try asking the author some challenging questions lest his interest stray! The forum and the archives of previous discussions will be accessible from the publisher's website as long as the book is in print.

about the author

MARK WINTERINGHAM is a quality engineer, course director, and the author of *Testing Web APIs*, with over 10 years of experience in providing testing expertise on award-winning projects across a wide range of technology sectors. He is an advocate for modern risk-based testing practices, holistic-based automation strategies, behavior-driven development, and exploratory-testing techniques. You can find him on Twitter @2bittester or at mwtestconsultancy.co.uk.

about the cover illustration

The figure on the cover of *Software Testing with Generative AI* is "Monténégrin," or "Man from Montenegro," taken from a book *L'Illyrie et la Dalmatie* by Balthazar Hacquet, published in 1815. Each illustration is finely drawn and colored by hand. In those days, it was easy to identify where people lived and what their trade or station in life was just by their dress. Manning celebrates the inventiveness and initiative of the computer business with book covers based on the rich diversity of regional culture centuries ago, brought back to life by pictures from collections such as this one.

## Part 1

Mindset: Establishing a positive relationship with LLMs

Before we start using large language models (LLMs) to assist our testing, we need to understand how LLMs work, what good testing looks like, and most crucially, how we combine the two to create value. As Marshall McLuhan once stated, "We shape our tools, and thereafter our tools shape us." This aphorism is also true when working with LLMs. Their behavior can give us the impression that they think and behave like humans, and therefore, we can rely on them to replace our work. However, this kind of thinking can lead us down a dangerous path, and not only slow down our work, but also bias us toward incorrect assumptions about the quality of both our work and our products.

This is why having a balanced mindset toward how LLMs work and how to select specific tasks within the context of testing is vital. We want to use the power of LLMs but also maintain a healthy skepticism about what they return and the influence they have on us during our work. With the correct mindset, the rest will fall into place much easier. So, let's learn what this mindset looks like.

1

Enhancing testing with large language models

This chapter covers

- How large language models can help us with testing
- How to develop a mindset toward working with large language models

In this book, we will be using large language models (LLMs) to enhance and accelerate our testing activities—and what is a better way to introduce ourselves to this technology than to ask an LLM to create an introduction for this book:

 Hello! I am ChatGPT, a language model designed by OpenAI to assist with a wide range of tasks and answer various questions.

Regarding the book, "How AI can be used to help support various software testing activities," I would recommend "AI-Driven Testing: Adding Intelligence to Your Software Testing Practice" by Julian Harty and Mahesh Sharma.

This book explores the application of artificial intelligence (AI) techniques to software testing and how it can help improve the effectiveness and efficiency of testing processes. The authors cover various topics related to AI-driven testing, including machine learning, natural language processing, and computer vision, among others.

Additionally, the book includes case studies, practical examples, and best practices for implementing AI-driven testing in different contexts. It is a valuable resource for software testers, developers, and anyone interested in leveraging AI to improve the quality of their software products.

This artificially generated response, which reads as if it were written by a human, was created by sending a one-sentence instruction, known as a *prompt,* to ChatGPT:

 ChatGPT, please introduce yourself and a book about how AI can be used to help support various software testing activities.

Defining what LLMs do and determining the potential they offer are both easy and difficult. To gain the most benefit from these tools, it is necessary to find a balance between the two. At first glance, LLMs work by simply taking instructions from a user and responding with an answer using natural language. But this simple explanation doesn't do justice to the potential an LLM can offer us as we test, nor does it explain the challenges that must be overcome to maximize their advantages. So, before we begin our journey to the world of LLMs and testing, let's find out how LLMs can help us and what we need to be aware of to successfully use them.

1.1   *Recognizing the effect of AI tools on testing and development*

In the past, an individual who wanted to take advantage of AI was required to have the skills to develop, train, and deploy an AI model or have access to a team of experts to complete these tasks, all of which would make use of AI in everyday activities an expensive and exclusive endeavor. With the recent advances in AI and publicly available LLMs such as ChatGPT and Gemini, open source generative models, and fine-tuning and retrieval methods for generative AI, we're now beginning to benefit from what some refer to as AI democratization.

The barrier to integrating AI into our everyday work has dropped dramatically. Social media managers can now use LLMs to generate catchy and engaging copy, analysts can summarize unstructured data into clear and concise reports, and customer support agents can rapidly generate bespoke responses to customers with a few simple prompts. The use of LLM is not limited to data scientists and AI scholars anymore, and it is also advantageous for those of us who work in testing and software development.

Good testing helps challenge assumptions and educate our teams on how our products truly behave in given situations. The more we test, the more we learn. But, as most professional testers will verify, there is never enough time to test everything we want. So, to be able to test more efficiently, we look for tools and techniques from automation to shift-left testing. LLMs offer another potential avenue to help us enhance the quality and scope of our testing so that we can discover and share more, which in turn can help our teams improve quality further.

What makes LLMs so useful is that they summarize, transform, generate, and translate information in a way that is easy for humans to understand and that professionals responsible for testing can use for their testing needs—all of which are available through simple chat interfaces or APIs. LLMs can assist us in rapidly creating test automation or provide support as we carry out testing ourselves. And if we develop the right skills to identify when LLMs can help and use them sensibly, we begin to test faster, further, and more effectively. To help illustrate this concept and what we'll be learning in this book, let's take a look at some brief examples.

1.1.1 Data generation

Creating and managing test data can be one of the most complex aspects of testing. Creating realistic, useful, and anonymized data can make or break the success of testing, and doing it effectively can be a drain on resources. LLMs offer the ability to generate and transform data rapidly, speeding up the test data management process. By taking existing data and converting it to new formats or using it to generate new synthetic data, we can utilize LLMs to assist us with our test data requirements and get more time to drive testing forward.

1.1.2 Automated test building

Similarly, LLMs' abilities to generate and transform can be used during the process of creating and maintaining automation. Although I would not advise having LLMs solely create automated tests for us, they can be used in targeted ways to help us create page objects, boilerplate classes, helper methods, and frameworks rapidly. By combining the knowledge of our products and our test design skills, we can identify the parts of the automation process that are algorithmic and structured in nature and use LLMs to speed up those segments of the automation process.

1.1.3 Test design

Perhaps a less commonly discussed topic is how LLMs can help us in the process of identifying and designing tests. Similar to automated testing, the value of LLMs lies not in completely replacing our test design abilities but rather in augmenting them. We can use LLMs to overcome biases and blind spots to expand and suggest ideas based on current test design ideas we might have. We can also summarize and describe complex ideas in ways that make them more digestible for us to springboard test ideas from.

We will explore such examples in this book and more to help us better appreciate when and where LLMs can be used and how to use them in a way that accelerates our testing. We'll explore how to build prompts to support us in building quality production and automation code, rapidly creating test data, and enhancing our test design for both scripted and exploratory testing. We'll also explore how we can fine-tune our own LLMs that will work as assistants to us in our testing, digesting domain knowledge and using it to help guide us toward building better-quality products.

1.2   *Delivering value with LLMs*

Testing is a collaborative process, and all team members are responsible for testing. How we contribute to the testing process differs based on our role and experience, but we all participate. Thus, throughout this book, we'll approach the use of LLMs with a critical mindset, discovering various ways in which we can use LLMs to help enhance the multiple types of testing we do. The intention is to give you the skills to identify and utilize LLMs to enhance and accelerate your testing, whether you are in a professional testing role or a developer who contributes to the testing process, all of which we can do by establishing some rules around the relationship between ourselves and the LLMs we want to use.

1.2.1   *A model for delivering value*

To get the most out of LLMs, we need to focus on three core principles this book has been structured around: the mindset, technique, and context (figure 1.1).

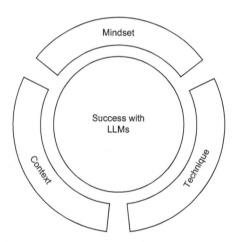

Figure 1.1   A model outlining the three tenets of success with generative AI

We'll explore these three core principles in depth in different parts of this book, starting with mindset. But to better appreciate why they are needed, let's discuss each of them briefly to understand what they mean and why they are required.

Mindset

This is perhaps the most essential of the three principles, as having the correct mindset toward how we utilize LLMs can dramatically increase or decrease their value. Having the correct mindset means having a clear sense of the purpose and value of testing, the capabilities of LLMs, and how to build a relationship between both in which LLMs are used in focused, targeted ways.

TECHNIQUE

While understanding where to use LLMs is vital, we also need the ability to work with them in a way that maximizes their value. In the context of LLMs, this means learning how to create and curate instructions that clearly communicate what we want an LLM to do, as well as ensuring that it responds in a way that is useful and avoids risks of misinformation. The ecosystem and abilities around LLMs have grown extensively, meaning learning about other techniques, such as integrating with API platforms for LLMs, and AI agents can help us identify and create more advanced opportunities with LLMs.

CONTEXT

As we progress, you'll notice how applicable the rule of garbage in, garbage out is to LLMs. If we prompt an LLM with a generalized, context-free request, we get a shallow, contextless response. Although technique can help us somewhat to maximize an LLM's response, the final piece of the puzzle is being able to provide an LLM with enough context so that it can respond in a way relevant to our needs. As you'll learn, there are different ways to approach this, such as retrieval-augmented generation (RAG) and fine-tuning, each having its challenges to consider and rewards to take advantage of.

As mentioned, this book has been structured in such a way that the three principles are explored in depth to help us get the most from LLMs. So, let's drill further into the concept of mindset and establish what a good mindset means before returning to technique and context later.

1.2.2 *Using both human and AI abilities*

Throughout this book, you'll learn not just how to use LLMs but also how to establish a working practice in which our testing benefits from our abilities, as well as from LLMs. The value of any tool, whether it's AI-based or not, comes not from its intrinsic features but rather from the relationship between the user and the tool. We can think of that relationship as an area of the effect model, as shown in figure 1.2.

This diagram demonstrates that to increase our influence, a healthy relationship with tools that focus on expanding and enhancing our core abilities is required. Without this balance, we become too dependent on tools or ourselves. We can certainly rely on our abilities, but our area of effect will be smaller, bound by constraints such as time, attention, and biases. Basically, without tools, we can do only so much. But also we cannot defer all the work to tooling. Without an individual at the core, tools lack direction. Yes, tools can be autonomous and set off to run by themselves, but if they aren't delivering feedback to a human, then no value is being extracted from them. The area of effect is missing its center. That's why this book aims to teach you about how to strike a balance in the use of LLMs in testing, focusing as much on our abilities to identify opportunities for LLM use as the skills to get the most value of them.

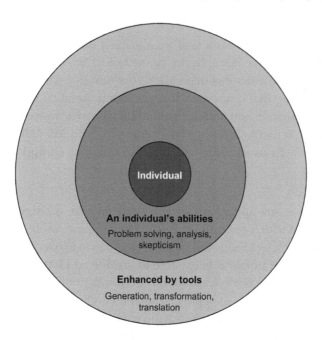

Figure 1.2   An outline of how tools enhance and extend the reach of testing

To help us better understand this relationship, let's consider an example in which we want to create tests for a file upload feature. First, we receive a user story like the following:

- As a paralegal, in order to store and share legal documents, I want to be able to securely upload documents.
- Acceptance criteria:
  - Upload should support the following common file formats: PDF, DOCX, TXT
  - The maximum file size should be 20MB
  - When a document is uploaded it should give a progress update to the user
  - Once uploaded, the document must initially be only accessible to the person who has uploaded it
  - A report of the upload and whether it was successful or not will be stored in the auditing feature

From this, we decide to simply rely on an LLM to generate the work for us—for example, sending a prompt like this:

 Create tests for a file upload feature

Sending this prompt to an LLM such as ChatGPT might return something like

1 Test for File Upload Functionality:

Test Case 1.1: Upload a Valid File

Input: Choose a file with a valid format (e.g., .jpg, .pdf).

Expected Outcome: The file is successfully uploaded, and a confirmation message is displayed.

Test Case 1.2: Attempt to Upload an Invalid File

Input: Choose a file with an invalid format (e.g., .exe, .html).

Expected Outcome: An error message is displayed, indicating that the file format is not supported.

2 Test for File Size Limit:

Test Case 2.1: Upload a File Below the Size Limit

Input: Choose a file smaller than the maximum allowed size.

Expected Outcome: The file is successfully uploaded, and a confirmation message is displayed.

Test Case 2.2: Attempt to Upload a File Exceeding the Size Limit

Input: Choose a file larger than the maximum allowed size.

Expected Outcome: An error message is displayed, indicating that the file exceeds the maximum size limit.

3 Test for File Overwrite Protection:

Test Case 3.1: Upload a File with the Same Name as an Existing File

Input: Upload a file with a name that matches an existing file in the system.

Expected Outcome: An error message is displayed, indicating that a file with the same name already exists.

4 Security Tests:

Test Case 4.1: Attempt to Upload a Malicious File (e.g., virus)

Input: Upload a known malicious file.

Expected Outcome: The system should detect the malicious file and prevent its upload, displaying a security warning.

5 UI and User Experience Tests:

Test Case 5.1: Check for a User-Friendly Interface

Input: Use the file upload feature and evaluate the user interface for clarity and ease of use.

Expected Outcome: The interface should be intuitive, with clear instructions and feedback for users.

Test Case 5.2: Check for Proper Error Messages

Input: Attempt various erroneous actions during the file upload process.

Expected Outcome: Error messages should be descriptive, helping users understand and resolve issues.

6   Integration Tests:

Test Case 6.1: Check File Upload with Other Features

Input: Test file uploads in conjunction with other features that depend on uploaded files (e.g., image processing, document storage).

Expected Outcome: Ensure the uploaded files are correctly processed and integrated with other system components.

7   Performance Tests:

Test Case 7.1: Upload a Large Number of Files Concurrently

Input: Simulate multiple users uploading a large number of files simultaneously.

Expected Outcome: The system should handle concurrent uploads without significant performance degradation or crashes.

8   Stress Tests:

Test Case 8.1: Upload Files Continuously for an Extended Period

Input: Continuously upload files for an extended period to assess system stability.

Expected Outcome: The system should not experience memory leaks, crashes, or performance degradation during this stress test.

At first glance, the response seems impressive. The LLM has provided us with a list of different tests to consider, which gives us the impression that we have everything we need to begin testing. However, if we start to consider the response more carefully, we can notice some problems:

- Test case 1.1 suggests testing with valid formats but offers examples of formats our user story doesn't support.
- The suggestions from number 4 onward are shallow. For example, the Security test offers a test to insert a malicious file but nothing else. Surely, there would be other security problems to consider.
- The expected outcomes are also very broad for each test case. For example, what does this response mean?

  Error messages should be descriptive, helping users understand and resolve issues

LLMs are designed to give a response regardless of what they've been asked to do, and although that might sound useful, it becomes problematic when the instructions it has been given are vague. The example we've looked at isn't being used to criticize the capabilities of LLMs but rather to help us appreciate that an LLM's response will be as detailed or as generic as the prompt it has been given. This means the responses we've received from the LLM are broad and vague because our prompt is vague. By not giving much thought to what we want to ask an LLM to do, the absence of any context or detail in the prompt means what has been returned is pretty useless—a classic example of garbage in, garbage out.

This is what the area of the effect diagram from earlier attempts to define. To get value from LLMs, we need to design prompts that are clear, contextual, and specific so that we can extract more value from an LLM. Instead of deferring all responsibility to a tool to create the response we desire, we instead appreciate that our understanding of a context and the ability to distill that understanding into clear instructions are required to create a prompt that will maximize the response from an LLM, leading to better-written prompts, such as

 Act as a professional software tester and suggest test ideas for the feature delimited by three hashes. All test ideas should be focused on discovering risks that impact the quality characteristics: Functionality, Data Integrity and Security

###

- As a paralegal, in order to store and share legal documents, I want to be able to securely upload documents.
- Acceptance criteria:

    Upload should support the following common file formats: PDF, DOCX, TXT

    - The maximum file size should be 20MB
    - When a document is uploaded it should give a progress update to the user
    - Once uploaded, the document must initially be only accessible to the person who has uploaded it
    - A report of the upload and whether it was successful or not will be stored in the auditing feature

###

which, when sent to an LLM, returns a response like this:

 Functionality:
- Format Compatibility Testing:
    - Verify that the upload feature supports the following file formats: PDF, DOCX, and TXT.
    - Attempt to upload files in various formats and ensure that the system handles them correctly.
- File Size Limitation Testing:
    - Test whether the system enforces a maximum file size limit of 20MB during the upload process.
    - Attempt to upload files larger and smaller than 20MB to validate the system's handling of these cases.

- Progress Update Testing:
  - Check that users receive real-time progress updates while a document is being uploaded.
  - Verify that these updates are clear and provide meaningful information to the user.

Data Integrity:

- Document Content Verification:
  - Upload files with known content and compare the content of the uploaded document with the original.
  - Ensure that the content remains intact and no data corruption occurs during the upload process.
- Document Privacy:
  - Test that uploaded documents are initially only accessible to the person who uploaded them.
  - Attempt to access the uploaded documents using another user's account to ensure that access control is enforced.
- Data Auditing Verification:
  - Confirm that the system accurately records all uploads in the auditing feature.
  - Verify that the audit logs include information such as the timestamp, uploader, document name, and whether the upload was successful.

Security:

- File Type Security Testing:
  - Attempt to upload files with malicious content, such as scripts or malware, and ensure that the system detects and rejects them.
- Access Control Testing:
  - Validate that the system properly enforces access control by ensuring that other users cannot access the documents uploaded by someone else.
- Secure Data Transmission:
  - Ensure that the document upload process uses secure communication protocols (e.g., HTTPS) to protect data during transmission.
- User Authentication and Authorization:
  - Verify that the system correctly authenticates and authorizes users before allowing them to upload or access documents.
- Secure Data Storage:
  - Assess how the system stores uploaded documents to ensure that they are encrypted or adequately protected against unauthorized access or data breaches.

- Session Management:
  - Test how the system manages user sessions, ensuring that sessions are terminated after a period of inactivity to prevent unauthorized access.

By creating a more focused and contextual prompt, we have created a response that offers a richer range of suggestions for our testing. This would not be achieved by an LLM alone but rather through the symbiosis of our skills to learn and frame our context into instructions that LLMs can take and rapidly expand on.

> **Activity 1.1**
>
> Try out the sample prompts we've explored in this chapter and see what responses you receive. To familiarize yourself with an LLM, read appendix A, which shares how to set up and send a prompt to ChatGPT.

1.2.3 *Being skeptical of LLMs*

Although a lot can be said about the potential of LLMs, we should be wary of taking their abilities for granted. For example, consider our introduction to this book from ChatGPT. It confidently recommended to us that we should read the book *AI-Driven Testing: Adding Intelligence to Your Software Testing Practice*. The problem is that this book doesn't exist and was never written by Julian Harty and Mahesh Sharma. The LLM simply made up this title. (We'll explore more about why this happens in chapter 2.)

LLMs offer much potential, but they are not a solution for every problem, nor are they a single oracle of truth. We will explore further in Chapter 2 how LLMs use probability to determine responses and how an LLM comes to a solution is not the same way humans do, which highlights the second aspect of our area of effect model. We must use our skepticism to determine what is and isn't of value from an LLM response.

To blindly accept what an LLM output is, at best, putting us at risk of slowing our work down rather than accelerating it—and at worst, influencing us to carry out testing that can have a detrimental effect on the quality of our products. We must remind ourselves that we—not LLMs—are the ones who are leading the problem-solving activity. This can be difficult at times when working with tools that communicate in a way that feels so human, but to do so exposes us to the aforementioned risks. That's why, in our area of effect model, we use our abilities to pick the elements from the LLM response that serve us well and reject and reevaluate how we instruct an LLM when it responds in a way that is not satisfactory.

As we progress through the book and learn more about LLMs and how they can contribute to testing, we will keep our area of effect model in mind so that you, the reader, can develop the ability to use LLMs in testing in a way that is sober, considered, and valuable to you and your team.

Summary

- Large language models (LLMs) work by taking a prompt we wrote and returning a response.
- The popularity of LLMs stems from the ease with which they offer access to powerful AI algorithms.
- LLMs have helped many people in different roles and can also help us in testing.
- We can use LLMs for a wide range of testing activities, from test design to automation.
- We want to avoid overusing LLMs and must always be critical of how they work.
- Success with LLMs comes from us appreciating the skills and abilities we bring to the process of using them.
- If our prompts to LLMs are shallow and generic, their response will be the same.
- Instead, we should use our skills to understand and frame a problem and use that to prompt LLMs to respond in the most valuable way possible.
- We must also be skeptical of the responses we get from LLMs to ensure the responses we get from them are of value to us.

Large language models and prompt engineering

This chapter covers

- The fundamentals of how large language models work
- The risks of using large language models
- A definition of prompt engineering
- Experimenting with prompt engineering to return various outputs
- How to solve problems using prompt engineering

In the previous chapter, we learned that it's important to take time and familiarize ourselves with new tools, and it's the very same mindset we'll be adopting in this chapter. Throughout this book, we'll be exploring how to use generative AI tools such as Open AI's ChatGPT and GitHub Copilot, which are built on large language models, or LLMs. There are many ways in which AI can be employed in testing, but what makes LLMs so interesting is their adaptability to different situations—hence, their rise in popularity. So, before we look at how we can incorporate LLM tools into our everyday testing, let's first learn a bit about what LLMs are, how they work, and how to get the most out of them by learning about the concept of prompt engineering.

What has made LLMs such as ChatGPT dominate tech headlines throughout 2023? Consider this sample interaction with ChatGPT that I had:

 Hello ChatGPT, can you introduce yourself briefly?

 Of course! I'm ChatGPT, an AI language model developed by OpenAI. I'm based on the GPT-3.5 architecture, which means I'm designed to understand and generate human-like text based on the prompts I receive. I've been trained on a diverse range of data sources, including books, articles, websites, and other text documents, up until September 2021. I can assist you with a wide array of topics, including answering questions, providing explanations, creative writing, and much more. Just let me know how I can help you!

 Nice to meet you.

 Nice to meet you too! I'm here to assist you with any questions or tasks you have. How may I help you today?

 I'm just getting to know you.

 That's perfectly fine! Feel free to ask me anything you'd like to know, whether it's about my capabilities, how I work, or anything else you're curious about. I'm here to provide information and help you out to the best of my abilities. Fire away with your questions!

Based on this quick conversation, we can see that

- It is possible to interact with ChatGPT using natural language. No traditional programming experience was required to get results from ChatGPT in this example.
- The output from ChatGPT is also in natural language. It's easy to understand and react to.

Advocates of LLMs are celebrating that these types of AI tools have democratized the use of AI, allowing anyone to use it to get results. However, this democratization is a double-edged sword. The nature in which we interact with LLMs can give us the illusion that we're talking with a machine that reasons in the same way we humans do. But making that assumption can affect our ability to get the most out of an LLM. So, to get the best results out of tools such as ChatGPT, we should know how they work (at least in general terms) to better understand how they can fit into our testing activities and how to extract the most value from them.

2.1 *LLMs explained*

How does a person with relatively little experience in building AI systems explain how a complex LLM system works? Fortunately, in the Computerphile video "AI Language

Models & Transformers" (www.youtube.com/watch?v=rURRYI66E54), Rob Miles offers an example that can help us gain a fundamental grasp on what LLMs do. (I strongly recommend watching all his videos on AI.)

Take out your phone and open a messaging app, or any other app that makes your keyboard appear. Above the keyboard, you'll likely see a range of suggested words to insert into your message. For example, my keyboard offers the following suggestions: *I, I am,* and *The.* Selecting one of these options, such as *I am,* causes the suggestions to update. For me, it offered the options *away, away for,* and *now.* Selecting the option *away for* once again updates the available options. So, how does the keyboard know which options to show?

In your keyboard, there is an AI model that behaves in a manner resembling LLMs. This description is an oversimplification, but at its core, the keyboard on your phone is applying the same machine learning approach as an LLM by using probability. Language is a complex and fluid set of rules, meaning any attempt to codify relationships explicitly is almost impossible. So instead, a model is trained on massive data sets to implicitly learn the relationships in language and create a probability distribution that is used to predict what the next word might be. This can best be described by visualizing the options available from the keyboard example, as shown in figure 2.1

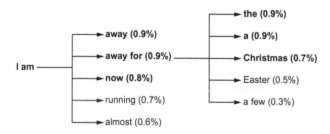

Figure 2.1 **Probability distribution in action**

As we can see, when we select the term *I am,* the model in our keyboard has been trained to assign probabilities to a vast range of words. Some of these will have a high probability of coming after *I am,* such as *away,* and some will have a low probability, such as *sandalwood.* As mentioned before, these probabilities come from a model that has completed a training process, known as unsupervised learning, in which vast amounts of data have been sent to an algorithm for processing. It's from that training process that a model is created with complex weights and balances that provide the model with its predictive abilities.

Supervised learning and unsupervised learning

When training AI, two of the more dominant techniques to use are supervised and unsupervised learning. Which learning approach is used will determine how data has been

Chances are good that if you play around with the predictive function on your keyboard, the output will differ from mine—even if we have the same phone and oper-
ating system. This is because once the model has been trained and is utilized in our
phones, it's still being fine-tuned by what we type into our phones. I travel for work,
so I must let people know when I am away and when I'm available. (It is perhaps a
damning indictment of my work–life balance!) So, words such as *I am* and *away* have
an increased probability as they are words I use more regularly. This is known as Rein-
forcement Learning with Human Feedback, or RLHF.

Again, comparing predictive messaging on a phone to an LLM is an oversimplification, but the comparison holds true. LLMs also use unsupervised learning and RLHF.
The difference, however, is that although an AI model on a phone can look at perhaps
the last five words typed to predict the next, LLMs use cutting-edge techniques, such as

- Generative pretrained transformers (which is what makes the GPT abbreviation
  in ChatGPT)
- Powerful hardware infrastructure using thousands of servers
- Training data on a scale that would dwarf what our humble keyboard model will
  have been trained on

Do we need to know the intricacies of each of these points? Not really, but it helps
us appreciate a key aspect of LLMs. The output of LLMs, no matter how powerful, is
probabilistic. LLMs are not a repository of information—there is structured knowledge stored within them like we would see on the wider internet. This means that how
it comes to conclusions differs from how we humans do (probability rather than experience), which is what makes them so powerful but also risky to use if we aren't vigilant
about how we use them.

2.2   *Avoiding the risks of using LLMs*

Having an AI predict what word goes after another isn't an easy task, and although
current LLMs have seen an explosion in ability, there are risks we need to be aware of.
Let's take a look at a few of them.

2.2.1   *Hallucinations*

The challenge with text prediction is to ensure that the output of an LLM makes sense and is rooted in reality. For example, back in chapter 1, when I asked ChatGPT to write an introduction to this book, it shared the following:

 Regarding the book, "How AI can be used to help support various software testing activities," I would recommend "AI-Driven Testing: Adding Intelligence to Your Software Testing Practice" by Julian Harty and Mahesh Sharma.

Initially, when LLMs were being developed, their output didn't make much sense. The text would be readable, but it lacked structure or grammatical sense. If we read this example, it parses perfectly well, and it makes sense. However, as I mentioned, the book that ChatGPT describes doesn't exist. In the context of an LLM, this is known as a *hallucination*. The LLM is able to output a clear statement in a way that grants it some authority, but what has been written is false.

LLM hallucinations can be caused by a range of factors, such as the quality of the data it was trained on, the degree to which a model has been trained on data (overfitting), or a model's propensity for giving an answer regardless of whether it is correct. One of the challenges of working with LLMs is that they act like a black box. It's difficult to monitor how an LLM reached a specific conclusion, which is compounded by its indeterminate nature. Just because I got an output that contained a hallucination doesn't mean that others will do the same in the future. (This is where the RLHF helps combat hallucinations: we can inform the model whether its output is false, and it will learn from that.)

The risk of hallucinations means we must always maintain an element of skepticism when interpreting the output of an LLM. We need to be mindful that what is being returned from an LLM is predictive and not always correct. We can't turn off our critical thinking just because a tool appears to be behaving in a way that mimics human behavior.

2.2.2   *Data provenance*

For most LLM users, it's not just how the model works precisely that is a black box to us, but also the data it has been trained on. Since ChatGPT's explosion in popularity, the conversation around data ownership and copyright has intensified. Companies such as X (formerly known as Twitter) and Reddit have accused OpenAI of stealing their data wholesale, and at the time of writing, a class action lawsuit against OpenAI has been filed by a collection of authors who accuse the company of breaching copyright law by training models on their works (https://mng.bz/1aBZ).

The results from these debates are yet to be seen, but if we bring this topic back to the world of software development, we must be mindful of what material an LLM has been trained on. For example, ChatGPT, at one point, would return nonsensical responses when specific phrases were sent to it, all because it had been trained on data from the subreddit r/counting, which is full of data that is seemingly nonsensical itself.

You can learn more about this weird behavior from Computerphile at www.youtube .com/watch?v=WO2X3oZEJOA). If an LLM has been trained on garbage, it will output garbage.

This becomes important when we consider tools such as GitHub Copilot, which uses the same GPT model that ChatGPT uses. Copilot has been fine-tuned differently, using the billions of lines of code stored in GitHub so that it can act as an assistant and suggest code snippets as we develop our codebase. We'll explore in later chapters how we can put Copilot to good use, but again, we should be critical of what it suggests and not blindly accept everything it offers as a suggestion. Why? Ask yourself, are you happy with the code you've created in the past? Do you trust all the code others have created? If a large population of engineers is prone to implementing bad patterns, then that is what tools like Copilot will have been trained on. The point is a little hyperbolic because a lot of good developers and testers out there do good work—good work that Copilot is trained on. But it's a thought exercise worth considering every now and then just to ensure that we remember who is in the driver's seat when building applications with LLMs.

2.2.3 *Data privacy*

Just as we need to be mindful of what an LLM outputs, we also have to consider what we enter into it. The temptation to share material with LLMs to find answers to problems we're facing will be strong. But we have to ask ourselves, where is the data we send being stored? As mentioned earlier, LLMs are being tweaked continuously through the RLFH feedback. Companies such as OpenAI and GitHub will take the information we share, store it, and use it for future model training (GitHub does offer some privacy controls over what it can store, though).

This can be problematic when working for companies (or for ourselves) who want to keep their intellectual property private. Take Samsung, for example, whose employees accidentally leaked confidential material through the use of ChatGPT, as described here by TechRadar (you can read about it at https://mng.bz/PN52):

> *The company allowed engineers at its semiconductor arm to use the AI writer to help fix problems with their source code. But in doing so, the workers entered confidential data, such as the source code itself for a new program and internal meeting notes data relating to their hardware.*

As the adoption of LLMs begins to increase across organizations, we may begin to see an increase in policies that restrict what we can and can't use LLMs for. Some may ban the use of third-party LLMs, and some organizations will opt to train and deploy their own internal LLMs for internal use (a topic we will explore in part 3). The result of those decisions will be highly contextual, but they will affect what type of LLMs we use and what data we can and cannot send, underlying our need to be mindful of what we send to LLMs.

It's also important to keep customer privacy in mind as we have an obligation not only to the companies we work for (especially for those who sign nondisclosure agreements) but also to our users. We have a legal and moral duty to protect user data from being spread into the wild, where we have no oversight.

In conclusion, although LLMs provide a wealth of opportunities, we must avoid the trap of anthropomorphizing them. Treating LLMs as if they have come to conclusions in the same way as we humans do is a fallacy. It can entrench a level of trust in the output that is dangerous and likely means that we aren't getting the most benefit out of them. However, if we learn to use the probabilistic nature of LLMs when we instruct them, we can increase our chances of creating outputs that can help us improve efficiency—which is where prompt engineering can help us.

2.3 *Improving results with prompt engineering*

We use natural language to prompt an LLM to return a desired outcome, but because they are probabilistic, we can communicate with them in a way that differs from normal interaction with humans. As LLMs have developed, a new field of engineering has appeared known as *prompt engineering*, which contains a collection of patterns and techniques that we can use to increase the likelihood of getting a desired output from an LLM.

> **What is a prompt?**
> In this book, we'll use the term *prompt* regularly as this will be our primary means of communicating with LLMs. When we use this term, we are simply referring to the natural language input that is sent to an LLM. For example, in the first example of this chapter, I sent the following prompt:
>
> Hello ChatGPT, can you introduce yourself briefly?
>
> which prompted the LLM to return this response to me:
>
> Hello! I'm ChatGPT, an AI language model developed by OpenAI. I can help with answering questions, providing information, brainstorming ideas, and more. Feel free to ask me anything!

In the coming chapters, we will use prompt engineering heavily to trigger LLMs to deliver a range of useful content for various testing activities. But before we begin, it's worthwhile learning the fundamentals of prompt engineering so that we can see how prompts are built to maximize output from LLMs.

To help us better understand what prompt engineering is, consider these two prompts sent to an LLM. The first is a general question:

 What risks should I test for when testing a Contact Us form?

The second is a more detailed prompt:

Assume the role of a professional software tester and suggest a list of risks for a Contact Us form using the following constraints:

\# Focus on the quality characteristics of accessibility, compliance and usability

\# Number each risk

\# Provide which quality characteristic the risk relates to

\# Use no more than 30 words to describe each risk

For example:

1 Semantic structure - Accessibility - The HTML structure of the form should follow WCAG A standards

Comparing the two, we can see that the second example is more detailed, with explicit requests and examples to outline what we might expect the LLM to return. Although the intention is similar, the output from each is drastically different.

Compare the output from the first example:

 Validation and Error Handling: Verify that the form correctly validates user input, such as email addresses, phone numbers, and required fields. Test for appropriate error messages when users submit incorrect or incomplete information.

Security: Ensure that the contact form is secure and protected against common vulnerabilities such as cross-site scripting (XSS) and SQL injection attacks. Validate that the form sanitizes or escapes user input to prevent malicious code execution.

Usability: Test the form's usability by evaluating factors such as the clarity of form fields, user instructions, and overall user experience. Make sure the form is intuitive, easy to navigate, and visually appealing.

against the second example:

 1 Keyboard accessibility - Accessibility - Ensure the form can be easily navigated and filled out using only a keyboard.

...

6 Consistent design - Usability - Verify that the form follows a consistent design pattern and matches the overall website design.

...

13 Consent checkboxes - Compliance - Ensure any consent checkboxes or privacy policy links are clearly presented and function correctly.

Imagine that we want to use the proposed risks in each example to guide our testing. The first example has output suggestions that are vague and abstract. We would still need to do a fair bit of work to break down the large topics, such as security risks, whereas, with the second example, we have specific, actionable risks that we could use easily. And the goal of using tools such as LLM is to *reduce* the workload, not increase it.

Our second prompt yields better results because the instructions it gives have been considered and are detailed and clear, which is what prompt engineering is essentially about. Although both prompts use natural language, with prompt engineering, we are aware of how an LLM works and what we want it to return to understand how to write a prompt so that we maximize the chances of a desired outcome. When using prompt engineering, we can see that although an LLM communicates in plain language, how it processes our request differs from how a human might do so, so we can adopt specific techniques to steer an LLM in the direction we want.

2.4 Examining the principles of prompt engineering

As LLMs have developed, so have the patterns and techniques of prompt engineering. Many courses and blog posts have been written around prompt engineering, but one notable collection of principles, which we'll explore shortly, has been created by Isa Fulford and Andrew Ng and their respective teams. A collaboration between OpenAI's LLM knowledge and Deeplearning.ai's teaching platform has created a course called ChatGPT Prompt Engineering for Developers, which features a series of principles and tactics that can be used in prompts to get the most out of LLMs. If you have the time, I encourage you to take the short course available at https://mng.bz/JNGp (https://www.promptingguide.ai/ is also a useful reference.) Although the course references ChatGPT specifically, the principles taught there can be applied across many LLMs. So let's explore these principles and tactics to get comfortable with prompting LLMs.

2.4.1 Principle 1: Write clear and specific instructions

This first principle might seem obvious at first glance—it's always sensible to provide instructions to others that are clear and specific. However, what this principle suggests is that we write prompts that are clear and specific *for an LLM*. And that means something different from what might be clear and specific to a human. To implement this concept, Fulford and Ng teach four tactics to achieve clear and specific prompts: use delimiters, ask for structured output, check for assumptions, and use few-shot prompting. In the next few sections, we'll examine each one in more detail.

2.4.2 Tactic 1: Use delimiters

When writing prompts, we may need to provide different content and data that serve different purposes. For example, the start of our prompt might include instructions on what we want an LLM to produce, whereas the end of our prompt might include raw data that we want to process. LLMs can guess our intentions for different sections of our prompts, but because our goal is to be as clear as possible, we can aid the process by using *delimiters*, which are characters used to separate strings, to state our intentions for different parts of our prompt. Take this prompt as an example. We open the prompt with a message that sets expectations:

(MW) You are a SQL data generator. Generate five rows of SQL for a MySQL database.

We use the * character to delimit rules:

* The table name is identified with a # sign.

* Each table column is identified with a % sign

* Each column is described in order of name, data type and data options using the | sign

* If a column data option says random, randomize data based on the suggested format and column name

We then use the #, %, and | delimiters that we set in rules to provide instructions:

Here are the instructions:

```
# rooms
% room_name | string | random
% type | string |  'single' or 'double'
% beds | integer | 1 to 6
% accessible | boolean | true or false
% image | string | random url
% description | string | random max 20 characters
% features | array[string] | 'Wifi', 'TV' or 'Safe'
% roomPrice |  integer | 100 to 200
```

When running this prompt within ChatGPT, I received the following output:

```
INSERT INTO rooms (room_name, type, beds, accessible, image,
    description, features, roomPrice) VALUES
        ('Room 1', 'single', 3, true, 'https://example.com/image1.jpg',
    'Lorem ipsum dolor', '["Wifi", "TV"]', 150),
        ('Room 2', 'double', 2, false, 'https://example.com/image2.jpg',
    'Lorem ipsum dolor', '["TV", "Safe"]', 180),
        ('Room 3', 'double', 4, true, 'https://example.com/image3.jpg',
    'Lorem ipsum dolor', '["Wifi", "Safe"]', 160),
        ('Room 4', 'single', 1, true, 'https://example.com/image4.jpg',
    'Lorem ipsum dolor', '["Wifi", "TV"]', 120),
        ('Room 5', 'double', 3, false, 'https://example.com/image5.jpg',
    'Lorem ipsum dolor', '["TV"]', 170);
```

As we can see, through the use of delimiters the correct table name `rooms` has been added, and the column names, formats, and ranges have been correctly randomized. This is made possible by the clear expectations and rules we set that are distinguished by various delimiters throughout the prompt.

The delimiters help to make the prompt clearer, but they also make it easy to modify. For example, if we want to reconfigure the generated data, we could enter another line, such as

```
% room_size | string | 20m2 to 50m2
```

So, when writing prompts that contain a large amount of data that changes context, we can use delimiters to make clear what is being provided in a prompt at a specific point.

> ### Activity 2.1
> Using the delimiter prompt example, we create new instructions—this time, for a booking that would include information about who made the booking, contact details, and check-in and check-out dates.

2.4.3 *Tactic 2: Ask for structured output*

One facet of LLMs that makes them useful is that they have the ability to provide outputs in structured formats. As we make our way through this book, we'll explore just how useful this ability is, but as a rule, we must always remember that we need to be clear in a prompt about what structured format we want to see used. Take this prompt as an example:

 Create a JSON object with random data that contains the following fields: firstname, lastname, totalprice, deposit paid. Also, include an object called booking dates that contains checkin and checkout dates.

We begin the prompt by clearly stating what format we want to see our object in, in this case, JSON, before we start outlining the structure of the object. When I sent this prompt to ChatGPT, the following result was returned:

```
{
  "firstname": "John",
  "lastname": "Doe",
  "totalprice": 150.50,
  "deposit_paid": true,
  "booking_dates": {
    "checkin": "2023-08-01",
    "checkout": "2023-08-10"
  }
}
```

As the prompt clearly states, the expected format and structure are two distinct instructions, meaning we can modify our instructions to quickly change the format by sending an additional prompt, such as

 Create this in a YAML format

Sending this prompt to ChatGPT returned the following output:

```
firstname: John
lastname: Doe
totalprice: 150.50
deposit_paid: true
booking_dates:
  checkin: 2023-08-01
  checkout: 2023-08-10
```

Notice the structure is the same (as well as the randomized data). By explicitly stating what format we desire, we can instruct an LLM with exactly what format we want at a given time and then alternate formats with ease.

> **Activity 2.2**
> Attempt to create an object that contains multiple parameters with different data types in different formats. Try prompting an LLM to convert your object from one format to another—for example, from JSON to XML.

2.4.4   *Tactic 3: Check for assumptions*

As we learned earlier, LLMs can hallucinate by generating output that contains information that is incorrect or disconnected from reality. It goes without saying that we want to reduce the risk of producing hallucinations, which is where our third tactic, checking for assumptions, can help. LLMs are more likely to hallucinate if they are provided with prompts that are focused on edge cases around a problem we want to solve. If an LLM is not properly instructed, it's more likely to make a guess at an answer than to outright inform us that it cannot provide a useful answer. So, if we want to avoid guesswork, we need to provide instructions in our prompt to allow the LLM to bail out if it cannot execute our request. Consider the following example. It provides initial instructions for the prompt, which includes a delimiter:

(MW)   You will be provided with a JSON object delimited by three hashes. Extract all emails that end with .com and write them out as a list.

We then check for assumptions and allow the LLM to bail:

(MW)   If no email addresses with a .com email address exist, simply write "No .com emails found"

Finally, we provide the data to process using ### as a delimiter:

(MW)
```
###
[{
  "firstname": "Bret",
  "lastname": "Averay",
  "email": "baveray0@apple.com"
}, {
  "firstname": "Annabel",
  "lastname": "Biswell",
  "email": "abiswell2@nsw.gov.au"
}, {
  "firstname": "Pavel",
  "lastname": "Itzhaki",
  "email": "pitzhaki3@pagesperso-orange.fr"
}, {
  "firstname": "Pail",
```

```
    "lastname": "Yandell",
    "email": "pyandell4@ning.com"
}, {
    "firstname": "Glennis",
    "lastname": "Pentecost",
    "email": "gpentecost6@yelp.com"
}]
###
```

Running this prompt with a collection of email addresses that can be extracted returned the following output:

 Here are the email addresses that end with ".com":

* baveray0@apple.com

* pyandell4@ning.com

* gpentecost6@yelp.com

But here's what happened when I ran the prompt again without email addresses:

 You will be provided with a JSON object delimited by three hashes. Extract all emails that end with .com and write them out as a list.

If no email addresses with a .com email address exist, simply write "No .com emails found"

```
###
[{
    "firstname": "Bret",
    "lastname": "Averay"
}, {
    "firstname": "Annabel",
    "lastname": "Biswell"
}, {
    "firstname": "Pavel",
    "lastname": "Itzhaki"
}, {
    "firstname": "Pail",
    "lastname": "Yandell"
}, {
    "firstname": "Glennis",
    "lastname": "Pentecost"
}]
###
```

I received the following:

 Here is the list of email addresses that end with .com extracted from the provided JSON object:

No .com emails found

This response from the LLM was a direct reference to this section of the prompt:

If no email addresses with a .com email address exist, simply write "No .com emails found."

which prevented the LLM from providing an output that was incorrect. For example, when I ran the prompt without the assumption check, the following was returned:

 Sure! I can help you with that. Here are the email addresses that end with ".com" from the provided JSON object:

```
["bret@example.com", "annabel@example.com", "pavel@example.com",
"pail@example.com", "glennis@example.com"]
```

Please note that I have used example.com as a placeholder domain for all the email addresses. Replace it with the appropriate domain if you have the actual email addresses.

This is an excellent example of an LLM hallucination. The object we provided contained no email addresses, so the LLM used guesswork and incorrectly started generating new email addresses based on existing data. However, with the assumption check in place, we prevented the hallucination from occurring.

Activity 2.3

Create a prompt that filters specific data out of a list of raw data and then outputs the results (for example, filter fruit from a list of different foodstuffs). Next, modify the data to include an edge case (for example, incorrect or missing data). Observe what the LLM outputs, and then attempt to correct the output by adding to the prompt some instructions that follow the check-for-assumptions prompt.

2.4.5   *Tactic 4: Few-shot prompting*

As we've progressed through this chapter and learned new concepts about LLMs and prompting, key points have been clarified using examples. They are essential tools when it comes to not just teaching but also communicating with one another. This is no different for LLMs. *Few-shot prompting* basically means providing explicit examples to clarify instructions (The word *few* in this context indicates how many examples you share. A prompt with no examples would be a *zero-shot prompt*). What follows is a prompt using examples. First, we provide the instructions in the prompt outlining the output format:

 You are an expert exploratory tester. Create three test charters for a booking system that focus on the risks around booking dates. The format should follow: Explore <Target> using <Resource> to discover <Information>

We provide examples to clarify the output format for the LLM:

For example:

* Explore user permissions using different users to discover permission risks
* Explore browser animations using different devices to discover how animations render

Sending this prompt to ChatGPT returned the following output:

 Explore date validation using various date formats to discover potential input errors.

Explore time zone handling using different geographical locations to discover discrepancies in booking times.

Explore booking conflicts using overlapping reservation requests to discover potential double-booking risks.

Consider the format of "Explore <Target> using <Resource> to discover <Information>." It is rule based, but it leans heavily on natural language to communicate the rules (unlike JSON or XML structures that rely on explicit delimiter rules). By providing examples in our prompt, we can help contextualize what we mean by `<Target>`, `<Resource>`, and `<Information>` and reduce the risk of the LLM guessing what that means.

> **Activity 2.4**
> Create a prompt that uses the few-shot tactic. In your prompt, provide the instructions you expect the LLM to follow and then add at least two examples to help guide it in providing a desired outcome.

2.4.6 Principle 2: Give the model time to "think"

It may seem a little unusual, given that we've been considering LLMs as probabilistic machines and not entities that can think, to see a principle that encourages us to give a model time to think. However, the best way to understand this principle is that we're not actually giving an LLM time to think but rather emulating how we would give someone time to think about a task in our prompt. In the ChatGPT Prompt Engineering for Developers course, Fulford gives a useful analogy as she introduces this principle: "If you give a model a task that's too complex to do in a short amount of time, . . . it may make up a guess which is likely to be incorrect."

She explains that the same situation would happen if humans were given a complex task with limited time to respond. We'd rely on educated guesswork and likely come up with a less-than-satisfactory answer. Thus, principle 2 offers tactics to help us write prompts that break down tasks and encourage LLMs to evaluate output to once again maximize the chances of a desired response.

2.4.7   *Tactic 1: Specify the steps to complete the task*

The first tactic is relatively straightforward once we are confident about using the tactics of principle 1 (write clear and specific instructions). By using delimiters, we can break a complex task into individual steps for an LLM to take to solve the larger task. Take a look at this prompt, where we first notify the LLM that a set of instructions is coming, followed by delimited data:

 You are going to be given a list of instructions to follow.

We then list each subtask clearly to instruct the LLM on what to do:

 1   Identify functional risks that might impact the text delimited by three hashes

2   Convert the risks into test charters

3   Format each charter into a Discover <feature> using <resource> to discover <information> format

Finally, we provide the data we would like to see processed:

 ###
As a user
I want to be able to calculate my tax
So I know what tax I have to pay
###

When sent to ChatGPT, it returned this result:

 Functional risks:

- Calculation accuracy: There is a risk that the tax calculation may be inaccurate, leading to incorrect tax amounts being calculated.

Test charters based on the identified risks:

- Test Charter 1: Validate the accuracy of tax calculations by inputting different test scenarios with known tax amounts and verifying that the calculated tax matches the expected values.

Formatting the charters into a "Discover <feature> using <resource> to discover <information>" format:

- Discover tax calculation accuracy using test scenarios with known tax amounts to validate the accuracy of the calculated tax.

This is a snippet from the output I received. It created many more risks and charters, but the first example from each section demonstrates the LLM responding to each subtask, one by one, to create an output.

Activity 2.5

Create a prompt that requires a complex task to be carried out. Attempt to break out the complex task into multiple subtasks that the LLM can carry out.

2.4.8 *Tactic 2: Instruct the model to work out its own solution first*

Our final tactic focuses not on the process of creating an output, but rather on evaluating the output itself. Similar to checking for assumptions, ask an LLM to evaluate the output to confirm that it aligns with what it has been instructed to produce. Let's check out an example to gain a better understanding of how this would work. First, take a look at a prompt that doesn't ask an LLM to work out its solution first but sets out the instructions for the LLM to follow:

(MW) You are a software developer in test that is experienced in writing Java. Create a unit test for the following method:

We then provide the code it needs to provide unit tests for:

(MW)
```java
public class AuthService {

    public HttpStatus deleteToken(Token token) throws SQLException {
        Boolean successfulDeletion = authDB.deleteToken(token);

        if(successfulDeletion){
            return HttpStatus.OK;
        } else {
            return HttpStatus.NOT_FOUND;
        }
    }

}
```

Sending this to ChatGPT, the following result was returned:

```java
import org.junit.jupiter.api.Test;
import static org.junit.jupiter.api.Assertions.*;

class TokenManagerTest {

    @Test
    void deleteToken_SuccessfulDeletion_ReturnsOK() throws SQLException
    {
        // Arrange
        TokenManager tokenManager = new TokenManager();
        Token token = new Token();

        // Act
        HttpStatus result = tokenManager.deleteToken(token);
```

```
            // Assert
            assertEquals(HttpStatus.OK, result);
        }
    }
```

This looks like reasonable Java code for a unit test, but if this were added to a suite of unit checks, it would fail because the method `authDB.deleteToken` in the production code provided has not been handled correctly. Specifically, if we wanted this unit check to work, we would need to mock `authDB.deleteToken`.

Now, if we run the prompt again but this time have it evaluate its solution before outputting a final answer, we get a different result. So first we change the prompt to a new prompt that asks the LLM to confirm that the result of the check works:

 You are a software developer in test that is experienced in writing Java. Create a unit test for the following method that will be shared. Before outputting the unit tests, check to see that the assertion of each unit check will return a deterministic result.

We then provide the code for which a unit test will be written:

```java
public class AuthService {

    public HttpStatus deleteToken(Token token) throws SQLException {
        Boolean successfulDeletion = authDB.deleteToken(token);

        if(successfulDeletion){
            return HttpStatus.OK;
        } else {
            return HttpStatus.NOT_FOUND;
        }
    }

}
```

Sending this to ChatGPT returned this result:

```java
import org.junit.jupiter.api.Assertions;
import org.junit.jupiter.api.Test;
import org.mockito.Mockito;

import java.sql.SQLException;

public class TokenDeletionTest {

    @Mock
    private AuthDB authDB;

    @Test
    public void testDeleteToken_SuccessfulDeletion() throws SQLException
    {
        // Mocking the behavior of authDB.deleteToken() to return true
        Token token = new Token();
        Mockito.when(authDB.deleteToken(token)).thenReturn(true);
```

```
            AuthService authService = new AuthService(authDB);
            HttpStatus result = authService.deleteToken(token);

            // Assertion: The method should return HttpStatus.OK
            Assertions.assertEquals(HttpStatus.OK, result);
        }
    }
```

This time, we can see that because we asked the LLM to evaluate its solution before returning a result, the output unit check uses `Mockito` to mock the `authDB.delete-Token`. So, if we observe problems with LLMs outputting erroneous solutions or they start hallucinating, we can add an instruction to evaluate solutions first to minimize the occurrence of hallucinations.

Activity 2.6

Create a prompt that requires an LLM to work out a solution to a problem. Observe its output and see if the solution it produces is correct. Then add instructions to have the LLM evaluate the solution. What happens? Does the solution change? Is it an improvement?

2.5　Working with various LLMs

So far, we've talked about LLMs in a broad sense while using OpenAI's ChatGPT in the previous examples to demonstrate how they work in general. However, ChatGPT is just one of the many different LLMs that we can use. So, before we conclude the chapter, let's familiarize ourselves with the ways in which LLMs differ from one another and learn about some of the currently popular models and communities so that we can increase our chances of finding the right LLM for the job.

2.5.1　Comparing LLMs

What makes an LLM good? How do we determine whether a model is worth using? These are not easy questions to answer. The complex nature of LLMs, how they're trained, and what data was used close these systems off to deep analysis, compromising an area that some researchers are trying to improve or shed light upon. However, that doesn't mean we shouldn't educate ourselves on some of the key aspects of LLMs and how they affect them. We might not all be AI researchers attempting to explore the deep inner workings of LLMs, but we are or will be their users and will want to know that what we spend resources on is giving us value. So, to help us break down some of the jargon and give us some grounding on how LLMs differ, let's go through some key attributes discussed in the world of LLMs.

PARAMETER COUNT

If you take a look at different LLMs, you'll likely see talk of LLMs having a 175-billion- or 1-trillion-parameter count. It can sometimes feel like marketing speak, but parameter count does not affect LLMs' performance. The parameter count essentially refers to the amount of statistical weights that exist in a model. Each individual weight provides a piece of the statistical puzzle that makes up an LLM. So, roughly speaking, the more parameters an LLM has, the better it will perform. The parameter count can also give us a sense of cost. The higher the parameter count, the more expensive it is to run, and there is a cost that may be, in part, handed down to users.

TRAINING DATA

LLMs require huge quantities of data to be trained on, so the size and quality of data will have an effect on the quality of an LLM. If we want an LLM to be accurate in how it responds to requests, it's not enough to just throw as much data as possible. It needs to be data that can help influence the probability of a model in a sensible manner. For example, the Reddit example we explored earlier in this chapter, in which the subreddit r/counting used to train ChatGPT caused it to hallucinate in strange ways, demonstrates that more isn't necessarily better. Still, similar to parameter count, the more high-quality data an LLM has been trained on, the better it will likely perform. The challenge is in knowing what data an LLM has been trained on—something that corporate creators of AI are keen on keeping a secret.

EXTENSIBILITY AND INTEGRATION

Just like with any other tool, the value of an LLM can be increased further if it can offer other features beyond its core abilities, such as integrating into existing systems or training models further for our specific needs. What features are available to integrate and extend LLMs depends largely on who was responsible for training.

For example, OpenAI offers paid-for API access to their models. But beyond an instruction feature that allows you to tweak output with a simple prompt, there is no ability to further fine-tune and deploy one of their GPT models for private use. Compare this to Meta's LlaMa model, which has been open sourced, allowing the AI community to download and further train to their own requirements, although they must build their own infrastructure to deploy the model.

As LLM platforms grow, we will see advances in not just their ability to respond to prompts but also the features around them and their access. Thus, it's necessary to keep said features in mind when evaluating what to work with.

QUALITY OF RESPONSES

Arguably, the most important factor to consider is whether an LLM provides responses that are legible, useful, and free (or as close to free) of hallucination as possible. Although criteria such as parameter count and training data are useful indicators of an LLM's performance, it's up to us to understand what we want to use an LLM for and then determine how each responds to our prompts and helps solve our specific problems. Not all challenges we face need the largest, most expensive LLM in the market. Thus, it's important that we take time to try out different models, compare their outputs, and then make a judgment for ourselves. For example, GPT models from OpenAI are found to perform better with code examples than Google Gemini. These details have been discovered through experimentation and observation.

The criteria we've explored are by no means an exhaustive list, but they demonstrate that there is more to consider about LLMs once we get past the initial glamour of how they respond. Different LLMs perform differently, helping us with various challenges. So let's take a look at some of the more popular currently available models and platforms.

2.5.2 Examining popular LLMs

Since OpenAI's launch of ChatGPT, there has been an explosion in releases of LLMs from various organizations. It's not to say that these models and related work weren't around before ChatGPT's release, but the public focus has certainly intensified, and an increasing number of marketing and release announcements have focused on companies releasing their LLM offerings. Here are some of the more common/popular LLMs that have been released since the end of 2022.

> **Keeping up with LLMs**
>
> It's worth noting that the situation with the launch of LLMs and their related features is extremely fluid and has grown at quite a fast pace. Therefore, it's likely that some of what we'll explore will differ from the time of writing in mid-2024 to the time you are reading this book. Fortunately, sites such as LLM Models (https://llmmodels.org/) share up-to-date lists to review. However, this list demonstrates that some of the bigger names in the LLM space are worth exploring.

OpenAI

At the time of writing, OpenAI is the most ubiquitous of organizations offering LLMs for use. Although OpenAI has been working on LLM models for quite some time, releasing their GPT-3 model in 2020, it was their release of ChatGPT in November 2022 that kick-started the popular wave of interest and use of LLMs.

OpenAI offers a range of different LLM models, but the two that stand out are GPT-3.5-Turbo and GPT-4o, which you can learn about more at https://platform.openai .com/docs/models/overview. These two models are used as *foundation* models or models that can be trained further for specific purposes, for a range of products such as ChatGPT, GitHub Copilot, and Microsoft Bing AI.

In addition to their models, OpenAI has offered a range of features such as API access to their direct GPT-3.5-Turbo and GPT-4 models and a collection of apps that integrate with ChatGPT (if you subscribe to their plus membership). It's by far the most popular LLM (for now) and has kick-started a race with organizations to release their own LLMs. Although we've already explored some prompts with ChatGPT, you can always access and experiment with ChatGPT at https://chatgpt.com/.

> **Sticking with OpenAI**
>
> Although there are many different LLMs that I encourage you to use, for the sake of consistency, we will stick with ChatGPT-3.5-Turbo. It's not necessarily the most powerful

(continued)
LLM at this time, but it is the most ubiquitous—and free. That said, if you want to try out these prompts with other LLM models, feel free to do so. However, keep in mind that their responses will likely differ from what is shared in this book.

GEMINI

Unsurprisingly, Google also has a stake in the Generative AI market with their own range of LLM models known as Gemini. Currently at the time of writing their most powerful model is Gemini 1.5 Pro, but they also offer other versions of their models such as Gemini 1.5 Flash and Gemini 1.0 Pro. Given it's Google the parameter counts for each model is not public knowledge, but they are relatively comparable in performance to other LLM models.

Similar to OpenAI, Google offers access to their Gemini models via their Google Cloud platform (https://ai.google.dev/) and has recently started offering apps that work similarly to OpenAI's ChatGPT apps, with the added integration into other Google Suite tools such as Google Drive and Gmail. You can access and experiment with Gemini at https://gemini.google.com/app.

LLAMA

LLaMa, which is the name for a collection of models, was first released by Meta in July 2023. What sets LLaMa apart from OpenAI's GPT models and Google's Gemini is that LLaMa is open source. In addition to the open source license, LLaMa comes in a range of sizes: 8 and 70 billion parameters, respectively. The combination of these sizes and their access means that LLaMa has been adopted by the AI community as a popular foundational model. The flip side of this access, though, is that Meta doesn't provide a public platform to train and run versions of LLaMa. So, data sets and infrastructure must be personally sourced for use.

More details on LLaMa can be found at the following links:

- https://ai.meta.com/blog/meta-llama-3/
- https://www.llama.com/llama-downloads/

HUGGING FACE

Unlike the other entries in our list, Hugging Face offers no proprietary model but instead facilitates an AI community that contains a wide variety of different models, most of which are open source. Looking at their index page of models available at https://huggingface.co/models, we can see hundreds of thousands of differently trained models that have come from different companies and research labs. Hugging Face also offers datasets for training, apps, and documentation that allows the reader to dive deeper into how models are built. All of these resources are available so that the AI community can access pretrained models, tweak them, and further train them for a specific use, which is something that we'll be exploring further in part 3 of this book.

The marketplace for LLMs has sizably grown in a short amount of time, both commercially and in open source, and similar to other areas of software development, being proactive in what new LLMs are appearing can be beneficial. However, it can also be overwhelming and not necessarily feasible to keep up with everything that is happening at once. So, instead of attempting to keep abreast of all the comings and goings in the AI community, we can opt to explore LLMs when we want to use LLMs to solve specific problems. Having a problem can help frame our criteria around which tools work best for us.

> **Activity 2.7**
> Either select an earlier prompt from this chapter or create one of your own and submit it to different LLMs. Note how each responds and compares. Do some of them feel more conversational? How do they handle receiving or sending code examples? Which ones provide the best response in your opinion?

2.6 *Creating a library of prompts*

One of the benefits of prompts is that once created, they can be used repeatedly. Consequently, a lot of collections of prompts for different roles and tasks are appearing online. For example, here are a few collections that I've seen shared recently:

- Awesome ChatGPT Prompts, GitHub (https://github.com/f/awesome-chatgpt -prompts)
- 50 ChatGPT Prompts for Developers, Dev.to (https://mng.bz/w5D7)
- ChatGPT Cheat Sheet, Hackr.io (https://mng.bz/q0PK)

This list is not at all exhaustive, and the sample collections aren't necessarily related to testing, but they are worth looking through to learn how others have created prompts, as well as giving us the opportunity to determine which prompts would be effective and which wouldn't.

Although prompt collections shared publicly can be useful, it's likely we'll end up creating prompts that are used for specific contexts. So, it's worthwhile getting into the habit of storing prompts that prove to be beneficial in some sort of repository for us and others to quickly use. Where you store these will depend on what and who they are used for. If they're for public use, then sharing a repository of prompts or adding to existing collections might be valuable. If we're creating and using them while developing company products, then we need to treat them in the same way as our production code and store them somewhere private so that we don't violate any policies around intellectual property. Finally, we may also consider version control so that we can tweak and track prompts as we learn more about working with LLMs and as the LLMs themselves evolve.

Wherever they are stored, the idea is to create a repository of prompts that are quick and easy to access so that once a prompt has been created for a specific activity, it can be reused multiple times rapidly so that we can get as much value from them to improve our productivity.

Activity 2.8

Create a space where you can store future prompts for you and your team to use.

Using prompts from this book

In the spirit of storing prompts for future use and to help you, the reader, with trying out the prompt examples in this book, you can find each prompt example at https://mng .bz/75mx.

This will enable you to quickly copy and paste the prompts into your chosen LLM as we go through each chapter, saving you the task of having to type the whole prompt manually. There will be sections in certain prompts where you will need to add your own custom content or context to use them. To make them clear, instructions on what is required to add to the prompt are provided in the prompt and will be formatted in all caps and inside square brackets.

2.7   Solving problems by using prompts

The tactics and tooling we've learned about in this chapter help provide us with a framework to use LLMs and design specific prompts for specific testing activities. We should be mindful, though, that although these tactics improve our chances of getting desired results, they are not foolproof. For example, when we ask an LLM to evaluate its output, the LLM isn't evaluating its output like a traditional application might. It's simply moving the predictive needle further toward an output that aligns with our requirements.

Single prompting vs. multi-prompting

Throughout this chapter, we've explored how to use principles and tactics to create individual prompts that are as effective as possible at maximizing desired output from an LLM. However, tools such as ChatGPT, Gemini, and Claude allow us to conduct conversations with LLMs, and the history of the conversations influences the output of future responses in said conversation. This raises the question of whether it would be easier to try multiple prompts in a conversation to tweak output. Although this can be effective, we do run the risk that the longer a conversation progresses, the higher the risk of hallucinations occurring as an LLM attempts to overfit responses to our requests. This is why tools such as BingAI are limited in the number of responses they can give in a conversation. However, more importantly, more doesn't necessarily mean better. The garbage in, garbage out rule is valid for both single and multiple prompts. Relying on multiple prompts in one conversation means we become less clear and precise in what we are asking for, which adds delays and increases hallucination, thus negating the value of using an LLM in the first place. In conclusion, whether we want to send a single prompt to get what we want or send multiple prompts, adopting the principles and tactics created by Isa Fulford and Andrew Ng will increase our productivity with LLMs.

Therefore, it is necessary to develop the skills to write prompts that help us solve our problems effectively and in a way that doesn't diminish the time saved using LLMs (for example, we don't want to spend hours tweaking prompts). This means being able to identify specific problems that LLMs can help with and then utilizing prompt engineering to maximize the chances of extracting valuable information from an LLM. This is what we'll explore throughout the rest of this book—when and how to use LLMs.

As we progress, we'll also learn that prompts come in many shapes and sizes. Throughout this chapter, we've looked at prompts that are manually written by us humans. But, as we'll learn, tools such as GitHub Copilot auto-generate prompts as we write our code. That doesn't mean we can't still infuse the principles and tactics into our ways of working, but it does take time, awareness, and practice to develop.

Activity 2.9

Before you continue reading this book and learn about different types of prompts for different testing activities, use the knowledge from chapters 1 and 2, consider a specific testing task that you do, and try to build a prompt that can help you with your work.

Summary

- LLMs are trained on vast amounts of data using sophisticated algorithms to analyze our requests and predict an output.
- The predictive nature of LLMs makes them quite adaptable but also means they come with some risks.
- LLMs can sometimes output *hallucinations*, or text that sounds authoritative and correct when, in fact, it is false.
- The data that LLMs are trained on may contain errors, gaps, and assumptions, and we must keep this in mind when using them.
- We must also be mindful of the data we share with LLMs so as not to cause unauthorized leaks of business or user information.
- Prompt engineering is a collection of principles and tactics used to maximize the chances of an LLM returning a desired output.
- We can use the knowledge that LLMs are predictive in nature and benefit from it by implementing prompt engineering.
- Using delimiters can help us clarify instructions and parameters in a prompt.
- An LLM can output data in various formats, but it requires us to explicitly state which structure format we want in a prompt.
- We can reduce hallucinations from LLMs by using the check-for-assumption tactic.
- Providing examples in a prompt can help ensure that an LLM provides an output in a desired format or context.

- Specifying specific subtasks in a prompt can help an LLM process complex tasks successfully.
- Asking LLMs to evaluate solutions to problems can also reduce errors and maximize outcomes.
- Knowing when to use LLMs and developing skills with prompt engineering is the key to success, regardless of the tool we use.

Artificial intelligence, automation, and testing

Before we delve deeper into the use of large language models (LLMs) in testing, let's ask ourselves the following questions:

- What is the purpose and value of testing?
- How can tooling help us?
- When is it appropriate to use AI tools?

It may seem that asking these fundamental questions is unnecessary. But if you are someone who sees testing merely as a confirmatory exercise, as in executing test cases to confirm a requirement is correct, then your mileage from the subsequent chapters will be limited. Understanding the value and performance of testing is critical for determining how tools can be used effectively. Thus, in this chapter, we're going to explore why a deeper understanding of testing can help us utilize tools.

That said, if you are someone who already has that deep understanding, feel free to skim through this chapter and move on. For the rest of us, let's go back to square one by asking why we test.

3.1   The value of testing

To help us appreciate having a clear understanding of why we need testing in software development, let's return to the common perspective that testing is a confirmatory exercise. By this, we mean that testing is viewed as something done to confirm the following conditions:

- Written requirements have been met.
- All critical paths have been covered in a system.
- The system works as expected.

Teams that hold this perspective tend to overly rely on the use of test cases/scripts that contain explicit instructions for a human, or machine, to follow and confirm whether an expected outcome has been met. The problem with this mindset and approach is less that it's utilizing test scripts and more that it only uses test scripts and nothing else, which results in edge cases being missed, more complex bugs or behavior left untested, and generally in a limited understanding of how our products behave. Many biases come from an overreliance on test scripts, but if we bring it back to the use of LLMs in testing, then it limits our appreciation of how these tools can help us. When tools such as ChatGPT grew in popularity, a large majority of demonstrations and debates around the use of LLMs in testing focused on one thing: test scripts. People would demonstrate how LLMs could generate test scripts to be executed manually by either a human or a test automation tool.

Although initially these might have had some use, the options for what else could be done with LLMs to help testing began to dry out. On the surface, this appears to be a limitation of the tooling in question, but instead, the real problem is the limited idea of what testing is and how it can help. So, if we are to expand our use of LLMs in testing, we have to first expand our understanding of what testing is and how it works.

3.1.1   A different way of thinking about testing

To help us establish a deeper understanding, let's explore a model of testing that I use to define what I believe testing is for and how it helps, which is shown in figure 3.1.

The model, based on one created by James Lyndsay in his paper "Exploration and Strategy" (https://mng.bz/mRdn), consists of two circles. The left circle represents imagination, or what we *want* in a product, and the right circle represents implementation, or what we *have* in a product. The purpose of testing is to learn as much as possible about what's going on in each of these circles by carrying out testing activities. The more we test in these two circles, the more we learn. We can then

- Discover potential problems that might affect the quality
- Overlap these two circles of information, ensuring we trust we are building the intended product

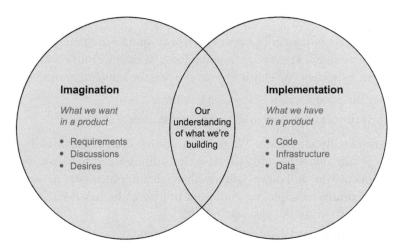

Figure 3.1 A model that helps describe the value and purpose of testing

To help describe this principle further, let's look at an example in which a team is delivering a hypothetical search feature that we want to ensure is delivered to a high degree of quality.

IMAGINATION

The Imagination circle represents what it is that we want from our product, and that includes expectations that are both explicit and implicit. So in this circle, our testing is focused on learning as much as possible about those explicit and implicit expectations. By doing so, we not only learn what has been explicitly stated in writing or verbally shared, but also dig down into the details and remove ambiguity over terms and ideas. Let's say a representative of the business or a user, such as a product owner, has shared this requirement with their team: "Search results are to be ordered by relevance."

The explicit information shared here tells us that the product owner wants search results ordered by relevance. However, a lot of implied information can be uncovered by testing the ideas and concepts behind what is being asked. This might come in the form of a series of questions, such as

- What is meant by relevant results?
- Who benefits from the results?
- What information is shared?
- How do we order results by relevancy?
- What data should we use?

By asking these questions, we gain a broader perspective of what is wanted, remove any misunderstandings and assumptions in our team's thinking, and identify potential risks that could affect those expectations. If we know more about what we are being asked to build, then we're more likely to build the right thing the first time.

IMPLEMENTATION

By testing the imagination, we get a stronger sense of what we are being asked to build. But, just because we might know what to build doesn't mean we end up with a product that matches our expectations. This is why we also test the implementation to learn

- Whether the product matches our expectations
- How the product might not match our expectations

Both goals are equally important. We want to ensure that we have built the right thing, but there will always be side effects, such as unintended behavior, vulnerabilities, missed expectations, and downright weirdness that might appear in our products. With our search results example, we could not only test whether the feature delivers results in the relevant order but also ask

- What if I use different search terms?
- What if the relevant results don't match the behavior of other search tools?
- What if part of the service is down when I search?
- What if I request results 1000 times in less than 5 seconds?
- What happens if there are no results?

By exploring beyond our expectations, we become more aware of what is going on in our product—warts and all. This ensures we don't end up making incorrect assumptions about how our product behaves and releasing a poor-quality product. It also means that if we find unexpected behavior, we have the choice to attempt to remove or readjust our expectations.

3.1.2 *A holistic approach to testing*

The described model of testing the imagination and implementation demonstrates that the testing goes beyond a simple confirmation of expectations and lays out a more holistic approach to testing. By implementing different activities that focus on the imagination and implementation spaces, through the testing we execute, we learn more about what we want to build and what we have built. The more we learn in these two areas, the more they align with one another. And the more they align, the more accurate our perception of quality becomes.

A team that is well-informed about their work has a better understanding of their product's quality. We are then also better equipped to decide what steps to take to improve quality. This enables us to focus our attention on specific risks, make changes in our product to align with users' expectations or determine what problems we want to invest time in to fix and which to leave alone. This is the value of good testing—to help teams get into a position where they can make these informed decisions and feel confident in the steps they are taking to develop a high-quality product.

To help us better appreciate this model, let's consider a sample context in which testing is required. For our example, we are responsible for the delivery of a fast-food ordering system. Users log on, find the restaurant they want to order from, place their order (which is sent to the restaurant), and then track the delivery of their order from within the product. A product like this one would need to be highly available, easy to use, and secure. So, to deliver a high-quality product, we might need to utilize different testing activities to focus on different types of risks, as shown in figure 3.2.

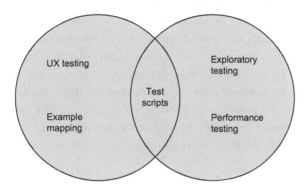

Figure 3.2 The imagination/ implementation model with sample activities shown

In the model, we can see a range of various activities that are placed in specific areas because they are focused on specific types of risks. For example, on the imagination side, we might be concerned with risks that affect the usability of a site. Therefore, we employ testing activities that focus on user experience testing and collaborative design. On the implementation side, we want to ensure the product is stable and minimize risks that might affect the product availability and application. Thus, we employ activities such as exploratory and performance testing. Finally, notice how in the area that overlaps, we have added test scripts. These are useful because they are informed by our explicit expectations (imagination) to mitigate risks around unexpected changes appearing in the product (implementation) as it grows and morphs over time, demonstrating that test scripting and automated checks are of use but are only one part of the holistic whole.

Each of these activities has different implementations, different challenges, and different ways in which tooling can help. But we wouldn't be able to easily identify these uses if we didn't understand that testing is an exercise in information gathering and knowledge sharing. With this model in place, an appreciation of the many different risks our work faces, and the testing activities that help mitigate them, we can begin to drill deeper into how tooling plays a part in testing.

3.2 How tools help with testing

You'll likely hear a tester say (or you may even have said it yourself) that there is never enough time to test everything. It will likely be repeated in this book a few times. Teams are always limited by time, budgets, meetings, staffing, and other factors, so to implement and execute effective, modern testing, we must rely on tools to help us. Tools are essential to testing, but they bring us to our next misconception around testing—that a tool, or machine, can test the way a human can.

3.2.1 Automation bias

To appreciate how machines and humans differ regarding testing, let's consider an example where both are used to test a website feature. The feature is a full-width banner for an e-commerce website with an image and some text to highlight the deal of the day. Initially, we test it manually, or in a human-led way, and observe the feature is working properly—the image is shown and all the text associated with it is correct. Then we decide to use tools to automate testing. We create code that will open the browser and assert that element A, which is where the deal of the day is loaded, exists. We run the automated test, and it passes. And then, one day, after another successful release in which all our automated tests pass, an end-user raises a bug and informs us they can't see the deal of the day. All they see is an empty white box at the top of the page.

What happened? During the process of creating the automated test, we have transferred our knowledge, which is built on implicit information based on mental heuristics and oracles, and made it explicit. We have stripped a complex understanding of a feature down to a single instruction: element A should exist on a web page. So, when the latest release of our product went out with a faulty function to retrieve the deal of the day, or the CSS was incorrect or broken, the automated test still passed because element A still exists. However, it takes a human a matter of seconds to see something is wrong.

The moral of this story isn't that tools are bad or unnecessary but that they are often misused or misinterpreted. This behavior is a type of *automation bias* that creeps into our perspective on the value of tooling, where we ascribe more value to the output of a tool than what it is relaying to us. That is, when we designed our automated test to look for element A, we assumed that all we as humans were doing was looking for element A. But we were considering many other factors, even if we weren't doing it consciously.

If we fall prey to automation bias, we run the risk of selecting and implementing tools that we believe can reveal and report information in the same way humans can, when in fact they don't, leading to misguided overconfidence in the products we're delivering, or generating a level of workload to have tools emulate human behavior that is unsustainable for a modern project. Tools cannot replace testing activities, and subscribing to that notion will ultimately lead to problems with quality and an increase in risks to a project. So instead, we have to shift our thinking more toward how tools can support our testing.

3.2.2 Being selective with tooling

Success with tools comes from situations in which some thought has been put into the problem we want to solve and what tools could potentially help. To better understand this, let's return to our deal-of-the-day feature and look closer at what a human is doing when they test a feature like this.

First, we consider different ways of testing the feature. We use our current understanding of said feature to formulate test ideas and select what we want to test first. Next, we need to set up our test. This might include setting up an environment or creating/ updating the necessary test data. (We might need to create a deal of the day to observe as well as test users to administer and view the deal.) With everything set up, we then need to execute our test, loading the browser or perhaps multiple browsers to verify that the deal renders correctly. Then once we've observed the results, we take notes or report our findings to our team, all of which would update our understanding of the feature, ready for us to start the process again. This flow can be summarized as shown in figure 3.3.

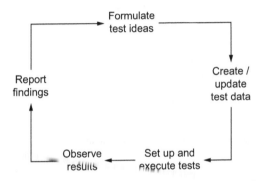

Figure 3.3 A visualization of the process of testing the deal-of-the-day feature

This cycle may be something that happens rapidly—for example, in an exploratory testing session. Or it may take place in a longer form, such as performance testing, in which each step has many details to consider. Regardless of the type of activity, to carry out the loop successfully, we need tools to complete the process. We would likely need to use tools such as database clients, test data managers, or infrastructure tools to set up state management. We would use note-taking tools, screenshot applications, and project management tools to report what has been learned. Figure 3.4 summarizes these tools used in testing by updating our initial visualization.

The visualization demonstrates how modern testing utilizes a range of tools for various tasks that occur rather than attempting to wrap the whole testing performance into the use of one tool. This is because there are many different activities at play when testing is carried out. A tool's ability to observe patterns, changes, and problems will always be limited compared to a human's observation skills. So instead, we get value from tools that do one job well, as opposed to a tool that does many things poorly.

What is so interesting about this kind of thinking is that when we take the time to consider it, it seems obvious to us. We all use tools to help us with distinct tasks that make up a larger activity. However, most of us do it without deliberate thought. Although we know that the use of tools in specific tasks is sensible, we need to develop the skills to start choosing and using tools intentionally. This means familiarizing ourselves with tools and being more in tune with what we're doing daily in our testing so that we can pick the right tool or, in the case of LLMs, the right prompt or enhancement. This is what the rest of this book will be focusing on, providing us with the skills needed to know when LLMs can help with specific tasks.

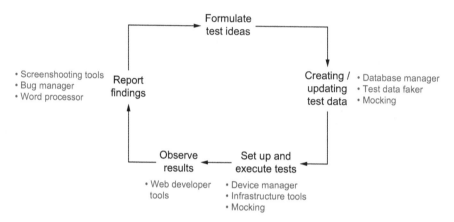

Figure 3.4   A visualization of the testing process, this time with the addition of tools

3.3   *Knowing when to use LLMs in testing*

We now understand how effective tool use in testing is about looking to enhance tasks within testing rather than replicating broad testing activities. But where do LLMs fit into this? Given their broad applications, let's take a look at some of the common ways in which LLMs are currently being used and see how each can be used to support testing.

3.3.1   *Generative capabilities*

In the vast field of artificial intelligence, LLMs fall under the banner of generative AI; that is, LLMs have been built with the purpose of generating content (which differs from other AI that may be used to predict or classify). For example, this means that if an LLM was asked to generate test cases for us, it would do so. However, just because it can generate material like test cases doesn't mean that those test cases are of value to us. We must remind ourselves that how an LLM generates outputs is based on a complex model of probabilities. This means its generative abilities differ from how we as humans might generate ideas.

If you recall, in chapter 1 we explored this concept when sending a prompt to an LLM:

(MW)   Create tests for a file upload feature

which might result in a response like this one (shortened for brevity):

 1. Test for File Upload Functionality:
- Test Case 1.1: Upload a Valid File
  - Input: Choose a file with a valid format (e.g., .jpg, .pdf).
  - Expected Outcome: The file is successfully uploaded, and a confirmation message is displayed.
- Test Case 1.2: Attempt to Upload an Invalid File
  - Input: Choose a file with an invalid format (e.g., .exe, .html).
  - Expected Outcome: An error message is displayed, indicating that the file format is not supported.

2. Test for File Size Limit:
- Test Case 2.1: Upload a File Below the Size Limit
  - Input: Choose a file smaller than the maximum allowed size.
  - Expected Outcome: The file is successfully uploaded, and a confirmation message is displayed.
- Test Case 2.2: Attempt to Upload a File Exceeding the Size Limit
  - Input: Choose a file larger than the maximum allowed size.
  - Expected Outcome: An error message is displayed, indicating that the file exceeds the maximum size limit.

How an LLM has generated these test cases is impressive, but they lack context and specificity for the feature or product we are testing. So instead, when working with LLMs, we need to make sure that how we prompt or extend them provides them with enough context to generate valuable outputs.

The consequence of ensuring that we provide sufficient context is that it's easier to use LLMs to generate outputs for very specific and targeted tasks. The alternative means we would have to provide a massive amount of input data that would result in a prompt that is expensive to build and maintain. For example, imagine the amount of context you would have to put into an LLM to obtain a test strategy relevant to our working context.

Instead, we can get more value from LLMs if we focus on using them to help with tasks such as

- *Test data generation*—When given explicit rules around data sets, LLMs can be used to generate rapid sets of data for use in a range of testing activities, from exploratory to performance testing.
- *Suggestions for risks and test ideas*—We should always avoid letting the output of an LLM be the sole arbiter of what to test. We can use them to suggest test ideas and risks that can be used as jumping-off points for new ideas or factored into our existing work.

- *Code snippets*—Similar to the earlier test case example, we gain little value from LLMs if we ask them to generate complete automated tests or frameworks. However, using them to generate smaller parts of automation or scripts used to support testing activities such as exploratory testing can be advantageous.

3.3.2 *Transformation capabilities*

Another benefit that LLMs offer is the ability to transform natural language from one structure to another. A common example of LLM transformation is language translation. Suppose that we sent something like this to an LLM:

 Convert the following text delimited by three hashes into French:

###

Hello, my name is Mark

###

Then it will return a response such as

 Bonjour, je m'appelle Mark

This is a useful way to illustrate how LLMs transform data, but we shouldn't be restricted to spoken languages only. LLMs are capable of transforming all types of data from one abstraction to another. Here are some examples that can help with testing:

- *Transforming test data*—Using LLMs to rapidly transform data from one structure to another can help speed up testing. For example, we might ask an LLM to convert plain-text test data into SQL statements or to convert SQL statements into helper functions that are called in test automation.
- *Converting code*—LLMs can convert functions, classes, and other data into new iterations of code. What makes this valuable is that LLMs can transform code into different languages but still keep the logic and flow of the original code in the newly translated output (although we should always test it to be sure).
- *Summarizing notes*—Although the conversion of data isn't as direct as, say, converting a code snippet from one language to another, we can use LLMs to transform and summarize at the same time. Also, we can use LLMs to take raw testing notes from testing activities such as exploratory or design testing sessions and have them converted into summary notes to be shared with others.

3.3.3 *Enhancing capabilities*

Finally, we can use LLMs to enhance and expand existing material. This usually means providing an LLM with a snippet of data and prompting the LLM to expand on it. This has some overlap with the generative capabilities because we're asking LLMs to generate a certain degree of new output, but in this situation, we're providing a lot more upfront context and instructing it to focus on existing material, as opposed to prompting an LLM to generate something completely new. This means we can use this ability to help us with testing tasks such as

- *Reviewing code*—Not all who conduct testing are confident coders, and even those who are comfortable with reading code can struggle at times to make sense of the code required to analyze or test. LLMs can enhance our understanding by taking code snippets and providing a natural language breakdown of how said code works, which can help with risk analysis, test design, and more.
- *Descriptive code*—Similar to reviewing code, we can use LLMs to help improve the descriptiveness of code—for example, rapidly creating code comments that can be easily created and maintained. This can be especially useful for automated testing, where communicating what our automation code is doing is important for maintenance.
- *Expanding analysis*—We can also use LLMs to expand our analysis activities, such as risk analysis and design testing (where we ask questions about requirements before the feature is built). By providing it with our current analysis data, we can ask LLMs to review and expand on it, suggesting new ideas that we can either incorporate into our analysis or ignore.

3.3.4 LLMs in use in testing

To put these different abilities of an LLM into context, let's return to our visualization of testing with the support of tools (figure 3.5).

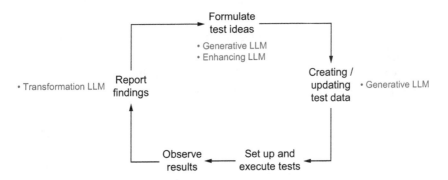

Figure 3.5   A visualization of the testing process, this time with the addition of LLMs

Here, we can see how LLMs can be inserted into distinct and specific tasks within the wider testing lifecycle. It brings us back to our area of effect model that we covered in chapter 1. Instead of attempting to use LLMs to replicate the full gamut of testing activities that exist within a lifecycle, we prioritize the best of our abilities as humans and the value we bring to testing. Then, we choose to add LLMs in select areas to expand our work so that we can move faster, learn more, and help ensure our teams are better informed so that they can build higher-quality products.

Summary

- If we have a limited understanding of what testing is, then the use of tools will also be limited.
- Testing is not a confirmatory exercise but rather a collection of different activities that help those seeking to learn about the imagination and implementation of a product.
- The imagination implies our understanding of what we want to build.
- The implementation implies our understanding of what we have built.
- As our understanding of both aspects increases, we bring them into alignment, which helps us deliver a higher-quality product.
- We run many different types of testing activities to focus on different types of risks and how they affect both imagination and implementation.
- Tools are an essential component of successful testing.
- LLMs can be used to generate, transform, and enhance outputs.
- LLMs should be used with smaller, specific tasks to generate outputs that provide value.
- LLMs can generate content that can help with specific tasks or create suggested content.
- LLMs can transform data to help convert raw data into useful formats or summarize it.
- LLMs can also enhance existing material, adding new suggestions or expanding details.
- We can insert LLMs into many distinct and specific testing tasks, which reflects the area of effect model we learned about in chapter 1.

## Part 2

Technique: Task identification and prompt engineering in testing

N ow that we've established a mindset that promotes a human-led approach, we can begin to build our techniques for using LLMs across a range of testing activities. In this part, we'll not only focus on ways in which LLMs can be employed to enhance specific tasks within testing through the use of prompt engineering and AI agents, but also learn how to identify tasks in which LLMs are beneficial. Focusing on this later skill is fundamental for success, and we'll learn why this is so by comparing examples of LLM use, focusing on broad, generalized tasks versus small, targeted tasks. By establishing clear goals and outputs with smaller tasks, we'll be better equipped for developing more valuable prompts that can be tweaked and improved using prompt-engineering techniques. All this can be utilized in an AI agent to create assistant tools that can support specific tasks. So, let's explore how task identification and prompt engineering can be applied to a wide range of testing tasks, such as development, automation, analysis, and exploration, to enhance the already valuable work we do to improve our product's quality.

AI-assisted testing for developers

4

This chapter covers

- Developing unit tests and production code with GitHub Copilot
- Developing unit tests and production code with ChatGPT

According to a poll on dev ecosystems conducted by JetBrains in 2022, 81% of respondents have a developer-to-QA ratio greater than one to one. Forty percent reported that they had "less than 1 QA per 10 developers," and only 1% reported that they had "more QAs than developers" (see www.jetbrains.com/lp/devecosystem-2022/testing.)

Understanding and building in quality is essential to delivering value to our users, yet the ratio between development and testing is nearly always imbalanced, and this is so for many reasons. Some organizational leaders choose to educate developers to build in quality with the support of quality coaches, and others simply don't want to invest in roles that advocate for testing and quality. Either way, this situation puts pressure on everyone on a team to deliver high-quality applications. So, how can artificial intelligence (AI) tools help relieve this pressure?

This chapter will specifically focus on how large language model (LLM) AIs, such as GitHub Copilot and ChatGPT, can help developers build quality into our work. Rather than thinking of these AI tools as replacements for developers and testers, we'll learn how they can guide us as we carry out activities that build in quality as we develop, as well as demonstrate how we can use AI tools to improve quality and identify risks when testing is a limited resource to take advantage of.

> **Setting up Copilot**
>
> In this chapter, we'll be looking at examples of GitHub Copilot in use. To familiarize yourself with Copilot before we try out these examples, you can find installation and operation instructions in appendix B.

4.1   *Examining the rise of the automated developer*

In April 2023, Similarweb, a market competition analysis company, reported that Stack Overflow's traffic in the preceding month had dropped by 14%. According to Similarweb, the cause was a rise in developers switching from Stack Overflow to tools such as GitHub's Copilot and ChatGPT (see https://mng.bz/5Oy4). Whether this is a sign of an ongoing trend of developers jumping ship or an anomaly that will eventually balance out, reports such as this one demonstrate the sweeping changes that LLM-based AI tools (LLMs) are introducing to the role of a developer.

As a tester, it's an interesting change to witness. For many years, as test automation tools became more advanced, I had discussions with developers about whether testing could be replaced by automated testing tools. Now, with LLMs that are trained against billions of lines of code from public and private repositories, conversations have turned toward whether developer roles can be automated. For example, a tool such as ChatGPT can be sent a prompt such as

 Write me some Java code that sends an HTTP request to a booking API

and it will then use its billions of trained weights and balances to return a working code example like this one:

```java
import java.io.BufferedReader;
import java.io.IOException;
import java.io.InputStreamReader;
import java.net.HttpURLConnection;
import java.net.URL;

public class BookingAPIClient {
    public static void main(String[] args) {
        String apiUrl = "https://api.booking.com/endpoint"; // Replace
with the actual API endpoint URL

        try {
            URL url = new URL(apiUrl);
```

```java
        HttpURLConnection connection = (HttpURLConnection)
        url.openConnection();

        // Set the request method (GET, POST, etc.)
        connection.setRequestMethod("GET");

        // Set request headers if required
        connection.setRequestProperty("Content-Type",
        "application/json");
        connection.setRequestProperty("Authorization",
        "Bearer YOUR_ACCESS_TOKEN");

        // Get the response code
        int responseCode = connection.getResponseCode();
        System.out.println("Response Code: " + responseCode);

        // Read the response
        BufferedReader reader = new BufferedReader(new
        InputStreamReader(connection.getInputStream()));
        String line;
        StringBuilder response = new StringBuilder();
        while ((line = reader.readLine()) != null) {
            response.append(line);
        }
        reader.close();

        // Print the response
        System.out.println("Response: " + response.toString());

        // Close the connection
        connection.disconnect();

    } catch (IOException e) {
        e.printStackTrace();
    }
  }
}
```

From just one basic prompt, we can use LLMs to create workable code (updating the apiUrl to a real API returned a positive result). So, it's not surprising that there are tools that combine prompts attempting to automate development work. Tools such as AutoGPT (https://github.com/Significant-Gravitas/AutoGPT) and MetaGPT (https://github.com/geekan/MetaGPT) have appeared to work as autonomous agents, generating their own prompts based on initial questions to solve complex problems. Although these tools are in their infancy, it's clear why the more hyperbolic claims of developers being automated out of their role are bandied about.

As someone who has spent much of his career explaining why test automation is not a suitable replacement, it's tempting to enjoy the schadenfreude of seeing developers defending their roles in the same way, but instead, it's more valuable to learn from the experiences of testers and the automation topic. Just as a tester's role can't be fully automated, neither can a developer's role. A development role is more than just the code that is produced. The solutions that developers create are a product of analytical skills, problem-solving, and design thinking. LLM tools give the impression of having these skills, which is not true.

Instead, developers find success with LLM tools by using them to enhance their own abilities: they may use tools such as Copilot to quickly and effectively create code that they want to build or seek advice from ChatGPT to solve issues or learn new APIs. These principles can also be applied to improving a developer's ability to build quality into an application. By combining techniques such as test-driven design (TDD) or the power of LLMs, developers can increase their productivity while ensuring that their analytical and design skills lead the charge. To help demonstrate this symbiosis, let's explore the following two examples:

- Using Copilot to rapidly generate unit checks and production code for TDD loops
- Emulating pairing with a simulated developer, courtesy of ChatGPT

Through the examples, you'll learn to set up and use these LLM tools, as well as appreciate the balance that is possible to strike between the power of AI and the abilities of developers.

> ### Experiences may vary
>
> Given that Copilot relies on predictive algorithms that are frequently trained on newly added code and updated APIs/libraries, it's worth highlighting that the output and experience you have when following the upcoming examples may be different from what has been recorded. Keep in mind that the goal of this chapter is not to replicate the examples 100%, but rather for you to become comfortable with using LLMs to assist our work in a way that helps us build in quality.

4.2 Pairing with LLMs

We've already seen that LLMs are probabilistic in nature, and as a result, it can be useful to think of them as outputting simulations of roles rather than inhabiting specific roles. An LLM has no more awareness of being a software tester than it does of being a restauranteur. But with prompt engineering, we can create prompts that frame an LLM's probabilistic output to simulate a role, helping us to create rubber ducks to interact with. This can be useful in a development capacity when testing resources are limited in either availability or capability. So, let's take a look at a couple of sample prompts we can use to elicit feedback that can help us improve the quality of our work and our products.

> ### Wait, what—rubber duck?
>
> When facing a problem that we have no solution for, it can help to verbalize the problem to others to find an answer. By articulating the problem to another person, we sometimes

find that the solution presents itself to us. However, there isn't always an opportunity to speak with colleagues; therefore, some developers will verbalize their issues to a rubber duck (or another item). Although we're sharing our challenges with an inanimate object, the experience is the same: verbalizing our challenges tricks our brains into finding solutions.

4.2.1 Analyzing ideas

Our first prompt is inspired by the shift-left testing mindset that some teams apply to help build quality into applications as early as possible. *Shift-left* testing means bringing testing analysis earlier into the development process, ideally around the point at which ideas are being discussed and details clarified. This process results in many questions being asked that help us identify issues earlier, deliver valuable features, and improve the quality of our products. Shift-left activities are an invaluable approach to improving quality and should be encouraged regardless of the use of AI in the development process. However, by introducing LLMs into the process, we can use prompts to generate questions that might reveal assumptions or misunderstandings or questions that we can simply disregard.

Let's take a look at a sample prompt that can be used to rapidly generate questions that might be useful. We use delimiters to inform the LLM where the data to analyze is found:

 You are a software testing expert. Analyze the text delimited by triple hashes and generate questions that will clarify ambiguities in the text.

We then set a series of rules around how questions are asked and output:

 * Questions will be generated by using the What, Where, Why, When, Who and How heuristic
* Multiple questions can be identified for each quality characteristic
* The quality characteristics we care about are: Accuracy, Security and Accessibility
* Output questions in the format of Question - Explanation

Few-shot prompting allows us to create an example of how we expect the output to look:

 Example:

What does relevant mean?

The acceptance criteria says relevant search results, but how do we determine what is relevant and what isn't?

We then enter the data for analysis into the delimited section of the prompt:

 ###

As a B&B owner

I want to be able to manage user access

So that I can allow different levels of access to multiple users

Features:

- DB is configured with an Admin user

- Guests are asked to create an account to make a booking

- Admin can see the accounts created on the platform and can delete them

###

The prompt outlines instructions for an LLM to analyze a user story and acceptance criteria and return a list of questions for us to consider. Notice how we also provide context in the quality characteristics instruction. If we want to focus on different characteristics, we can update these as well.

Entering this prompt into ChatGPT returned the following result:

 Accuracy:

1 What criteria are used to determine the accuracy of user access management?

Explanation: The text mentions managing user access, but it doesn't specify how accuracy is ensured in granting different levels of access to multiple users.

2 How is the system ensuring that the right access levels are assigned to users?

Explanation: The text refers to allowing different levels of access to multiple users, but it doesn't explain the mechanism for guaranteeing the accuracy of access permissions.

Security:

1 Who has access to the database configured with an Admin user?

Explanation: The text mentions configuring the database with an Admin user, but it doesn't specify who has access to this Admin account and how its security is maintained.

2 How is the platform protecting user account information and data?

Explanation: The text talks about guests creating accounts for bookings, but it lacks details about the security measures implemented to safeguard user data.

3 What security measures are in place to prevent unauthorized access to user accounts?

Explanation: The text mentions that Admin can see and delete accounts, but it doesn't explain how unauthorized access to such account management functionalities is prevented.

Accessibility:

1 What levels of accessibility are provided to different types of users?

Explanation: The text mentions managing user access with different levels, but it doesn't clarify what those levels are and how they vary based on user types.

2 How are guests guided to create accounts for booking, and is the process accessible to all users?

Explanation: The text states that guests are asked to create accounts, but it doesn't specify how this process is carried out and if it meets accessibility standards.

3 What measures are taken to ensure the platform's accessibility for users with disabilities?

Explanation: The text doesn't provide information on how accessibility is addressed for users with disabilities, and it's essential to understand the measures taken to accommodate their needs.

4 Where can we find information about the platform's accessibility features?

Explanation: The text mentions nothing about the platform's accessibility features, so it would be helpful to know where this information is available.

Reading through the response, we can see that there is an interesting collection of questions ranging in quality. For example, consider this question:

 How are guests guided to create accounts for booking, and is the process accessible to all users?

Explanation: The text states that guests are asked to create accounts, but it doesn't specify how this process is carried out and if it meets accessibility standards.

This is a helpful question that encourages us to consider in more detail the statement "Guests are asked to create an account to make a booking, "found in our user story. We could consider this question and think about how we would design the booking process to make it accessible to all types of users.

However, other questions are perhaps not quite as good. For example,

 What criteria are used to determine the accuracy of user access management?

Explanation: The text mentions managing user access, but it doesn't specify how accuracy is ensured in granting different levels of access to multiple users.

What makes this question problematic is its reference to the quality characteristic *accuracy*. Typically, accuracy would be more focused on the accuracy of data processed or stored (think bank interest rate calculations). Instead, the phrase "accuracy of user access" feels like an odd way to describe the rules set around users and what they can access. Ultimately, it's up to us to evaluate each question for suitability and use. Some questions can encourage us to build products that are more closely aligned with what a user wants and help us avoid errors, whereas other generated questions will either make little sense or cover topics already considered.

We'll come back to this prompt and how we might use it during the development of a feature, but first, let's take a look at how we can repurpose this prompt to review our code.

4.2.2   *Analyzing code*

Just as we can prompt an LLM to analyze written-down ideas, we can also have it review code and help us identify risks. Using this prompt is akin to simulating the role of a developer or tester that you are pairing with by having them analyze your work as you develop to offer suggestions for consideration. Let's check out a prompt that could be of use for this type of activity. We use delimiters to signal where the code will be, as well as check for assumptions if no code is given:

 You are a software testing expert. Analyze the code delimited by triple hashes and identify risks that might impact the code. If no code is provided, respond with "No risks could be found."

We then provide instructions around quality characteristics and output structure:

 * Risks must be related to the quality characteristics: Performance, security and interoperability

* Multiple risks can be identified for each quality characteristic

* Output identified risks in the format of Risk - Quality Characteristic - Explanation

Few-shot prompting allows us to give an example of output structure:

 Example:

Overflow - Security - Adding in large integers as parameters might cause the method to trigger a buffer overflow.

Code is provided within the instructed delimiters:

```
###
public BookingResult createBooking(Booking bookingToCreate) throws
➥SQLException {
    if(dateCheckValidator.isValid(bookingToCreate.getBookingDates())) {
        if (bookingDB.checkForBookingConflict(bookingToCreate)) {
            return new BookingResult(HttpStatus.CONFLICT);
        } else {
            CreatedBooking createdBooking =
            ➥bookingDB.create(bookingToCreate);

            if(bookingToCreate.getEmail() != null &&
            ➥bookingToCreate.getPhone() != null){
                MessageBuilder messageBuilder = new MessageBuilder();
                Message message = messageBuilder.build(bookingToCreate);

                messageRequests.postMessage(message);
            }

            return new BookingResult(createdBooking,
```

```
        HttpStatus.CREATED);
      }
   } else {
      return new BookingResult(HttpStatus.CONFLICT);
   }
}
}
###
```

After I sent the prompt with the sample code and quality characteristics to ChatGPT, the following output was returned:

 Based on the provided code snippet, let's analyze the potential risks that might affect the quality characteristics of Performance, Security, and Interoperability:

- Performance - Nested Validation:
    - Risk: The nested validation checks (`dateCheckValidator.isValid` and `bookingDB.checkForBookingConflict`) may lead to performance issues, especially when dealing with a large number of bookings.
    - Explanation: If the system has to process a substantial amount of bookings, the nested validation can result in increased execution time and resource consumption.

- Performance - Message Posting:
    - Risk: The message posting (`messageRequests.postMessage`) might introduce performance bottlenecks, affecting the overall system responsiveness.
    - Explanation: If the message posting process involves network communication or I/O operations, it could slow down the execution of the `createBooking` method.

- Security - SQL Injection:
    - Risk: The code is susceptible to SQL injection attacks as it directly uses the `bookingToCreate` object in the database queries.
    - Explanation: Malicious input in the `bookingToCreate` object could manipulate the SQL queries and compromise the integrity and security of the database.

- Security - Inadequate Authorization:
    - Risk: The code does not perform explicit authorization checks before creating bookings, potentially allowing unauthorized users to create bookings.
    - Explanation: Lack of proper authorization checks can lead to unauthorized access and misuse of the system's booking creation functionality.

- Interoperability - Platform Dependencies:
    - Risk: The code might have dependencies on specific platforms or libraries, limiting its interoperability with other systems or environments.
    - Explanation: If the `MessageBuilder` or `messageRequests` rely on platform-specific features or external libraries, it could cause issues when running the code in different environments.

- Interoperability - Error Codes:
  - Risk: The code returns HTTP status codes directly, which may not be compatible with other systems that expect different error code formats.
  - Explanation: If external systems expect error codes in a different format (e.g., JSON or XML), using HTTP status codes may hinder interoperability.

Similar to the previous prompt, which generated questions around written requirements, the quality of these different risks varies. For example, the risk "Performance - Message Posting" feels quite abstract, as we can see in its explanation:

 If the message posting process involves network communication or I/O operations, it could slow down the execution of the `createBooking` method.

Suggesting risks around network communication or I/O operations feels vague because it might refer to a range of implementations, some of which might relate to our work and some that might not.

However, other risks are more concrete and potentially useful—for example, "Security - Inadequate Authorization," which highlights the following:

 The code does not perform explicit authorization checks before creating bookings, potentially allowing unauthorized users to create bookings.

This risk feels more concrete because it refers to actions that are carried out in our method and the absence of potentially important checks within it. Of course, we may carry out authorization checks elsewhere, but the information it has given highlighted an explicit activity that we might need to discuss further to improve the security of our booking feature.

Generating more ideas

So far, we've looked at singular prompts to send to LLMs, which gives us useful responses to review. But what if we want to solicit more questions and risks? We simply ask by submitting an additional prompt, such as "Generate more questions" or "Identify further risks." Be wary, though, as this has diminishing returns. An LLM will try to fulfill our requests at the risk of increasing hallucinations. So, as options start to dry out, we may see more suggestions that are less connected to the ideas and code we wanted feedback on in the first place.

4.2.3   Recognizing that a simulation is better than nothing at all

When testing is discussed, the focus is typically on the production and execution of test cases. But a highly trained and experienced tester delivers value by using their critical and lateral thinking skills and asks questions that help view solutions in new ways and reveal potential problems. The prompts we've looked at can offer a simulation of that process. However, it's important to remember that LLMs don't have these critical and lateral thinking skills and that the questions and risks generated come from the instruction of our prompts. Instead, these types of prompts can offer a lightweight way to simulate the experience of pairing with testers or other developers when the opportunity to pair is unavailable. The key is to develop an eye for generated questions to determine which are of use.

4.3 Building in quality with AI assistance

So far, we've looked at prompts as singular activities, but now, let's turn our attention to how the prompts we've recently learned and other LLM assistant tools can be used in conjunction with TDD to help us build in quality.

Although TDD is not strictly a testing activity when compared to other testing activities, TDD that is carried out correctly helps guide developers to build quality into products. To recap, the process of TDD is to use unit-checking tools to first create failing checks and then just enough production code to make the check *pass* (and fix any other checks that may have failed). Once all our checks are passing, we can refactor our production code

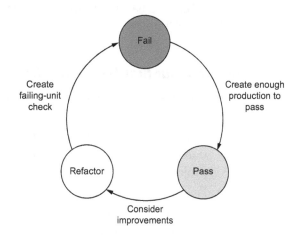

Figure 4.1 The red/green/refactor TDD cycle

while ensuring all our checks are green. Once that's complete, we start the loop again until our work is complete, as demonstrated in figure 4.1.

> ### What's all this about checks?
>
> In our Automation in Testing training, Richard Bradshaw and I make a distinction between human-led and tool-led testing. We call the latter type *automated checking* because the tools can only assert explicit actions or data that we codify into our automation. This distinction helps us better appreciate that automated tools such as unit-checking frameworks are excellent at rapidly checking small, specific changes in a product but are unable to tell us more about a system beyond its assertions. Humans, however, are slower and less deterministic in testing, although we are much more efficient at identifying many events happening simultaneously. Hence, this is why tools check and humans test. One is not better than the other, and hopefully, this book will demonstrate that we can have the best success when combining both.

This approach enables us to design products that are highly testable while ensuring we deliver what the business or end user desires.

Although its benefits are manifold (improving code design, making it more testable, and most importantly, improving its quality), some developers find it hard to adopt the TDD approach, believing that it slows down development as we create unit checks for each specific section of production code added to our system. However, with tools such as Copilot, we can learn how to establish a balance in which the tools enable us to rapidly create unit checks and build in quality.

> **Setting up Copilot**
>
> This chapter assumes that you have installed and configured the Copilot plugin within your IDE. If you haven't already completed the setup process, you can find installation instructions in appendix B.

4.4 Creating our first TDD loop with LLMs

To demonstrate, let's undergo the process of creating part of a feature for a sample timesheet manager:

- As a timesheet user, I want to be able to track time against specific projects so that I can keep a history of how much time I have spent working on individual projects.
- Features:
  - Time is tracked in half hour units.
  - To complete a timesheet, a project and amount of time must be entered.
  - Only I should be able to see my tracked time.

You can review the test and production code created as part of this example in the following GitHub repository: https://mng.bz/6YMG.

4.4.1 Preparing the work

Before starting to create my timesheet manager feature, I wanted to think about how I would go about building it. To get help with this process and encourage me to think about the solution from various angles, I took the first prompt we explored earlier in this chapter and entered my context into it. Specifically, I changed the quality characteristics to accuracy and consistency and added the user story into the delimited section at the bottom of the prompt:

 You are a software testing expert. Analyze the text delimited by triple hashes and generate questions that will clarify ambiguities in the text.

- * Questions will be generated by using the What, Where, Why, When, Who and How heuristic
- * Multiple questions can be identified for each quality characteristic
- * The quality characteristics we care about are: Accuracy and Consistency
- * Output questions in the format of Question - Explanation

Example:

What does relevant mean?

The acceptance criteria say relevant search results, but how do we determine what is relevant and what isn't?

###

As a timesheet user

I want to be able to track time against specific projects

So that I can keep a history of how much time I have spent working on individual projects

Features:

- Time is tracked in half hour units

- To complete a timesheet a project and amount of time must be entered

- Only I should be able to see my tracked time

###

Sending this prompt to ChatGPT returned the following response:

 Accuracy:

- What is the required precision for tracking time in half-hour units? - The text mentions that time is tracked in half-hour units. It's important to know the level of accuracy required for this tracking.

- How will the system handle invalid time entries? - Since time must be entered to complete a timesheet, what measures are in place to ensure that only valid time entries are accepted?

- What validation mechanisms are in place to prevent users from entering incorrect time data? - To maintain accuracy, it's essential to know how the system will validate and handle potential data entry errors.

- How will the system handle time zone differences for users in different locations? - This is important to ensure that the tracked time is consistent and accurate for users in various time zones.

Consistency:

- Where will the history of tracked time be stored and accessed? - To ensure consistency, it's important to know where the data will be stored and how users can access it.

- What are the rules for displaying and formatting tracked time information? - Consistency in displaying the tracked time across the system is crucial for a seamless user experience.

- Who is responsible for verifying and maintaining the consistency of tracked time data? – It's essential to assign responsibility for data integrity and consistency to avoid discrepancies.

- When and how often will the timesheet data be synchronized or updated? - Ensuring consistency in real-time updates or scheduled syncs is vital to avoid discrepancies between users' data.

- How will the system handle potential conflicts if multiple users try to update the same project's timesheet simultaneously? - Maintaining consistency in data updates when multiple users are involved is critical to prevent data loss or inaccuracies.

- What security measures are in place to protect the data and ensure its integrity? - Consistency also involves safeguarding the data from unauthorized access or tampering.

> **What are quality characteristics?**
>
> Quality means very different things to different people and is a multifaceted concept. Therefore, when attempting to understand what quality means to a stakeholder or end user, we break out ways of thinking about it into different characteristics. For example, quality characteristics might include look and feel, usability, compliance, and much more. Different projects will have different quality characteristics that we prioritize, and it's up to us as teams to identify what quality characteristics are of priority to us and our users.

From here, I read each of the questions sent back to me and noted the ones that stood out as raising points I hadn't considered. Let's go through some of them and explore my thinking behind each one:

 How will the system handle invalid time entries? / What validation mechanisms are in place to prevent users from entering incorrect time data?

These two questions felt very similar, but they highlighted that I will, at some point, need to add date–time handling into the code to prevent problems around invalid entries.

 How will the system handle time zone differences for users in different locations?

It's a good question, but not relevant to this work as I plan to just track the amount of time carried out and not when it was carried out (at least for now).

 What are the rules for displaying and formatting tracked time information?

Connected to the previous question, I opted for simply tracking the amount of time that had elapsed and not specifically when it had occurred, meaning that the displaying of information is relatively straightforward.

How will the system handle potential conflicts if multiple users try to update the same project's timesheet simultaneously?

At this time, there is no multiple-user feature, although it might be introduced later, so I make a note to consider this for future iterations.

Many more questions could be asked and addressed, but what this process demonstrates is that, by generating different questions, I am required to think about various aspects of this feature's design. Some I can choose to rule out, or shelve for later conversation, and some help me to improve the quality of my feature by raising my awareness to validation and date–time formatting.

4.4.2 Loop 1: Save a timesheet entry

With the questions from the previous prompt in my mind, I start my first loop by creating an empty maven project within my IDE before heading to the pom.xml to add my required dependencies. I require JUnit 5 to build my unit checks, so I entered the comment

```
<!--    Junit jupiter engine-->
```

Copilot returns the following code block:

```
<dependencies>
    <dependency>
        <groupId>org.junit.jupiter</groupId>
        <artifactId>junit-jupiter-engine</artifactId>
        <version>5.8.2</version>
        <scope>test</scope>
    </dependency>
</dependencies>
```

At the time of writing, the proposed version of `junit-jupiter-engine` is an older version, so I update to `5.9.2` as shown here:

```
<dependencies>
    <dependency>
        <groupId>org.junit.jupiter</groupId>
        <artifactId>junit-jupiter-engine</artifactId>
        <version>5.9.2</version>
        <scope>test</scope>
    </dependency>
</dependencies>
```

This required update is a good example of how data provenance can affect what is being suggested. While constantly being trained on code that is being pushed to GitHub, Copilot runs the risk of lagging behind the latest versions of libraries and APIs. So, we need to be vigilant when adding in dependencies via AI code assistants to ensure they are suggesting the version we want.

Furthermore, what is demonstrated here is how the Copilot IDE plugin will take code (or in this case a code comment) I have written, add it to a prompt, and then send it to the Copilot LLM to process. The LLM then sends back to the IDE plugin a suggestion of what to enter next, and the plugin then presents me with the suggestion. I now have the option to either accept the suggestion by hitting Tab or continue to write my own code.

Much like other LLMs, Copilot is triggered by prompts. But unlike a chat-based LLM (such as ChatGPT), Copilot is tuned to process code-based rather than text-based prompts. This distinction is important because it highlights both the benefits of different types of fine-tuned LLMs for different activities, as well as the need to write prompts that work for different prompt types. This is why TDD and AI assistants are an interesting combination to work with. The unit checks we create not only frame the design of our work but also serve as prompts to inform how we want to implement features.

For example, for our first check, I prompt Copilot to create my first unit check for me by adding the following comment into a new class titled `TimesheetTest` in `src/test/java`:

```
// Test that when a timesheet is submitted with a project name
 and hours it returns true
```

This triggers Copilot to suggest the following unit check:

```
@Test
public void testSubmitTimesheetWithProjectNameAndHours() {
    Timesheet timesheet = new Timesheet();
    boolean result = timesheet.submitTimesheet("Project 1", 8);
    assertEquals(true, result);
}
```

Looking at this suggested check, we see that it has the necessary details we require. It's given the class I intend to build a sensible name of `Timesheet` and suggested the method `submitTimesheet` with the correct parameters of project name and hours. This check is enough of a prompt that when I create a new class `Timesheet` in `src/main/java`, Copilot suggests

```
public boolean submitTimesheet(String projectName, int duration) {
    return true;
}
```

The unit check served as a prompt to Copilot to create my production code, and although what has been produced is not exactly exciting, the check has been fulfilled. We can also see that Copilot works by building prompts on prompts to get to what we want. First, I created a prompt in the form of a code comment to help Copilot suggest the code for the unit check, and then that unit check served as a prompt for the suggested production code. As the unit checks grow, so will the prompts and directions to Copilot on what to build. Now, let's look at how I used this process to build out the `submitTimesheet` method.

4.4.3   *Loop 2: Retrieve a timesheet entry*

With the first loop, I created the skeleton of my project, but at the moment, the actual production code bears little fruit. So, with the second loop, I looked to add more features to the `Timesheet` class to help flesh out the `submitTimesheet` method. Again, I start by adding a new comment prompt to `TimesheetTest`:

 `// Test that when timesheets are added they can be retrieved as a list`

And upon creating a new line, Copilot returned the following check as a suggestion:

```
@Test
public void testAddTimesheetsToList() {
    Timesheet timesheet = new Timesheet();
    timesheet.submitTimesheet("Project 1", 8);
    timesheet.submitTimesheet("Project 2", 8);
    timesheet.submitTimesheet("Project 3", 8);
    assertEquals(3, timesheet.getTimesheets().size());
}
```

This time, the generated check is using the `submitTimesheet` method to create some data that I can then verify using the newly created `getTimesheets` method. So, heading over to the `Timesheet` class, I use Copilot to generate the necessary `getTimesheets` method, which returns

```
public Collection<Timesheet> getTimesheets() {
    return null;
}
```

Although it's helpful that it created the method signature for me, the internals of the method are not so useful. However, I add the following to the top of the class:

```
private HashMap<String, Integer> timesheets = new HashMap<>();
```

Then I return to the `submitTimesheet` method and remove `return true` from inside the method. When I enter the keyword `if` into the statement, Copilot returns

```
public boolean submitTimesheet(String projectName, int duration) {
    if (projectName != null && duration > 0) {
        timesheets.put(projectName, duration);
        return true;
    } else {
        return false;
    }
}
```

This is a useful demonstration of how a project requires a degree of warmup before the LLM can return more accurate suggestions when working with Copilot. By returning to the `submitTimesheet` method, removing its contents, and then waiting for Copilot to respond, I get a refreshed response from Copilot based on the new details I've provided. Just as a prompt for a chat LLM requires clear and explicit details, so does Copilot. The initial stock methods that were returned from Copilot for `Timesheet` are likely because there is little context to work with. Essentially, the prompts sent to Copilot lack information. But as I create new unit checks and additional code to show our intent in our code, the suggestions become more useful.

This is also demonstrated when I delete the `getTimesheets` method entirely. With the new `HashMap` added to the class, my updated code prompts Copilot to return an updated version of the method:

```
public Collection<Integer> getTimesheets() {
    return timesheets.values();
}
```

Running both of my unit checks after this loop, I can see both checks are passing and now have working code that is a bit more feature rich than when I started the loop.

4.4.4   Loop 3: Calculating times for a project

For the final loop, I went back to the questions returned from ChatGPT and thought about the question:

MW How will the system handle potential conflicts if multiple users try to update the same project's timesheet simultaneously?

Although there is no functionality for multiple users at this point in the project, the question from ChatGPT did make me think about how to handle multiple timesheet submissions to the same project. So, I created my third unit check to handle this scenario by once again creating a code comment to prompt Copilot for another unit check:

MW `// Test that the total hours worked can be calculated from a list` `of timesheets from one project`

It returned the following unit check:

```
@Test
public void testCalculateTotalHoursWorked() {
    Timesheet timesheet = new Timesheet();
    timesheet.submitTimesheet("Project 1", 8);
    timesheet.submitTimesheet("Project 1", 8);
    timesheet.submitTimesheet("Project 1", 8);
    assertEquals(24, timesheet.getTimesheets().stream()
.mapToInt(Integer::intValue)
.sum());
}
```

This time, the suggested check is close, but I want the `Timesheet` class to return a total, not have a total processed within the unit check itself. So, I opted to update the check to explicitly state there is a method for getting total timesheet hours:

```
@Test
public void testCalculateTotalHoursWorked() {
    Timesheet timesheet = new Timesheet();
    timesheet.submitTimesheet("Project 1", 8);
    timesheet.submitTimesheet("Project 1", 8);
    timesheet.submitTimesheet("Project 1", 8);

    int total = timesheet.getTotalTimesheetHours("Project 1");

    assertEquals(24, total);
}
```

Heading back over to `Timesheet` and waiting for Copilot, the LLM returns the following code:

```
public int getTotalTimesheetHours(String projectName) {
    return timesheets.get(projectName);
}
```

This allows the code to compile, but my new unit check fails because the project count isn't being updated. Instead, because I am using a `HashMap`, the count is being overwritten. I need to update `submitTimesheet` to handle duplicate projects, which I do by dropping the following comment into `submitTimesheet`, just after the initial `if` statement:

```
// Check to see if project already exists
```

Dropping in the code comment returns the following suggested code:

```
if (timesheets.containsKey(projectName)) {
    // If it does, add the new duration to the existing total
    duration += timesheets.get(projectName);
}
```

This expands the `submitTimesheet` function to allow it to increase the duration of existing projects in a timesheet:

```
public boolean submitTimesheet(String projectName, int duration) {
    if (projectName != null && duration > 0) {
        // Check to see if project already exists
        if (timesheets.containsKey(projectName)) {
            // If it does, add the new duration to the existing total
            duration += timesheets.get(projectName);
        }
        timesheets.put(projectName, duration);
        return true;
    } else {
        return false;
    }
}
```

A final run of my three-unit checks confirms that they are all passing and that I have all the features I want in my Timesheet class. However, the code is starting to become more complex, so I turn my attention to refactoring my code with the use of ChatGPT.

4.4.5 *Refactoring code*

One benefit of pairing with others is the ability for a pair partner to see potential problems and risks that we might not see. However, in the absence of a pair partner, I chose to use the second of the prompts we explored earlier in this chapter—specifically, the prompt that analyzes code and returns suggestions. Taking the prompt and adding my code and the quality characteristics' accuracy and consistency, I sent the following prompt to ChatGPT. I slightly updated the instructions to make it clear I am providing Java code:

 You are a software testing expert. Analyze the Java code delimited by triple hashes and identify risks that might impact the code. If no code is provided, respond with "No risks could be found"

I update the additional instructions with my quality characteristics:

 * Risks must be related to the quality characteristics: Accuracy and Consistency

* Multiple risks can be identified for each quality characteristic

* Output identified risks in the format of Risk - Quality Characteristic - Explanation

An example is provided to demonstrate the format of the response:

 Example:

Overflow - Security - Adding in large integers as parameters might cause the method to trigger a buffer overflow.

The code I created from my earlier loops is added in the delimited section:

```
###
public class Timesheet {

    private HashMap<String, Integer> timesheets = new HashMap<>();

    public boolean submitTimesheet(String projectName, int duration) {
        if (projectName != null && duration > 0) {
            // Check to see if project already exists
            if (timesheets.containsKey(projectName)) {
                // If it does, add the new duration to the
                // existing total
                duration += timesheets.get(projectName);
            }
            timesheets.put(projectName, duration);
            return true;
        } else {
            return false;
```

```
        }
    }

    public Collection<Integer> getTimesheets() {
        return timesheets.values();
    }

    public int getTotalTimesheetHours(String projectName) {
        return timesheets.get(projectName);
    }
}
###
```

Sending the prompt returned the following risks that I might want to consider:

 Risk 1 - Accuracy - `submitTimesheet` method can overwrite existing duration:

The `submitTimesheet` method allows adding a new duration to an existing project's total if the project already exists in the timesheets. However, this approach may not always ensure accuracy. If the user intends to submit a correction or update the duration for a specific project, this method will not provide accurate results. It merely adds the new duration to the existing one without considering the possibility of editing or deleting a previous entry.

Risk 2 - Consistency - Null key in timesheets HashMap:

The timesheets HashMap allows null keys. This might lead to inconsistency issues when querying for timesheet information by project name. If a project with a null name is mistakenly added to the timesheets, it may cause issues in subsequent operations, leading to unexpected behavior.

Risk 3 - Consistency - Lack of validation for project names:

The `submitTimesheet` method does not validate the project name before adding it to the timesheets HashMap. This lack of validation might result in inconsistent data, such as duplicate or improperly formatted project names. For example, if two different variations of the same project name (e.g., `"ProjectA"` and `"projecta"`) are added, the system might treat them as separate projects, leading to inconsistencies in reporting or querying.

Risk 4 - Accuracy - `getTotalTimesheetHours` method may throw `NullPointer-Exception`:

The `getTotalTimesheetHours` method directly calls `timesheets.get(project-Name)`, which may throw a `NullPointerException` if the given `projectName` is not present in the timesheets HashMap. This can lead to inaccurate results if the method is used without checking for the existence of the project name in the timesheets before calling this method.

Risk 5 - Accuracy - Return type of `getTotalTimesheetHours` method:

The `getTotalTimesheetHours` method returns an int data type, which might lead to accuracy issues if the actual total timesheet hours for a project exceed the maximum value that an int can hold. This can result in data loss due to overflow if the sum of durations for a project exceeds `Integer.MAX_VALUE`.

Risk 6 - Consistency - Lack of synchronization in a multi-threaded environment:

If this `Timesheet` class is used in a multi-threaded environment, there is a risk of inconsistent behavior since the methods of this class are not synchronized. This can lead to data corruption or incorrect calculations if multiple threads concurrently access and modify the timesheets HashMap.

Unlike the questions prompt, this response appears to call out specific items of my code and gives reasons for how things might go wrong. With this response, I have the following options:

1 Review each risk on a case-by-case basis and then mitigate the ones I feel are important and ignore the others.

2 Ignore the proposed risks entirely, or perhaps send another prompt to ChatGPT to see whether there are more risks.

3 Use the response from ChatGPT as a prompt in and of itself to help me refactor my code.

For the purposes of this demonstration, I chose to go with the third option and send an additional prompt to ChatGPT:

MW   Refactor the code to mitigate the risks suggested. Check to see that each risk has been mitigated before outputting the solution.

Notice how I used the time-to-think principle to get the LLM to check whether each risk has actually been mitigated by the refactored code it suggested. This helps increase the likelihood that the code that's returned will be useful. Sending this prompt to ChatGPT returned the following code:

```java
import java.util.Collection;
import java.util.concurrent.ConcurrentHashMap;

public class Timesheet {                                    Changes HashMap to
                                                            ConcurrentHashMap
    private ConcurrentHashMap<String, Long> timesheets =
new ConcurrentHashMap<>();

    public boolean submitTimesheet(String projectName, long duration) {
        if (projectName != null && duration > 0) {
            // Perform validation on project name by converting it to
            // lowercase
            projectName = projectName.toLowerCase();              Adds in additional
                                                                  code to lowercase
                                                                  project names
            // Check to see if project already exists
            timesheets.put(projectName, timesheets
            .getOrDefault(projectName, 0L) + duration);
            return true;
```

```
        } else {
            return false;
        }
    }

    public Collection<Long> getTimesheets() {
        return timesheets.values();
    }

    public long getTotalTimesheetHours(String projectName) {
        return timesheets.getOrDefault(projectName.toLowerCase(), 0L);
    }
}
```

Converts the int
data type to long

To check whether these modifications hold up, I copied the suggested code into `Timesheet`, modified `testCalculateTotalHoursWorked` to take a `long` instead of an `int` in `TimesheetTest`, and discovered that my checks still pass and I refactored my code.

However, has this improved my code? To confirm, I run the original code analysis prompt with my updated code again and receive new risks:

 Risk - Accuracy - Case Sensitivity Issue:

Explanation: The method `submitTimesheet` converts the `projectName` to lowercase before using it as a key in the timesheets map. This conversion might lead to inaccurate data retrieval if there are projects with the same name but different letter cases (e.g., `"ProjectA"` and `"projecta"` will be considered the same project).

Risk - Consistency - Inconsistent Data Entry:

Explanation: The `submitTimesheet` method does not enforce consistent data entry for `projectName` values. If different users enter project names in various formats (e.g., `"Project A"`, `"project-A"`, `"project_A"`), it could lead to multiple entries for what should be the same project in the timesheets map.

Risk - Accuracy - Missing Validation for Duration:

Explanation: Although the method `submitTimesheet` checks for a positive duration, it does not handle cases where the duration is 0 or negative. This could lead to incorrect data being recorded in the timesheets map.

Risk - Consistency - Lack of Input Sanitization:

Explanation: The `submitTimesheet` method does not sanitize the `projectName` input, which could lead to inconsistent data due to invalid characters or unexpected inputs.

Risk - Accuracy - Potential Data Loss:

Explanation: The method `submitTimesheet` returns a boolean value, but it does not provide any feedback or error handling mechanism if the submission fails. This lack of feedback could lead to data loss if the submission fails silently, and the user is not aware of the issue.

What is interesting in this response is I can confirm that some risks have been mitigated such as

 Risk 5 - Accuracy - Return type of `getTotalTimesheetHours` method:

The `getTotalTimesheetHours` method returns an int data type, which might lead to accuracy issues if the actual total timesheet hours for a project exceed the maximum value that an int can hold. This can result in data loss due to overflow if the sum of durations for a project exceeds `Integer.MAX_VALUE`.

However, it appears that there are still some risks that haven't mitigated. For example, in the first list of risks I received the following risk:

 Risk 3 - Consistency - Lack of validation for project names:

The `submitTimesheet` method does not validate the project name before adding it to the timesheets HashMap. This lack of validation might result in inconsistent data, such as duplicate or improperly formatted project names. For example, if two different variations of the same project name (e.g., `"ProjectA"` and `"projecta"`) are added, the system might treat them as separate projects, leading to inconsistencies in reporting or querying.

It was handled by ChatGPT implementing a `lowerCase` method to help sanitize the project name. However, on the second analysis, I was returned the following:

 Risk - Consistency - Inconsistent Data Entry:

Explanation: The `submitTimesheet` method does not enforce consistent data entry for `projectName` values. If different users enter project names in various formats (e.g., `"Project A"`, `"project-A"`, `"project_A"`), it could lead to multiple entries for what should be the same project in the timesheets map.

This risk is very similar to the original, allegedly mitigated, risk. It feels like this additional risk around inconsistent data entry should have been handled properly when my code was refactored. I could once again ask the LLM to refactor my code for me, but instead given the potential for going around in circles with the LLM, it would be sensible for me to take the lead and fix the problems myself. This is an important skill to develop—knowing when to rely on an LLM and when to take charge.

The reason this choice is important can be highlighted by one of the other suggested risks that came from the second round of analysis. Specifically,

 Risk - Accuracy - Missing Validation for Duration:

Explanation: Although the method `submitTimesheet` checks for a positive duration, it does not handle cases where the duration is 0 or negative. This could lead to incorrect data being recorded in the timesheets map.

This sounds like a convincing risk, but it's a demonstration of a hallucination. As the code stands, if the duration is ≥0, the method simply returns false and bails out of the timesheet storage:

```
if (projectName != null && duration > 0)
```

LLMs can be biased sometimes to prioritize giving an answer regardless of its quality, meaning the more times we ask an LLM to analyze our code, the more likely it will start to generate hallucinations to give the impression that it's producing useful results rather than returning with a response that no useful information can be shared. This is why we must keep careful tabs on when it's beneficial to use an LLM.

At this point, I chose to stop the use case as what we've covered demonstrates the way in which different types of LLMs can help me in different ways. Copilot offers the ability to rapidly generate code, but it requires code-based prompts to help it with its suggestions. What this means is that if we're working on a fresh project that has very little production code for our LLM to analyze, we're more likely to get results from Copilot that aren't useful to us. So, to improve the quality of the output from Copilot, we give it more context using unit checks. This helps not only guide Copilot in the building of our code, but also provides us with the benefits of TDD including well-designed, testable code.

With ChatGPT, we've demonstrated that it can be a useful tool for analysis when prompted correctly. Building prompts able to analyze ideas and code and suggest risks and improvements can rapidly offer us alternative perspectives to consider, which we can then either act upon or reject. Utilizing the LLM as a simulation of a role that advocates quality can help us improve our work.

4.5 *Improving documentation and communication with LLMs*

It might not seem so, but communicating the work we've done through code comments and release notes can contribute significantly to product quality. By sharing new developments and changes to code bases, we can help fellow developers understand how our work affects theirs, guide testers in what to focus on when testing our work, and even help how users view our products (for example, Slack's early release notes helped market their tooling with their clear communication and humor).

Despite these benefits, documentation and release notes are sometimes left to languish at the end of a development cycle or are ignored entirely. This makes sense, given the time required to write and maintain code comments and release notes that are useful and relevant, especially when there is time pressure to be constantly delivering new features. However, with the use of LLMs, we can reduce that time overhead while ensuring we generate useful documentation that creates value for future readers. So, let's take a look at some useful prompts that can rapidly generate documentation for us.

4.5.1 *Generating code comments*

Although we should always strive to create code arranged in a way that is fluent and easy to parse, regardless of experience with a code base, code comments can provide the extra detail that prevents code misuse and speeds up development. This is even more important if we're releasing APIs that will be used by others. (I've on many occasions wasted time trying to understand how a library works from poorly documented API docs.) The challenge is to get the right balance in code comments: too few, and the person reading your code is left to fend for themselves; too much, and we create more work for ourselves in maintaining code and comments to ensure they align.

So, instead, let's take a look at a prompt that can take care of the process of annotating our work with comments for us. I use the check-the-solution tactics to ensure the code is not altered:

 You are a Java Developer. Update the code delimited by three hashes and add in code comments to explain how the code works. Check that no parts of the code have been changed before outputting the completed code commented code.

Next, I use delimiter tactics to state where the code is:

```
###
import java.util.*;
import java.util.concurrent.ConcurrentHashMap;

public class Timesheet {

    private ConcurrentHashMap<String, Long> timesheets = new
    ConcurrentHashMap<>();

    public boolean submitTimesheet(String projectName, long duration) {
        if (projectName != null && duration > 0) {
            projectName = projectName.toLowerCase();

            timesheets.put(projectName,
            timesheets.getOrDefault(projectName, 0L) + duration);
            return true;
        } else {
            return false;
        }
    }

    public Collection<Long> getTimesheets() {
        return timesheets.values();
    }

    public long getTotalTimesheetHours(String projectName) {
        return timesheets.getOrDefault(projectName.toLowerCase(), 0L);
    }

}
###
```

In this prompt, we use the usual delimiter tactics to provide our code that we would like to see commented, but we also want to ensure that the LLM doesn't change our code to make it align with the comments it creates. So, we also make it explicit within the prompt to check that no parts of the code have been changed before outputting the completed commented code. Sending this prompt with our example code from earlier to ChatGPT returned the following commented code:

```java
import java.util.*;
import java.util.concurrent.ConcurrentHashMap;

public class Timesheet {

    // ConcurrentHashMap to store project timesheets where the key is
    // the project name (in lowercase) and the value is the total duration.
    private ConcurrentHashMap<String, Long> timesheets = new
    ConcurrentHashMap<>();

    // Method to submit a timesheet entry for a project.
    public boolean submitTimesheet(String projectName, long duration) {
        if (projectName != null && duration > 0) {
            // Normalize the project name to lowercase to ensure case
            // insensitive matching.
            projectName = projectName.toLowerCase();

            // Update the timesheet entry for the project by adding
            // the submitted duration.
            timesheets.put(projectName,
            timesheets.getOrDefault(projectName, 0L) + duration);
            return true; // Submission successful
        } else {
            return false; // Invalid input, submission failed
        }
    }

    // Method to retrieve all timesheet durations.
    public Collection<Long> getTimesheets() {
        return timesheets.values();
    }

    // Method to get the total hours for a specific project.
    public long getTotalTimesheetHours(String projectName) {
        // Retrieve the total duration for the specified project
        // (case-insensitive) or return 0 if not found.
        return timesheets.getOrDefault(projectName.toLowerCase(), 0L);
    }
}
```

As we can see, the methods and sections of code within them have now been annotated with comments to give us more detail. What stands out most are comments such as

```java
// ConcurrentHashMap to store project timesheets where the key is the
// project name (in lowercase) and the value is the total duration.
private ConcurrentHashMap<String, Long> timesheets = new
ConcurrentHashMap<>();
```

The comment provides not only references to what `ConcurrentHashMap` is used for, but also highlights that all project names will be stored in lowercase, a reference to part of the code inside `submitTimesheet`, which does stand in contrast to comments like these that feel a little unnecessary:

```
// Method to submit a timesheet entry for a project.
public boolean submitTimesheet(String projectName, long duration)
```

Once again, we choose what to use. Although the prompt we've used has provided us with comments, we've observed that some are probably more useful than others. Thus, our role changes from being the author of comments to an editor, selecting and tweaking the comments that seem the most useful.

Maintaining code comments with prompts

What makes this process so useful is that when we inevitably come to a point in which our code changes and our comments need updating, we simply can run the prompt again with our updated code to regenerate our comments to incorporate our changes.

A final observation is that although the comments can be useful for someone reading our code directly, what if we want to provide more structured documentation in the form of, say, Javadoc? In that case, we can modify the prompt and use structured data tactics to create a prompt. We'll use an updated prompt with structured data tactics for Javadoc:

You are a Java Developer. Update the code delimited by three hashes and add in code comments in a Javadoc format to explain how the code works. Check that no parts of the code have been changed before outputting the completed code commented code.

We then provide the code using delimiter tactics:

```
###
import java.util.*;
import java.util.concurrent.ConcurrentHashMap;

public class Timesheet {

    private ConcurrentHashMap<String, Long> timesheets =
    new ConcurrentHashMap<>();

    public boolean submitTimesheet(String projectName, long duration) {
        if (projectName != null && duration > 0) {
                projectName = projectName.toLowerCase();

            timesheets.put(projectName,
            timesheets.getOrDefault(projectName, 0L) + duration);
            return true;
        } else {
            return false;
        }
    }
}
```

```
public Collection<Long> getTimesheets() {
    return timesheets.values();
}

public long getTotalTimesheetHours(String projectName) {
    return timesheets.getOrDefault(projectName.toLowerCase(), 0L);
}

}
###
```

Sending this prompt with our example code to ChatGPT produces

```
import java.util.*;
import java.util.concurrent.ConcurrentHashMap;

/**
 * Represents a timesheet management system for tracking hours spent on
 * different projects.
 */
public class Timesheet {

    // A concurrent hash map to store project names and their
    // corresponding total hours
    private ConcurrentHashMap<String, Long> timesheets = new
    ConcurrentHashMap<>();

    /**
     * Submits a timesheet entry for a project.
     *
     * @param projectName The name of the project.
     * @param duration    The duration in hours to be submitted.
     * @return true if the submission was successful, false otherwise.
     */
    public boolean submitTimesheet(String projectName, long duration) {
        if (projectName != null && duration > 0) {
            // Normalize the project name to lowercase for consistency
            projectName = projectName.toLowerCase();

            // Update the total hours for the project or add a new
            // entry if it doesn't exist
            timesheets.put(projectName,
timesheets.getOrDefault(projectName, 0L) + duration);
            return true;
        } else {
            return false;
        }
    }

    /**
     * Retrieves a collection of all total timesheet hours for all
     * projects.
     *
     * @return A collection of total hours for all projects.
     */
```

```
    public Collection<Long> getTimesheets() {
        return timesheets.values();
    }

    /**
     * Retrieves the total timesheet hours for a specific project.
     *
     * @param projectName The name of the project.
     * @return The total hours spent on the specified project, or 0
     * if the project is not found.
     */
    public long getTotalTimesheetHours(String projectName) {
        // Normalize the project name to lowercase for consistency
        // and retrieve the total hours
        return timesheets.getOrDefault(projectName.toLowerCase(), 0L);
    }
}
```

Using this prompt, we've improved the quality of some of the comments and also created Javadoc-friendly comments that can be used to document our code for external users. Now we only have to tweak and edit at the points we see fit.

4.5.2   Generating release notes

Just as we can use a LLM to modify our code to add comments, we can also use LLMs to transform our code base into release notes that can be consumed by others in the team and beyond. To do this, we create a new prompt with the following details; we check the solution tactics to ensure the release notes are legible:

 You are a Java Developer. Convert the code delimited by three hashes into a bullet-pointed set of release notes that describes how the code works. Check that the release notes can be read by someone who has no experience with the code created before outputting it.

We add an additional instruction to reduce the wordiness of the release notes:

 * Only output the release notes.

Then we use delimiter tactics to state where the code is:

```
###
import java.util.*;
import java.util.concurrent.ConcurrentHashMap;

public class Timesheet {

    private ConcurrentHashMap<String, Long> timesheets =
    ➥new ConcurrentHashMap<>();

    public boolean submitTimesheet(String projectName, long duration) {
        if (projectName != null && duration > 0) {
                projectName = projectName.toLowerCase();
```

```
                timesheets.put(projectName,
                    timesheets.getOrDefault(projectName, 0L) + duration);
                return true;
            } else {
                return false;
            }
        }

        public Collection<Long> getTimesheets() {
            return timesheets.values();
        }

        public long getTotalTimesheetHours(String projectName) {
            return timesheets.getOrDefault(projectName.toLowerCase(), 0L);
        }

    }
    ###
```

The prompt follows a similar pattern to the previous code comment-focused prompt, but this time, instead of asking it to inject comments into our code, we instruct that the code be transformed into natural language release notes. For example, sending the prompt with the sample code to ChatGPT returned

 Release Notes:

* The code defines a Java class named `Timesheet` that is used to manage timesheet data.

* It uses a `ConcurrentHashMap` to store timesheet entries, where project names (in lowercase) are associated with their respective durations (in hours).

* The `submitTimesheet` method allows users to submit timesheet entries. It requires a project name and a positive duration as parameters. If these conditions are met, it stores the duration associated with the project name in the map. If not, it returns false.

* The `getTimesheets` method returns a collection of all recorded timesheet durations.

* The `getTotalTimesheetHours` method allows users to retrieve the total duration for a specific project name (case-insensitive). If the project name is not found, it returns 0.

Note: Ensure that project names are provided in lowercase when using the `submit-Timesheet` method to avoid case sensitivity issues when retrieving total timesheet hours.

The result we get is in a completely different format compared to our original code that attempts to detail what our code base does. Reviewing the output, it does feel quite technical, which makes sense considering we've asked for detailed notes on a small amount of code. However, even these release notes can be of use because we can adapt an earlier prompt for suggesting risks to analyze the notes. We use delimiters to signal where the release notes will be:

 You are a software testing expert. Analyze the release notes delimited by triple hashes and identify risks that might impact the code. If no code is provided, respond with "No risks could be found."

We then provide instructions around quality characteristics and output structure:

 * Risks must be related to the quality characteristics: Performance, security and interoperability

* Multiple risks can be identified for each quality characteristic

* Output identified risks in the format of Risk - Quality Characteristic - Explanation

Few-shot prompting allows us to give an example of output structure

 Example:

Overflow - Security - Adding in large integers as parameters might cause the method to trigger a buffer overflow.

Release notes are provided within the instructed delimiters:

 ###

Release Notes:

* The code defines a Java class named `Timesheet` that is used to manage timesheet data.

* It uses a `ConcurrentHashMap` to store timesheet entries, where project names (in lowercase) are associated with their respective durations (in hours).

* The `submitTimesheet` method allows users to submit timesheet entries. It requires a project name and a positive duration as parameters. If these conditions are met, it stores the duration associated with the project name in the map. If not, it returns false.

* The `getTimesheets` method returns a collection of all recorded timesheet durations.

* The `getTotalTimesheetHours` method allows users to retrieve the total duration for a specific project name (case-insensitive). If the project name is not found, it returns 0.

Note: Ensure that project names are provided in lowercase when using the `submit-Timesheet` method to avoid case sensitivity issues when retrieving total timesheet hours.

###

Using this prompt in ChatGPT returned the following suggested risks:

Concurrent Modification - Performance - The use of `ConcurrentHashMap` may not be suitable for high concurrent access, leading to performance bottlenecks if there are frequent modifications to the timesheet entries by multiple users simultaneously.

Lack of Input Validation - Security - The `submitTimesheet` method lacks proper input validation. It only checks for positive durations but does not validate the project name, making it vulnerable to injection attacks or other malicious input.

Case Sensitivity - Interoperability - The requirement to provide project names in lowercase may lead to interoperability issues when integrating with systems that expect case-insensitive input or have different naming conventions.

No Authentication/Authorization - Security - The release notes do not mention any authentication or authorization mechanisms, which can pose security risks if unauthorized users can submit or access timesheet data.

Data Exposure - Security - The `getTimesheets` method provides access to all recorded timesheet durations, which might expose sensitive information if not properly restricted or authenticated.

Of course, this might be an unnecessary step if we can directly ask an LLM to suggest risks based on the code directly, but it does demonstrate the power of LLM's ability to transform data from one format to another.

4.6   *Maintaining a balance with code assistants*

The perspective on the value that tools such as Copilot and ChatGPT offer depends on individuals. For some, it means the automation of development and the loss of many roles, and for others, it's nothing but an advanced tool that randomly picks suggested code. What this chapter demonstrates is the ongoing theme that their worth and usefulness lie somewhere between those two extremes.

These models, trained on masses of data from Stack Overflow and GitHub repositories, are very sophisticated in what they suggest for both production and test code. But they still require direction from us humans—direction that is guided by our abilities to communicate with stakeholders, analyze requirements, and design implementation. How well we can use AI tools in development depends on honing our complementary skills, which can be summarized by using the area-of-effect model shown in figure 4.2.

A balanced approach can help us deliver features faster but still ensure that we build in quality. So, our goal is to maintain that balance in situations in which we may need to rely on our own abilities or the features of our tools. Sometimes, code assistants won't be able to suggest the correct implementation, and we need to take charge. This gives us more control but does sacrifice speed. At other times, we can rely on code assistant tools to reference vast amounts of data to suggest new design ideas through unit checks or conversations. However, we want to ensure that we keep our TDD loops focused on design and not on test coverage. Too many unit checks, and we lose sight of our design and end up in a box-checking activity.

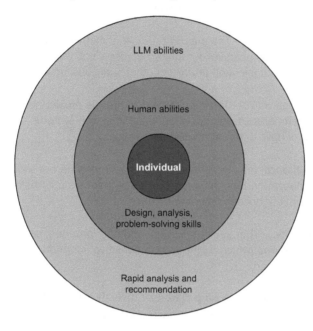

Figure 4.2   **An area-of-effect model, updated to demonstrate the skills of a human and the abilities of code assistant tools**

Summary

- The majority of generative AI tools currently on the market rely on LLMs trained with vast amounts of data scraped from the internet.
- LLMs are sophisticated algorithms that apply statistical analysis to our requests to determine what output they should respond with.
- Copilot is a coding assistant tool that uses the OpenAI GPT-4 and is trained on code stored on GitHub.
- Copilot works within an IDE and reads your code as a prompt to suggest what to add next into test code and production code.
- Tools such as Copilot can work well with the TDD red/green/refactor loop to help us rapidly create unit checks and production code.
- To help Copilot return code that is valuable, we need to guide it with prompts.
- Success with AI code assistants depends on our understanding of our abilities and the features of code assistant tools.
- There is push–pull relationship between how much we are leading versus the tooling leading design.
- We must be aware of the tradeoffs when the balance shifts from humans to tools leading.

5
Test planning with AI support

This chapter covers

- How the value of models is associated with the use of LLMs
- Using models with LLMs in test planning
- Evaluating the suitability of suggestions generated by LLMs

Now that we've started to see how large language models (LLMs) can help support quality in development, it's time to tackle the question of whether LLMs can generate test cases. On the surface, the answer is simple: yes, they can. But the deeper and more important question is why would you want them to generate test cases? What are we hoping to achieve by generating swathes of test cases without thought or direction? Just because we can create test cases doesn't necessarily mean it's the right thing to do in a given situation.

The motivation behind the question comes from a desire to use LLMs to direct the required testing for a feature, an epic, or a project. Although LLMs may be valuable in terms of advising us what testing we should carry out, there are concerns about how trusting we should be and how much we should rely on LLMs. Much like other activities we've explored and will explore, there is a balance to be struck. On one hand, we must keep a healthy skepticism in place whenever we use LLMs to aid in testing, but we shouldn't outright dismiss their potential value (as long as we keep that critical eye for when they might lead us astray). Therefore, this chapter will explore two questions at the core of how LLMs can guide the direction of the testing, focusing on how test planning is conducted:

- Can LLMs support us in our test planning?
- How can LLMs be used effectively to support said planning?

Specifically, we'll be looking at the activities we need to carry out when determining what type of testing is necessary for a feature, an epic, or a project. To do this, we'll examine what test planning looks like in a modern software development team. But before that, we will identify how LLMs can best support us during the planning phase.

5.1 Defining test planning in modern testing

For most of us, a test plan implies detailed documentation that attempts to meticulously define how we will carry out our testing. But if you are someone who works in a modern, agile, software development team, ask yourself: When was the last time you documented a test plan for upcoming work? If so, what did it look like?

Test planning these days comes in a myriad of forms. Some of us might say that we haven't written a test plan for a long time, and others might capture key details in a one-page test plan or rely on acceptance criteria to determine what testing takes place. Others may still create formal test plans following stringent test plan templates. Whether our planning is conducted formally or informally, what drives a test plan are the risks to our product and project, and this relationship is illustrated in figure 5.1.

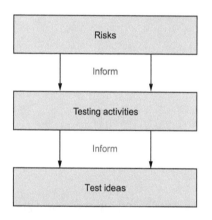

Figure 5.1   A diagram showing the relationship of risk and test planning

Therefore, when we are planning the testing we intend to carry out, our core goal is to define and mitigate specific, measurable risks. The risks we define inform us of what testing we will do, and depending on the type of intended testing, we can consider different test ideas.

5.1.1 Test planning, LLMs, and area of effect

Considering that risk is at the core of our testing, we need to establish a relationship with LLMs that helps elevate a risk-based planning approach, while ensuring that we aren't too biased by an LLM's output. A lot of discussion has been around how LLMs can be used to direct our testing by having them generate test cases for us. (For the

sake of this discussion, we'll include both automated and nonautomated test cases.)
But just because an LLM can generate test cases doesn't mean that they are necessary
or relevant to mitigating the risks we care about. The result may be that some suggested test cases are of value, but using an LLM greatly increases the risk of running
wasteful or misleading testing.

We want to be directed and efficient in our testing, so focusing on using an LLM
to support us in identifying risks is key. First, it opens up how we conduct our testing.
Asking an LLM to generate test cases ties us to one type of testing activity, and although
there is a case for using test cases as part of a holistic strategy of different testing techniques, we shouldn't rely on a monoculture of test cases alone. Instead, we should focus
on risks to explore different concerns we might have without the bias of choosing a testing technique. Once we understand what risks we care about, we can select a suitable
testing activity to mitigate said risks.

Second, and most importantly, focusing on risk changes the way we use an LLM. In
figure 5.2, the area of effect model demonstrates how we can tell the LLM what features
we are focusing on and what risks we have identified already.

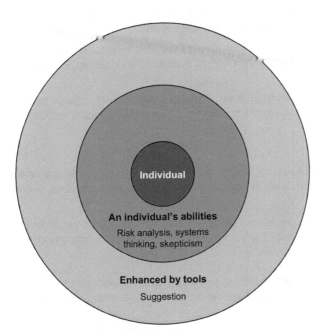

**Figure 5.2　Area of the effect model
demonstrating the core roles of the
human and the LLM as an assistant**

As demonstrated in the figure, the LLM serves as an assistant that expands our ideas
around risk and potentially help us uncover new risks that hadn't been considered
already, helping us expand our risk coverage, while ensuring we control the direction
of our testing.

5.2   *Focused prompts with the use of models*

If we want to use LLMs to help us identify risks, we need to be aware of the hazards of an overreliance on them when determining what to focus on. To better understand this, let's take a look at a common example of how LLMs are said to help with testing, why they can be problematic, and how we can better direct our use of LLMs to increase their value and decrease the risk of misdirected testing.

5.2.1   *Weak prompts mean weak suggestions*

Throughout Part 1 of this book, we've seen how poorly framed prompts such as

  Create tests for a file upload feature

return a generic list of actionable results not rooted in a context, which means that they require a large amount of reworking or risk affecting the quality of our testing (reduced in size for readability):

  Implementing a file upload feature can introduce several risks, including:

1 Security Risks:

   – Malicious Files: Users might upload files containing malware or viruses, which can infect the system and compromise security.

   – Injection Attacks: If the system doesn't properly validate file types and content, it could be vulnerable to injection attacks such as cross-site scripting (XSS) or SQL injection.

   – Denial of Service (DoS) Attacks: Attackers may upload large or numerous files to overwhelm the system's storage or processing capacity, leading to a denial of service.

2 Privacy Risks:

   – Sensitive Data Exposure: Users might inadvertently upload files containing sensitive information, such as personal identification, financial data, or confidential documents.

   – Data Leakage: Improper handling of uploaded files could result in unintended exposure of data, especially if the files are accessible to unauthorized users.

3 Compliance Risks:

   – Regulatory Compliance: Failure to comply with regulations like GDPR or HIPAA regarding the handling of personal or sensitive data could result in legal consequences.

   – Copyright Infringement: Users may upload copyrighted material without permission, exposing the platform to potential legal actions for copyright infringement.

4 Performance Risks:

   – Bandwidth and Storage: Large file uploads can consume significant bandwidth and storage resources, potentially impacting system performance and scalability.

– Concurrency: Multiple users uploading large files simultaneously could strain server resources and degrade system responsiveness.

If we put garbage in, we get garbage out, and if we're not critical of how we're interacting with LLMs, then trouble will ensue. We already know that to obtain value successfully from an LLM, we need to create prompts that are specific to the problem we want solved. When generating suitable risks, the challenge is being able to create those specific prompts for a complex system. The skills required to get to this point don't lie in our ability to write a prompt but to break down a system into more manageable chunks. By doing this, we can then create more targeted and focused prompts. So, the question then turns to breaking a system down to create better prompts.

5.2.2   *What are models and why can they help*

Before we go into the process of using models to help us with our prompting, let's clarify what is meant by models. When we use the term *model* in the context of testing and software development in general, we are referring to an abstract representation of some information. It can be something that is visualized (for example, a data flow diagram of an application), or it can be something held in our mind. We say that it is abstract because although it is based on information found in reality, a model usually simplifies, accentuates, or ignores certain aspects of the information it's based upon. It provides a partial representation of the truth. This is why the aphorism "All models are wrong, but some are useful," based on a quote from George Box, is used when discussing models. Models tend to be used to focus on specific attributes or concepts within a wider context. This might seem like criticism, but when put to good use, it can help us with problem-solving. For example, consider the model of an application shown in figure 5.3.

This visual model of an application has been designed to help its reader ascertain the dependencies between APIs. Notice

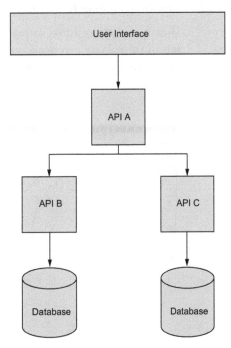

Figure 5.3   A basic visualization of a model of a system

how it doesn't contain every detail of the platform. The APIs are abstracted into boxes that summarize the details of what code lives inside each API, and the front end of the system is simply summarized into a box titled "User interface." This model is flawed because it doesn't give us an accurate picture of every aspect of the platform, but it is still useful because it accentuates the details that the reader cares about—the relationships between APIs on a platform. If the reader wants to understand APIs dependencies, then this model has value. However, if the reader wants to understand the implementation of the front end or the specific behavior of functions within each API, the model is worthless.

So, when creating a model, we lean into the idea of a model giving us only a partial picture by highlighting the information we want and discarding other details. This approach to modeling systems can help us make our prompts generate suggested risks that are more contextual and valuable.

5.3   Combining models and LLMs to assist test planning

Now that you better understand the dangers of creating prompts that aren't focused on a specific part of a system, let's look at how we can mitigate this risk by using models. To demonstrate our model-based approach, let's imagine we are using an LLM to help inform our test-planning process.

5.3.1   Creating a model to identify prompts

Unsurprisingly, our first step is to create a model of the application. We'll explore different formats we can use to create models shortly, but in the meantime, let's imagine we've created a model that looks like the one shown in figure 5.4.

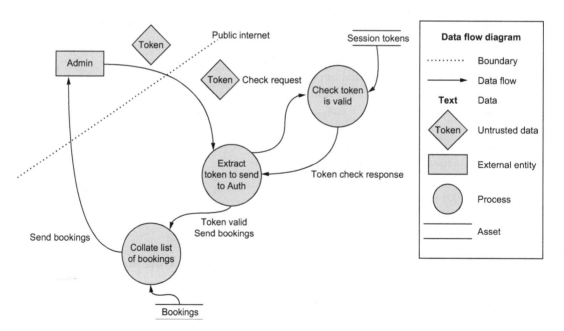

Figure 5.4   A visual model of an application

The model uses a data flow diagram to outline how data is handled in the process of requesting a collection of bookings from API. The model itself is not of an entire system, but of a specific piece of functionality that exists in a wider B&B/hotel booking management system. To break down what the model is specifying, when an administrator wants to see the lists of bookings stored in the database, the following steps take place:

1　A request is sent to view the list of bookings, and a token is attached to the request.
2　The token is then extracted from the initial request and sent to be validated against a list of valid sessions.
3　If the token is confirmed as a valid session, then a positive response is returned to part of the system that is managing the view bookings request.
4　The list of bookings is then collated and sent back to the administrator.

Considering this flow, let's first look at the type of response we might get from an LLM if we were to build a prompt that attempts to encompass everything in the model at once. First, we would create a prompt:

 You are an expert software tester. Generate a list of risks for an application that uses session-based tokens to authorize access to view a list of bookings.

When the prompt is sent to an LLM, such as ChatGPT, we receive something like the following response:

 Session Token Generation Flaws: The process of generating session tokens may have vulnerabilities, such as predictable token patterns, leading to token guessing attacks.

Session Token Leakage: Session tokens might inadvertently get exposed in logs, error messages, or through insecure transmission channels, potentially leading to unauthorized access.

Session Token Storage: Improper storage of session tokens, such as in cookies without secure flags or local storage susceptible to XSS attacks, could result in token theft.

Session Hijacking: Lack of proper mechanisms to prevent session hijacking attacks, such as session fixation, where an attacker sets a user's session token, or session replay attacks.

Session Expiration: Inadequate session timeout configurations might lead to prolonged session exposures, increasing the window of opportunity for attackers to exploit stolen tokens.

Session Fixation: Failure to invalidate and regenerate session tokens upon authentication events or significant state changes, enabling attackers to fixate sessions to known tokens.

Insufficient Token Entropy: Session tokens generated with insufficient entropy may be susceptible to brute-force or dictionary attacks.

Token Lifetime Management: Lack of proper mechanisms to manage token lifetimes, including revocation, renewal, and rotation, could result in prolonged exposure and increased risk of unauthorized access.

Insecure Token Transmission: Session tokens transmitted over insecure channels, such as HTTP instead of HTTPS, are prone to interception and sniffing attacks.

Cross-Site Request Forgery (CSRF): Inadequate CSRF protection could allow attackers to forge requests, leading to unauthorized actions using valid session tokens.

Session Token Injection: Lack of proper input validation and output encoding might expose the application to session token injection attacks, allowing attackers to manipulate session states.

Insecure Session Termination: Improper session termination mechanisms, such as failing to invalidate session tokens upon logout or session expiration, may lead to lingering session vulnerabilities.

Session Data Integrity: Absence of integrity checks on session data may allow attackers to tamper with session parameters or payloads, leading to unauthorized access or data manipulation.

Insufficient Logging and Monitoring: Inadequate logging of session-related events and insufficient monitoring for suspicious activities may impede timely detection and response to session-based attacks.

Session Token Forensics: Lack of forensic capabilities to trace and investigate session-related incidents may hinder post-incident analysis and remediation efforts.

The returned list looks quite long at first glance, but after reading it, there appear to be some problems. First, looking over the list of suggested risks, they are predominantly focused on security risks. Although security risks are important to consider, there are minimal risks focused on the interaction between the auth and booking components, or the compilation of the booking list. The LLM has taken the token portion of the prompt and focused too heavily on it. So, let's consider a prompt created by focusing on a specific slice of the model we created:

 You are an expert software tester. Generate as many risks as possible for the behavior delimited by three hashes.

###
A Booking API that, once authorized, sends a list of bookings that are stored within a database to a user for review.
###

With this prompt, we're attempting to describe a specific part of the system that has been captured in our model. Instead of asking for suggestions that cover all parts of the functionality at once, we select one part of the system to see if we can get better suggestions. This means that if we send this to an LLM such as ChatGPT, we might see the following list of suggestions (again reduced for readability):

1 Data Security Risks:

- Unauthorized access to sensitive booking data due to insufficient authentication or authorization mechanisms.
- Risk of data breaches if the API doesn't encrypt data transmission between the server and the user, leaving data vulnerable to interception.
- Risk of SQL injection attacks if the API doesn't sanitize inputs properly, leading to unauthorized access or manipulation of the database.

2 Data Accuracy Risks:

- Inaccurate or outdated booking information being transmitted to users if the API doesn't synchronize properly with the database.
- Risk of data corruption during transmission, leading to inconsistencies between the database and the information sent to users.

3 Performance Risks:

- Slow response times or timeouts if the API doesn't handle a large volume of booking requests efficiently.
- Risk of service degradation or downtime if the API cannot handle concurrent requests effectively, leading to performance bottlenecks.

4 Scalability Risks:

- Inability to handle increased traffic during peak booking periods, leading to system overload or crashes.
- Risk of resource exhaustion if the API doesn't scale dynamically to accommodate growing user demands, resulting in degraded performance.

5 Dependency Risks:

- Risk of service disruptions if the API relies on external dependencies (e.g., third-party APIs, libraries, or services) that may experience downtime or changes in functionality.
- Risk of version incompatibility if the API is built on outdated or deprecated frameworks, leading to compatibility issues with other systems or libraries.

6 Error Handling Risks:

- Inadequate error handling mechanisms that may result in ambiguous or misleading error messages, making it difficult for users to diagnose and troubleshoot issues.
- Risk of exposing sensitive system information in error messages, potentially aiding attackers in exploiting vulnerabilities.

7 Concurrency Risks:

- Risk of data corruption or race conditions if the API doesn't handle concurrent access to the database properly, leading to inconsistencies or data loss.
- Inconsistent behavior or unexpected outcomes if the API doesn't implement proper locking mechanisms to manage concurrent access to shared resources.

8 Regulatory Compliance Risks:
  - Risk of non-compliance with data protection regulations (e.g., GDPR, HIPAA) if the API doesn't adhere to industry standards for handling sensitive user data.
  - Potential legal consequences if the API fails to comply with industry-specific regulations (e.g., PCI DSS for payment data).

9 Load Testing Risks:
  - Risk of performance degradation or system failure under heavy load if the API hasn't been adequately tested for scalability and endurance.
  - Inaccurate capacity planning leading to under-provisioning or over-provisioning of resources, resulting in suboptimal performance or unnecessary costs.

10 Documentation Risks:
  - Risk of misunderstanding or misusing the API functionality if the documentation is incomplete, outdated, or unclear.
  - Potential delays in development or troubleshooting efforts if developers cannot rely on accurate and up-to-date API documentation.

Let's compare this response against the previous one we got from ChatGPT and see if there is an improvement. First, there was the problem of the initial prompt focusing too much on specific aspects of the functionality and ignoring other parts. Given that we've explicitly selected a distinct part of the system based on our model, it makes sense that a lot of focus in the new prompt response is on ways to test booking lists. We asked it to do that. But what stands out is the diversity of suggestions. In the initial prompt, most of the suggestions were based on different states that a token could be in; this prompt offers not only more suggestions, but also a mix of ideas around the correctness of bookings, boundaries, invalid data, and caching. Next, there was the problem of some suggestions being too vague to be actionable. Reviewing the suggestions that sit under each header, we can see they are more explicit—for example, the negative test suggestions mention specific types of status codes to consider.

The results are improved because LLMs respond better when more context is added to a prompt, and by using a model, we can slice up the behavior, focus on specific components, and capture and communicate the context in our prompt. This does mean we are ignoring other components in the model in favor of being focused so that we can communicate how a part of the system works. But if we iterate this process, we can change up which part of a model we want to create a prompt for. For example, we could run a second prompt that focuses exclusively on the token validation portion of the system to create a prompt like this:

 You are an expert software tester. Generate as many risks as possible for the behavior delimited by three hashes.

###

An Authorization API that will take a token from a different API and check to see if the token is valid and in date before either responding positively or negatively depending on the result.

###

When sent to an LLM like ChatGPT, it would return something like this:

1   Token Validation Failure: The Authorization API may fail to properly validate the token received from the different API, leading to unauthorized access.

2   Expired Token: The Authorization API may not accurately detect expired tokens, allowing access to users who should no longer have permissions.

3   False Positive/Negative Responses: There is a risk of the API providing incorrect responses, either granting access to unauthorized users or denying access to authorized ones.

4   Performance Degradation: If the token validation process is resource-intensive, it may lead to performance degradation or even downtime during high traffic periods.

5   Dependency Failure: If the different API providing tokens experiences downtime or issues, the Authorization API may not be able to perform its function correctly.

6   Security Vulnerabilities: The Authorization API could be susceptible to security vulnerabilities such as injection attacks or improper access control mechanisms.

7   Lack of Logging/Monitoring: Without proper logging and monitoring, it may be challenging to identify unauthorized access attempts or diagnose issues with token validation.

8   Inadequate Error Handling: Poor error handling could result in ambiguous or misleading error messages, making it difficult for developers to troubleshoot integration issues.

9   Token Spoofing: Malicious actors may attempt to spoof tokens to gain unauthorized access, exploiting weaknesses in the token validation process.

10 Token Replay Attacks: Attackers could intercept valid tokens and replay them to gain unauthorized access, highlighting the importance of implementing measures to prevent token replay attacks.

11 Token Expiry Race Condition: A race condition may occur if a token expires between the time it's validated and the time access is granted, potentially allowing unauthorized access.

12 Inconsistent Token Validation Logic: If the token validation logic differs between the Authorization API and the different API, it could lead to inconsistencies and unexpected behavior.

13 Regulatory Compliance Issues: Failure to properly secure and validate tokens could result in non-compliance with industry regulations or data protection laws.

14 Scalability Concerns: As the number of users and tokens increases, the scalability of the Authorization API may become a concern, potentially leading to performance issues or service disruptions.

15 Integration Challenges: Integrating the Authorization API with the different API and other systems may present technical challenges, such as compatibility issues or data format mismatches.

We would then pick suggestions from this list and add them to those we selected from the previous prompt response to build a list of risks that we might want to consider in our test planning.

This demonstrates that to improve the quality of risk suggestions from an LLM, we need to understand system under test. Simply picking a requirement or feature and asking an LLM to generate risks will not work. The lack of context being provided to an LLM means it will rely on common patterns of behavior in similar feature requirements it has been trained on, which results in vague responses and hallucinations. To get something of value from an LLM, we need to be specific so that we provide rich contextual information for it to use, which we can get using models. By creating a model of the system, we not only improve our understanding of what we're testing, but also compartmentalize parts of the system into specific areas that we can use to inform the type of prompts we write. We can then iterate through each part of the system, creating prompts to return suggestions that build up a collage of risks that are more relevant and more targeted on specific components and how they might behave.

All of this can once again be summarized using the area of effect model, as shown in figure 5.5.

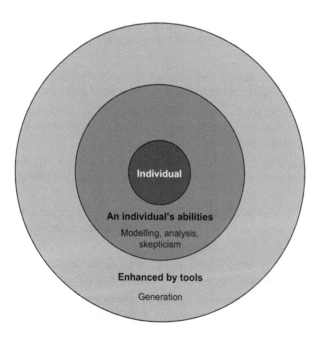

Figure 5.5   Area of effect model showing the skills required to get valuable outputs from an LLM

The area of effect model shows how our modeling and analysis skills are what drive the LLM's ability to provide value. If our understanding is weak, then so are our prompts, which means the results we get will be weak.

> **Activity 5.1**
>
> Pick a part of a system you are testing and create a model of how it works. Either create a data flow diagram or pick a different modeling technique. Once you've created your model, pick a specific part of the model and use it to create a targeted prompt to generate suggested risks.

5.3.2 *Experimenting with different model types*

In the example we have just explored, we used a data flow diagram approach to model how our system worked. However, as mentioned before, models are flawed, meaning the model we used previously helped us identify potential prompts from the perspective of how data is being handled in our application, but it omits other perspectives in the process. It's therefore useful to experiment with different types of models to help us consider how our application works from different perspectives, which allows us to prompt an LLM to suggest a wide range of risks to use. So, let's take a look at a few different types of modeling techniques to help us expand our work.

FORMAL MODELING TECHNIQUES

When using the data flow diagram format (DTD), we employ explicit symbols and rules that belong to that format so that our model can visually explain what is happening as clearly as possible. DTDs, however, are just one of many different types of formal models that we can borrow and steal from to create models that work for us. For example, UML, or Unified Modeling Language, contains many different modeling approaches to look at an application from different perspectives. Structural UML diagrams such as component diagrams can be used to break down a system's architecture and help us use LLMs to generate risks focused on specific parts of the system. For example, figure 5.6 demonstrates how we might interpret our booking list functionality as a component diagram.

It would result in a prompt that looks something like this:

 You are an expert software tester. Generate as many risks as possible for the behavior delimited by three hashes.

###

A `BookingRequest` class that sends out a request to an Auth API to confirm whether `BookingService` can complete its request

###

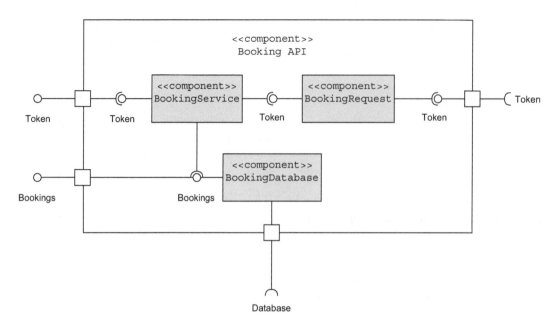

Figure 5.6   A component diagram of the booking list functionality

We can also use behavioral diagrams such as sequence and use case diagrams to help us capture user flows through a system and create prompts that generate user-focused prompts (for example, a model like the one in figure 5.7).

It might help us create a prompt like this:

 You are an expert software tester. Generate as many risks as possible for the behavior delimited by three hashes.

###

A user wants to view a list of bookings after logging into an application. They have logged in with the correct credentials and are requesting the booking list before their authorization has expired.

###

The options for formal-based models and diagrams are vast, so experimentation is recommended. Exploring how different models work and what types of prompting they trigger can help us determine the ones more suitable for us. We can also use what we learn from formal modeling techniques to build custom models that work for us.

MENTAL MODELS

Although different formal modeling techniques can help us analyze our system from different perspectives, it is an expensive activity to carry out. Taking the time to model a system in different ways takes time and requires us to carry out extensive research to build up enough knowledge to frame our application in different ways. However, we can approach interpretations of models from another angle, in which we focus on changing our perception of a single model using heuristics.

If we return to figure 5.7, the model is designed to walk us through the flow of how conditional actions determine what happens next. So, we create prompts that focus on those conditions because that's what the model is designed to highlight. But what if we were to change our perception by adopting a different mental model? One example would be to use the mnemonic SFDIPOT, sometimes known as San Francisco Depot. Created by James Bach as part of the Heuristic Test Strategy Model (https://mng.bz/o0lN), SFDIPOT is designed to help us consider a product from different perspectives; each letter in the mnemonic stands for a different perspective:

- *Structure*—What the product is made of
- *Function*—What the product does
- *Data*—What the product processes
- *Interfaces*—Ways in which the product can be interacted with
- *Platform*—What the product depends on
- *Operations*—How the product will be used
- *Time*—How time affects the product

Although this mnemonic can be used on a strategic level, we can also apply it to smaller sections of a system, as shown in figure 5.7. We can use these different types of perspectives to re-evaluate our product through different lenses. For example, we might review figure 5.7 by asking how time might affect our functionality. It might inspire a prompt such as the following, which sets out initial instructions to generate risks and use the delimiter tactic:

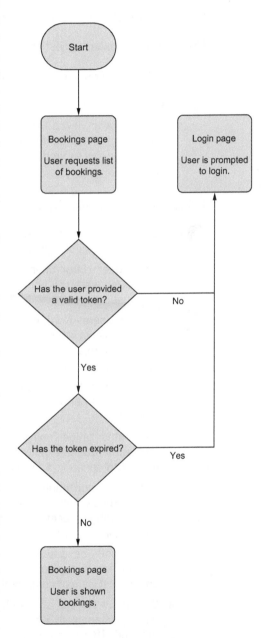

Figure 5.7   A user flow diagram of the booking list functionality

You are an expert software tester. Generate as many risks as possible for the behavior delimited by three hashes.

Focus on risks around the speed at which the user is using the system (fast or slow) and the amount of users who are using the system at a point in time.

We can use the time to think of tactics to avoid off-topic suggestions:

 Check that each suggestion matches the time conditions before outputting them.

Then we'll provide the context to work from:

 ###

A user wants to view a list of bookings after logging into an application. They have logged in with the correct credentials and are requesting the booking list before their authorization has expired.

###

Using a prompt like this can result in the following response:

1. Single User - Normal Speed: One user logs in, accesses the booking list immediately after successful login, ensuring it displays within an acceptable response time.
2. Single User - Slow Speed: A single user, with a slower internet connection, logs in and requests the booking list, examining how the system handles a delayed response.
3. Multiple Users - Normal Speed: Multiple users simultaneously log in and request the booking list within a short time frame to observe if the system slows down or if there's any impact on response time due to concurrent requests.
4. Multiple Users - Slow Speed: Simulate multiple users accessing the system with slower connections, attempting to view the booking list concurrently to assess the system's performance under slower network conditions and concurrent user requests.
5. User Authorization Timing: A user attempts to access the booking list right before their authorization expires to verify if the system allows access or handles the request appropriately in this critical time window.
6. Expiry of Authorization During Access: Simulate a scenario where a user's authorization expires while they are viewing the booking list to ensure the system handles this expiration gracefully without crashing or showing sensitive information after the authorization has lapsed.
7. Heavy Load Scenario: Generate a heavy load by increasing the number of simultaneous users significantly and assess how the system manages to provide the booking list without compromising response time or crashing due to the load.
8. Concurrent Access and Authorization Renewal: Multiple users access the system simultaneously while some of their authorizations are expiring and getting renewed. This test verifies the system's behavior when dealing with concurrent access and authorization renewal processes.

9 Intermittent User Access: Users log in at different intervals, some requesting the booking list immediately after login while others perform various activities first. This test ensures that the system maintains consistent response times despite varied user behaviors.

10 Randomized Access Timing: Randomly timed user requests for the booking list to emulate real-world scenarios, testing how the system copes with unpredictable and irregular access patterns.

The results of this response are much more focused on how a user or users might interact with a system. They are also much more detailed than some of the earlier high-level suggestions of load testing. The prompt includes explicit information about how the system is expected to work, but we've added focus for the prompt based on a shifted perspective of how we think the functionality in figure 5.7 would work over time.

Using heuristics such as SFDIPOT means we can quickly iterate over the same part of a model, but also shift our perspectives and read models in different ways to help us identify new instructions we can add to our prompts.

> **Activity 5.2**
>
> Create a new model using a different modeling technique of the same feature modeled in the earlier activity, or use the mental modeling technique to re-evaluate your existing model. Use them to come up with new prompts that can suggest unique ideas for the previous prompts that you created.

5.4 LLMs and test cases

We began this chapter by asking whether LLMs can be used to generate test cases. Instead, we've taken a journey using risk as our guide to determine what type of testing we might do. The purpose was to show that we are in control of the direction we want our testing to take. Based on the risks that we identified and the ones suggested by an LLM, we might determine that the testing we carry out doesn't need to rely on test cases at all.

However, if our planning has identified that test cases are indeed required, whether they are run manually or through automation, we have done the due diligence in identifying smaller, more focused segments of a feature through modeling that we can use in our prompts. For example, we might create a prompt that combines the modeling work we've done earlier, risks we've identified, and even example test cases we've already captured. We use the delimiter tactic to outline two sections of data:

 You are an expert software tester. Generate suggested test cases based on the behavior delimited by three hashes and the test cases delimited by three back ticks.

Focus on risks around the speed at which the user is using the system (fast or slow) and the amount of users who are using the system at a point in time.

We can take the time to think to stop repetition and focus on risk:

Check that each suggestion matches the proposed risks before outputting them and that they are not a repeat of the test cases found in the section delimited by three backticks.

We then provide a capture area in the delimited section:

 ###

A user wants to view a list of bookings after logging into an application. They have logged in with the correct credentials and are requesting the booking list before their authorization has expired.

###

Finally, we provide test cases in delimited section:

  ```

Test Case 1: Single User - Normal Speed:

- Test accessing the booking list immediately after logging in with valid credentials, within a typical speed range.
- Verify that the booking list is displayed correctly without any delay or errors.

Test Case 2: Single User - Slow Speed:

- Simulate a slow network connection or system performance.
- Attempt to access the booking list immediately after logging in with valid credentials, but at a slower pace.
- Ensure that the system responds appropriately, perhaps with a loading indicator or progress bar, and eventually displays the booking list without timing out or crashing.

Test Case 3: Multiple Concurrent Users:

- Have one user login and request the booking list while another user performs a different action (e.g., making a booking).
- Verify that the system can handle concurrent requests without performance degradation or conflicts.

```

When sent to ChatGPT, it returned the following proposed test cases for me:

 Test Case 4: Single User - Fast Speed:

- Test accessing the booking list immediately after logging in with valid credentials, but at a very fast pace.
- Verify that the system can handle rapid requests without causing errors or unexpected behavior.

Test Case 5: Multiple Concurrent Users - Normal Speed:

- Have multiple users log in simultaneously and request the booking list.
- Ensure that each user receives the correct booking list without delays or interference from other users' requests.

Test Case 6: Authorization Expiry:

- Login with valid credentials and wait until the authorization expires.
- Attempt to access the booking list again.
- Verify that the system denies access or prompts the user to reauthenticate instead of displaying the booking list.

Again, the goal here isn't to blindly generate an exhaustive list of test cases but to critically evaluate what is suggested and see if it generates useful, novel ideas or inspires us to identify new test cases of our own.

5.4.1 *Having a healthy skepticism of generated risks and test cases*

Codifying explicit steps about how to approach the testing of an application is no match for the complex, intuitive testing we do as humans. Test cases can help to a certain point, especially in the automation space, but we must avoid a monoculture of test cases that runs the risk of affecting the quality of our products rather than helping improve it. Therefore, we must be mindful that LLMs provide value as an assistant to our test-planning activities and are not an authority on what to test. The alternative is overrelying on LLMs to do our work, which makes users naively think that they can be trusted completely to replicate our testing, which in turn may make us generate thousands of test cases rapidly without thought and/or value. However, the danger doesn't stem from LLMs alone. Instead, we must think carefully and methodically about what we are asking LLMs to create for us and be skeptical of what is returned.

Summary

- Test planning can range from informal notes to formal documentation on how testing will take place.
- All test planning, however, is rooted in the risks we care about in our testing.
- Generic and vague prompting can harm our planning rather than assist it. Instead, we need to develop more accurate and specific prompting to generate useful suggestions.
- Using visual and mental models can help us break down a system to create better prompts.
- All models are flawed, but this can be used to our advantage to create models that accentuate details we care about to help us solve problems.
- Creating models allows us to break down a feature or segment of a system to better understand how its parts work.

- Building prompts based on specific parts of a model can help us produce valuable, accurate, and actionable suggestions.
- We can use a range of different modeling techniques to obtain different perspectives on a system's behavior.
- Experimenting with different formal modeling approaches can help us generate different types of prompts.
- Reviewing a single model with different mental models can help us shift our own internal biases and perspectives regarding what types of prompts to write.
- We should focus on what to test and use LLMs to suggest ideas, not the other way around.

Rapid data creation using AI

6

This chapter covers

- Generating basic test data using LLMs
- Changing the format of test data
- Using complex data sets to prompt LLMs to create new data sets
- Integrating LLMs as a test data manager for automated checks

Managing test data is one of the most challenging aspects of testing and software development. Typically, data requirements grow with the complexity of a system. Having to synthesize data relevant to our context for automated checks and human-driven testing that handles complex data structures and anonymizes at scale and on demand can impose a huge drain on testing time and resources, which could be better spent on other testing activities.

However, we need test data. It is simply not possible to carry out most testing activities if we lack the necessary data to trigger actions and observe behavior. That's why this chapter shows how we can use large language models (LLMs) to generate test data, providing different prompts to create both simple and complex data structures and integrate LLMs into our automation frameworks via third-party APIs.

6.1   *Generating and transforming data with LLMs*

Given that LLMs are powerful, probabilistic, text generators, it sounds logical that, with the right prompting, they can generate and transform test data easily. This is true, but it depends on writing clear prompts that communicate our data requirements explicitly, so that we get the right data we want, in the correct format and without any errors caused by hallucinations. There are many ways in which we can approach this, but let's begin by looking at some basic prompts we can use casually to create test data for a range of testing activities.

6.1.1   *Prompting LLMs to generate simple data sets*

To start, let's explore how we can create basic data set examples such as this one:

```
{
  "room_name": "Cozy Suite",
  "type": "single",
  "beds": 1,
  "accessible": true,
  "image": "https://example.com/room1.jpg",
  "description": "Charming room",
  "features": ["Wifi", "TV"],
  "roomPrice": 150
}
```

As we can see, the JSON data set has a mixture of data types using a fairly straightforward structure. We'll see how to work with more complex structures later in the chapter, but for now, let's return to a prompt that we used back in chapter 2 to create some sample test data. First, we set out the main instructions for the prompt and use the time-to-think principle to improve the quality of the output JSON:

 You are a JSON data generator. Generate 5 JSON objects in an array and check that 5 JSON objects have been created before outputting the results.

We use different delimiters to set out the rules for our data requirements:

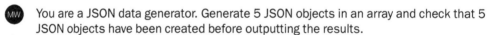 * Each parameter is identified with a % sign.

* Each column is described in order of key, value data type and options using the | sign.

* If a column data option says random, randomize data based on the suggested format and column name.

Then we provide the data we want to be created following our delimited rule set:

 Here are the instructions:

```
% room_name | string | random
% type | string |  'single' or 'double'
% beds | integer | 1 to 6
% accessible | boolean | true or false
% image | string | random url
% description | string | random max 20 characters
% features | array[string] | 'Wifi', 'TV' or 'Safe'
% roomPrice |  integer | 100 to 200
```

This prompt relies on a range of prompt-engineering tactics to set out explicitly what we want to see generated. We use the format tactic to declare what format we want our test data to be returned in. The delimiter tactic is used to set the rules for how we structure our data and what format values should be in. Also, we instruct the LLM to work out the solution before outputting it to reduce the risk of hallucinations.

Sending this prompt to ChatGPT returned the following data set:

```
[
  {
    "room_name": "Cozy Suite",
    "type": "single",
    "beds": 1,
    "accessible": true,
    "image": "https://example.com/room1.jpg",
    "description": "Charming room",
    "features": ["Wifi", "TV"],
    "roomPrice": 150
  }
  {
    "room_name": "Deluxe Room",
    "type": "double",
    "beds": 2,
    "accessible": false,
    "image": "https://example.com/room2.jpg",
    "description": "Luxury abode",
    "features": ["Wifi", "Safe"],
    "roomPrice": 180
  },
  {
    "room_name": "Economy Stay",
    "type": "single",
    "beds": 1,
    "accessible": true,
    «image»: «https://example.com/room3.jpg»,
    "description": "Budget-friendly",
    "features": ["TV"],
    "roomPrice": 120
  },
  {
    "room_name": "Family Suite",
    "type": "double",
    "beds": 3,
    "accessible": true,
    "image": "https://example.com/room4.jpg",
```

```
      "description": "Spacious and comfy",
      "features": ["Wifi", "TV", "Safe"],
      "roomPrice": 200
   },
   {
      "room_name": "Executive Loft",
      "type": "single",
      "beds": 1,
      "accessible": false,
      «image»: «https://example.com/room5.jpg»,
      "description": "Modern design",
      "features": ["Wifi", "Safe"],
      "roomPrice": 170
   }
]
```

There are a few observations to make from this generated data. We can see that in places where the prompt has been explicit in data expectations, we get generated data that is close to our expectations—for example, the features accessible and room-Price. There are, however, some weaker areas where our prompt has left the LLM to determine what to output. Two notable areas are the image URLs that have opted for example.com and the relationship between beds and type. The image URLs, although valid, don't point to actual images. Depending on our requirements, we may need to tweak our prompt further to make the URLs more explicit. The other relationship is interesting as well, as one of the records states that the room type is double but it offers three beds. It's a good start though, and there are times when this type of generated data is enough to support our testing.

But what if we want this data in a different data structure? This can be handled by quickly reworking the prompt. For example, this prompt is requesting the same data, but this time in an XML format. We begin by rewording the initial instructions to create the data in an XML format:

 You are an XML data generator. Generate 3 XML entries in an array and check that 3 XML objects have been created before outputting the results.

We add an initial instruction to handle a root XML node:

 * The root node element name is identified with a # sign

   * Each element is identified with a % sign

   * Each column is described in order of element name, data type and options using the | sign

   * If a column data option says random, randomize data based on the suggested format and column name

Then we provide the same data steps as before:

 Here are the instructions:

```
# rooms
% room_name | string | random
% type | string |  'single' or 'double'
% beds | integer | 1 to 6
% accessible | boolean | true or false
% image | string | random url
% description | string | random max 20 characters
% features | array[string] | 'Wifi', 'TV' or 'Safe'
% roomPrice |  integer | 100 to 200
```

Although it's not necessarily common to have to handle different data formats in one application, the prompt demonstrates one of the advantages of working with LLMs to generate data. Using the structured output tactic, we're able to keep most of the prompt the same as the JSON prompt example and simply modify it to give us XML; when I sent it to ChatGPT, I got the following result:

```xml
<rooms>
    <room>
        <room_name>A1</room_name>
        <type>single</type>
        <beds>3</beds>
        <accessible>true</accessible>
        <image>https://example.com/room_a1.jpg</image>
        <description>Cozy room</description>
        <features>
            <feature>Wifi</feature>
            <feature>TV</feature>
        </features>
        <roomPrice>150</roomPrice>
    </room>
    <room>
        <room_name>B2</room_name>
        <type>double</type>
        <beds>2</beds>
        <accessible>false</accessible>
        <image>https://example.com/room_b2.jpg</image>
        <description>Spacious suite</description>
        <features>
            <feature>TV</feature>
            <feature>Safe</feature>
        </features>
        <roomPrice>180</roomPrice>
    </room>
    <room>
        <room_name>C3</room_name>
        <type>single</type>
        <beds>1</beds>
        <accessible>true</accessible>
        <image>https://example.com/room_c3.jpg</image>
        <description>Modern design</description>
        <features>
            <feature>Wifi</feature>
            <feature>Safe</feature>
```

```
        </features>
        <roomPrice>130</roomPrice>
    </room>
</rooms>
```

Again, the output has similar attributes as the previous examples. The structure of the XML is valid, and the rules determining what data to use have been followed. But, similar to the JSON example, we have some unusual choices being made. Single rooms with three beds, oddly named rooms, and dummy URLs are used. With both prompts, we could add more information to mitigate these problems, but we run the risk of having to create a lot of rules in our prompt to manage the relationship between data points. There are, however, other choices we can make with our prompts to handle more complex rule sets, but first, let's explore another way in which LLMs can help us thanks to their ability to transform data.

> **Activity 6.1**
>
> Using the prompt shared in this section, change the data structure to create either new XML or JSON test data.

6.1.2 *Transforming test data into different formats*

One of the core benefits of LLMs, which has been highlighted by advocates of the technology, is its ability to translate text from one language to another—for example, from French to English and back again. We can also use this approach to transform data and code from one structure or language to another. For example, take a look at the following prompt that transforms some JSON into a SQL statement. We use the delimiter tactic and instructions to start the prompt:

 You are a JSON to SQL transformer. Convert the JSON object delimited by triple hashes into a SQL statement that will:

1 Create a SQL table to insert the transformed records into
2 Create insert statements to add each record to a database

Next, we instruct the model to check the solution to improve the output:

 Check that each SQL statement covers all aspects of the JSON before outputting the results

Then we provide the data that we want to see transformed:

```
###
[{
    "firstname": "Sally",
    "lastname": "Wilson",
    "totalprice": 229,
    "depositpaid": false,
```

```
        "bookingdates": {
            "checkin": "2017-02-20",
            "checkout": "2019-07-05"
        },
        "additionalneeds": "Breakfast"
    },{
        "firstname": "Jim",
        "lastname": "Jones",
        "totalprice": 871,
        "depositpaid": false,
        "bookingdates": {
            "checkin": "2017-08-11",
            "checkout": "2021-06-30"
        },
        "additionalneeds": "Breakfast"
    },{
        "firstname": "Mary",
        "lastname": "Ericsson",
        "totalprice": 558,
        "depositpaid": true,
        "bookingdates": {
            "checkin": "2018-07-04",
            "checkout": "2022-09-25"
        }
    }]
    ###
```

In this prompt, we're asking an LLM not only to take a JSON object and convert it into a SQL `INSERT` statement that we could run, but also create the necessary `CREATE` statement to allow us to insert our data in the first place. Sending this to ChatGPT returned the following SQL statement:

```
-- Create the table
CREATE TABLE bookings (
    id SERIAL PRIMARY KEY,
    firstname VARCHAR(255),
    lastname VARCHAR(255),
    totalprice DECIMAL(10, 2),
    depositpaid BOOLEAN,
    checkin DATE,
    checkout DATE,
    additionalneeds VARCHAR(255)
);

-- Insert the records
INSERT INTO bookings (firstname, lastname, totalprice, depositpaid,
 checkin, checkout, additionalneeds)
VALUES
    ('Sally', 'Wilson', 229.00, false, '2017-02-20', '2019-07-05',
 'Breakfast'),
    ('Jim', 'Jones', 871.00, false, '2017-08-11', '2021-06-30',
 'Breakfast'),
    ('Mary', 'Ericsson', 558.00, true, '2018-07-04', '2022-09-25',
NULL);
```

What stands out in this response is not just that correct SQL has been generated to create and insert our data into a database, but that it has honored the values from the original JSON object. It demonstrates the importance of tactics such as these that go into a prompt:

 Check that each SQL statement covers all aspects of the JSON before outputting the results

The prompt helps ensure that the data parameters themselves are not modified during the transformation process.

These quick prompts demonstrate that LLMs can be used to rapidly generate and transform data with prompts that can be reused multiple times by replacing the data object inside the delimited portion of each prompt. This can prove useful for testing activities such as exploratory testing and debugging, where we require data fast to help us progress with our testing. But, as demonstrated, we can quickly come across either inconsistent or invalid data as our requirements become more complex.

> **Activity 6.2**
>
> Build a prompt that attempts to convert a piece of XML into either a SQL or JSON data structure. Ensure that the test data within the XML is transferred across without problems.

6.2   *Processing complex test data with LLMs*

In the original prompts to generate data, we set the rules and expectations in plain language. It means we are required to decode the structure of our data and its relationships before explicitly stating the learned rules in our prompt—a task that can quickly become quite complicated. Thus, instead of attempting to work out those rules ourselves, let's take a look at how we can send different data specifications formats or existing data to prompt an LLM to create more complex data.

6.2.1   *Using format standards in prompts*

Let's begin by looking at how we can employ data specification formats such as OpenAPI v3 and XSD that outline the structure and rules our data has to follow. These types of specifications can be useful for a few reasons:

- *Ready-to-go solutions*—Creators of specification frameworks have already handled the heavy lifting when it comes to communicating data structures in different formats. Consider the prompts we created earlier with the delimited rules that outline data names and types. All of this has already been considered and set out in specification frameworks. Therefore, it makes sense to use them rather than build our own.
- *Ubiquity*—The frameworks we'll use are standardized and have been adopted by lots of teams and organizations. This increases the likelihood that LLMs have

been trained on specification frameworks, which will maximize our chances of obtaining a desired output when we send a prompt.

- *Free use*—If we are working in teams that use tools such as OpenAPI and XSD to specify data structure or APIs, then the specifications are already available for us to use. The work is already done in the design phase for a feature or application.
- *Intrinsic testability*—Employing a commonly used structure means that an LLM has likely been exposed to it more in its training than if we were using proprietary structures. This means that an LLM is likely to increase the probability of a higher-value output and assist our testing further.

Given that this approach has a few benefits, let's take a look at how they can be added to prompts to generate data for us.

JSON WITH OPENAPI

We'll start by creating a prompt that uses the OpenAPI 3.0 format to create JSON data, resulting in the following prompt, which sets out the prompt instructions using the delimiter, format, and work-our-solution tactics

 You are a JSON data generator. Generate a JSON array with 3 randomized JSON objects based on the OpenAPI schema delimited by three hashes. Confirm that all 3 JSON objects match the OpenAPI schema rules before outputting the results.

We then provide the OpenAPI specification for processing:

```
###
openapi: 3.0.0
components:
  schemas:
    Room:
      title: Room
      type: object
      properties:
        accessible:
          type: boolean
        description:
          type: string
        type:
          type: string
          pattern: Single|Double|Twin|Family|Suite
        features:
          type: array
          items:
            type: string
            pattern: WiFi|TV|Radio|Refreshments|Safe|
        image:
          type: string
        roomNumber:
          type: string
        roomPrice:
          type: integer
          format: int32
```

```
          minimum: 0
          maximum: 999
          exclusiveMinimum: true
          exclusiveMaximum: false
        roomid:
          type: integer
          format: int32
      required:
        - accessible
        - description
        - features
        - image
        - roomNumber
        - roomPrice
###
```

Notice how the prompt indicates at the start that we intend to use the OpenAPI format to outline our data requirements. We use this to set our expectations of how the resulting data should be structured, which we can see when submitting the prompt to ChatGPT and receiving the following output:

```
[
  {
    "accessible": true,
    "description": "Cozy single room with a view",
    "type": "Single",
    "features": ["WiFi", "TV"],
    "image": "single_room.jpg",
    "roomNumber": "101",
    "roomPrice": 75,
    "roomid": 1
  },
  {
    "accessible": false,
    "description": "Spacious double room with amenities",
    "type": "Double",
    "features": ["WiFi", "TV", "Refreshments"],
    "image": "double_room.jpg",
    "roomNumber": "202",
    "roomPrice": 120,
    "roomid": 2
  },
  {
    "accessible": true,
    "description": "Family suite with a view and entertainment",
    "type": "Family",
    "features": ["WiFi", "TV", "Radio", "Refreshments", "Safe"],
    "image": "family_suite.jpg",
    "roomNumber": "305",
    "roomPrice": 180,
    "roomid": 3
  }
]
```

Compared to the previous data we generated, this data feels more accurate. The descriptions are more detailed and cite other attributes of the room found elsewhere. For example, the family suite description references the data related to the room type and features.

The image attributes are questionable as they simply provide an image name, but that might suffice if images are stored within our application. However, what our use of the OpenAPI language allows us to do is to set more detailed rules, meaning that we could update the image section of the specification from

```
image:
  type: string
```

to the following, in which the pattern points to test images we might have generated earlier:

```
image:
  type: string
  items:
    type: string
    pattern:
https://realdomain.com/image_1.png|https://realdomain.com/image_2.png
```

If we were to add this pattern into our prompt and send it to an LLM, it would return objects such as this one:

```
{
    "accessible": true,
    "description": "Cozy single room with a city view",
    "type": "Single",
    "features": ["WiFi", "TV"],
    «image»: «https://realdomain.com/image_1.png»,
    "roomNumber": "101",
    "roomPrice": 89,
    "roomid": 12345
}
```

By utilizing different specification rules used in OpenAPI, we can control our output more successfully.

XML AND XSD

The same process can be applied to other formats. Consider the following prompt that uses the same approach as the previous one but takes an XML Schema Definition (XSD) instead. We use format, delimiter, and work-out-solution tactics to outline the prompt to take an XSD format:

 You are an XML data generator. Generate 3 randomized XML objects based on the XSD schema delimited by three hashes. Add all the XML objects to parent element of rooms. Confirm that all 3 XML subobjects match the XSD schema rules before outputting the results.

Next, we provide the XSD format to set how we want data output:

```
###
<?xml version="1.0" encoding="UTF-8"?>
<xs:schema xmlns:xs="http://www.w3.org/2001/XMLSchema">

    <xs:element name="room">
        <xs:complexType>
            <xs:sequence>
                <xs:element name="accessible" type="xs:boolean"/>
                <xs:element name="description" type="xs:string"/>
                <xs:element name="type">
                    <xs:simpleType>
                        <xs:restriction base="xs:string">
                            <xs:enumeration value="Single"/>
                            <xs:enumeration value="Double"/>
                            <xs:enumeration value="Twin"/>
                            <xs:enumeration value="Family"/>
                            <xs:enumeration value="Suite"/>
                        </xs:restriction>
                    </xs:simpleType>
                </xs:element>
                <xs:element name="features">
                    <xs:complexType>
                        <xs:sequence>
                            <xs:element name="feature"
                                type="FeatureType" minOccurs="0"
                                maxOccurs="unbounded"/>
                        </xs:sequence>
                    </xs:complexType>
                </xs:element>
                <xs:element name="image" type="xs:string"/>
                <xs:element name="roomNumber" type="xs:string"/>
                <xs:element name="roomPrice" type="xs:decimal"/>
                <xs:element name="roomid" type="xs:integer"/>
            </xs:sequence>
        </xs:complexType>
    </xs:element>

    <xs:simpleType name="FeatureType">
        <xs:restriction base="xs:string">
            <xs:enumeration value="WiFi"/>
            <xs:enumeration value="TV"/>
            <xs:enumeration value="Radio"/>
            <xs:enumeration value="Refreshments"/>
            <xs:enumeration value="Safe"/>
            <xs:enumeration value="Views"/>
        </xs:restriction>
    </xs:simpleType>

</xs:schema>
###
```

The prompt works in a manner similar to the one before. This prompt comes with an additional step to ensure that our test data is grouped by storing it under a single root node. But the rest of the prompt works the same, resulting in an XML output that is similar to the previous prompt that generated JSON data, as demonstrated in the response I got when I prompted ChatGPT for XML test data:

```xml
<?xml version="1.0" encoding="UTF-8"?>
<rooms xmlns:xsi="http://www.w3.org/2001/XMLSchema-instance"
 xsi:noNamespaceSchemaLocation="schema.xsd">
    <room>
        <accessible>true</accessible>
        <description>Cozy single room with a view</description>
        <type>Single</type>
        <features>
            <feature>WiFi</feature>
            <feature>TV</feature>
            <feature>Views</feature>
        </features>
        <image>single_room.jpg</image>
        <roomNumber>101</roomNumber>
        <roomPrice>89.99</roomPrice>
        <roomid>1001</roomid>
    </room>
    <room>
        <accessible>false</accessible>
        <description>Luxurious suite with all amenities</description>
        <type>Suite</type>
        <features>
            <feature>WiFi</feature>
            <feature>TV</feature>
            <feature>Safe</feature>
            <feature>Refreshments</feature>
            <feature>Views</feature>
        </features>
        <image>suite_room.jpg</image>
        <roomNumber>201</roomNumber>
        <roomPrice>349.99</roomPrice>
        <roomid>1002</roomid>
    </room>
    <room>
        <accessible>true</accessible>
        <description>Spacious family room for a comfortable
stay</description>
        <type>Family</type>
        <features>
            <feature>WiFi</feature>
            <feature>TV</feature>
            <feature>Radio</feature>
            <feature>Safe</feature>
        </features>
        <image>family_room.jpg</image>
        <roomNumber>301</roomNumber>
        <roomPrice>179.99</roomPrice>
        <roomid>1003</roomid>
```

```
    </room>
</rooms>
```

These types of prompts can be extremely useful when we need to create test data for NoSQL databases. I remember once working on a project with XML documents that included more than 1,000 elements. It was practically impossible to generate all the test data we required, so we had to compromise. But with an LLM and a prompt similar to the ones we've just looked at, the process of creating XML documents would have taken a matter of minutes.

> ### Activity 6.3
> Use either an OpenAPI or XSD specification to create new test data. If you have access to the specifications, try them out. Alternatively, locate example specifications and try them out in a prompt to generate test data.

6.2.2 *SQL exports as prompt guides*

The prompts we've explored so far have created data entities that exist as a single entity, but it's just as common to work with applications in which data is split into separate locations. For example, how would we prompt an LLM to create data for a SQL-based database that contained data distributed across multiple tables?

One method is to take an alternative approach using the few-shot tactic (providing examples to a prompt) and provide the structure of a database, along with examples, to demonstrate what data is created and where. Take for example the following prompt requesting SQL data to be generated across two different tables. First, we set out the initial instructions for the prompt using delimiter and structured format tactic:

 You are a SQL generator. Take the sql statement delimited by three hashes and create a SQL statement that generates 5 new records that follow the format of the provided statement.

We then have the LLM work out the solution before sharing the output:

 Check that each new entry doesn't match the provided SQL statement before outputting the newly generated data and that the SQL can be executed successfully before outputting it.

Finally, we provide the SQL for each table for the LLM to process

```
###
CREATE TABLE rooms (roomid int NOT NULL AUTO_INCREMENT, room_name
  varchar(255), type varchar(255), beds int, accessible boolean,
  image varchar(2000), description varchar(2000),
  features varchar(100) ARRAY, roomPrice int, primary key (roomid));

INSERT INTO rooms (room_name, type, beds, accessible, image,
  description, features, roomPrice) VALUES ('101', 'single', 1,
```

```
true, 'https://www.mwtestconsultancy.co.uk/img/testim/room2.jpg',
'Aenean porttitor mauris sit amet lacinia molestie. In posuere
accumsan aliquet. Maecenas sit amet nisl massa. Interdum et
malesuada fames ac ante.', ARRAY['TV', 'WiFi', 'Safe'], 100);

CREATE TABLE bookings (bookingid int NOT NULL AUTO_INCREMENT, roomid
int, firstname varchar(255), lastname varchar(255),
depositpaid boolean, checkin date, checkout date,
primary key (bookingid), FOREIGN KEY (roomid) REFERENCES
ROOMS(roomid));

INSERT INTO bookings (roomid, firstname, lastname, depositpaid,
checkin, checkout) VALUES (1, 'James', 'Dean', true, '2022-02-01',
'2022-02-05');
###
```

In this prompt, we've provided SQL statements for two different tables connected via the `roomid`. The first is the `rooms` table, which has the following attributes (laid out in a more readable format):

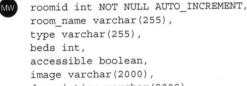

```
roomid int NOT NULL AUTO_INCREMENT,
room_name varchar(255),
type varchar(255),
beds int,
accessible boolean,
image varchar(2000),
description varchar(2000),
features varchar(100) ARRAY,
roomPrice int,
primary key (roomid)
```

And the second is the `bookings` table:

```
bookingid int NOT NULL AUTO_INCREMENT,
roomid int,
firstname varchar(255),
lastname varchar(255),
depositpaid boolean,
checkin date,
checkout date,
primary key (bookingid),
FOREIGN KEY (roomid) REFERENCES ROOMS(roomid)
```

Providing the LLM with both `CREATE` and `INSERT` statements helps maximize the desired output, ensuring not only that the correct type of test data is created, but also that the relationship between data sets is correct. If we were to provide only insert statements, we'd be providing less context and increasing the risk of foreign keys being populated with relationships to nonexistent records.

Sending this prompt to ChatGPT returned the following response:

```
-- Generate new rooms records
INSERT INTO rooms (room_name, type, beds, accessible, image,
```

```
description, features, roomPrice) VALUES
 ('102', 'double', 2, true, 'https://www.example.com/image1.jpg',
'Lorem ipsum dolor sit amet, consectetur adipiscing elit.',
ARRAY['TV', 'WiFi'], 150),
 ('103', 'single', 1, false, 'https://www.example.com/image2.jpg',
'Nulla facilisi. Sed at lorem nec elit rhoncus tristique.',
ARRAY['WiFi', 'Safe'], 120),
 ('104', 'suite', 3, true, 'https://www.example.com/image3.jpg',
'Pellentesque fermentum tortor a dui interdum, ut efficitur felis
pharetra.', ARRAY['TV', 'Safe', 'Minibar'], 220),
 ('105', 'double', 2, false, 'https://www.example.com/image4.jpg',
'Vestibulum non tortor sit amet lacus mattis efficitur.',
ARRAY['WiFi'], 160),
 ('106', 'single', 1, true, 'https://www.example.com/image5.jpg',
'Fusce ut ligula nec ligula auctor tincidunt vel sit amet dui.',
ARRAY['TV', 'WiFi'], 130);

-- Generate new bookings records
INSERT INTO bookings (roomid, firstname, lastname, depositpaid,
checkin, checkout) VALUES
 (2, 'Emma', 'Watson', true, '2023-08-15', '2023-08-20'),
 (3, 'John', 'Smith', false, '2023-09-01', '2023-09-05'),
 (4, 'Sophia', 'Johnson', true, '2023-08-25', '2023-08-30'),
 (5, 'Michael', 'Williams', false, '2023-09-10', '2023-09-15'),
 (6, 'Olivia', 'Brown', true, '2023-09-20', '2023-09-25');
```

The test data inserted is similar to the responses from other prompts, but there is now the addition of `roomid` values using ids that connect the bookings to existing rooms, which have also been generated in the response.

What these prompts have demonstrated is that if we have data that contains complex relationships or many different parameters, we can use existing documentation to assist test data generation. This is not only a great time saver but also an approach that ensures our test data generation can stay in lockstep with the structure of our data at any given time, saving us even more time in test data maintenance.

Don't forget data privacy

In the examples provided in this chapter, we've used dummy data structures and specifications, but when we create test data for our applications it's likely that we'll rely on either our organization's intellectual property or user data. If we are to use those items to create our test data, we need to make sure that we aren't violating internal policies for sharing intellectual property or laws around user data privacy. Depending on what we can and can't share will determine how we frame our prompts.

Activity 6.4

Use the SQL prompt to create your own test data. Try either locating SQL from an application you are working on or using example SQL to see what happens.

6.3 Setting up LLMs as test data managers

We've examined how to create data by sending prompts through tools such as ChatGPT. But how can we go about integrating these types of prompts into our automated checks? Let's take a look at the potential of accessing LLMs via API platforms by enhancing this simple UI automated check with data generation from an LLM model:

```
@Test
public void exampleContactUsFormTest() throws InterruptedException {
```

We use Selenium to open a webpage:

```
driver.get("https://automationintesting.online/#/");
```

Next, we complete the Contact Us form on the webpage:

```
ContactFormPage contactFormPage = new ContactFormPage(driver);
contactFormPage.enterName("John Smith");
contactFormPage.enterEmail("john@example.com");
contactFormPage.enterPhone("01234567890");
contactFormPage.enterSubject("Test Subject");
contactFormPage.enterDescription("This is a test message");
contactFormPage.clickSubmitButton();
```

Then we assert that the contact form page has been submitted:

```
assert contactFormPage.getSuccessMessage().contains("Thanks for getting
    in touch");
```

With this automated check, we're going to replace the hardcoded strings used to complete the contact form and instead connect to the OpenAI API platform and prompt one of their LLM models to create test data that we can then parse and use in our check. Examples of the initial and completed OpenAI integrated check can be found in the supporting repository at https://mng.bz/n0dv.

6.3.1 Setting up an OpenAI account

Before we can start sending prompts using the OpenAI API platform, we'll need to set up an account. This can be done by registering via https://platform.openai.com/.

> **OpenAI platform costs**
>
> OpenAI charges based on the number of tokens you send to and receive from an LLM. A *token* is essentially a word or collection of smaller words. For example, "Hello ChatGPT" would count as two tokens. The more tokens you use, meaning the bigger the prompts and content you receive back, the more it costs. If you are registering for a new account with OpenAI at this point, they will give you $5 in free credit that can be used during your first three months. This is more than enough for what we need to complete our exercise. However, since the free credit expires after three months, if you have no free credits left,

(continued)

you will need to provide billing details before you can send and receive prompts: https://mng.bz/vJRx. Also, you are strongly advised to set a usage limit that works best for you so that you don't end up with a surprising bill: https://platform.openai.com/account/billing/limits.

Once registered, we need to generate an API key that we'll provide in our requests to authenticate ourselves. This can be done via https://platform.openai.com/account/api-keys and clicking the Create New Secret Key button, which asks us to give our API key a name. Upon entering a name and clicking the Create key, we'll be given an API key, as shown in figure 6.1.

Figure 6.1   A newly created API key for the Open API platform

As the instructions state, we need to record this API key elsewhere for future use as we'll not be able to view it again. So, we make a note of the key and then click Done to make sure our key has been saved, as shown in figure 6.2.

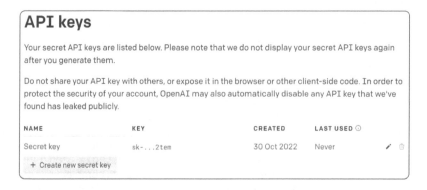

Figure 6.2   Screen shot of the API key manager for the OpenAI API platform

With our key created and recorded, we're ready to begin work on integrating OpenAI into our project.

6.3.2 Connecting to OpenAI

Our first step is to build the necessary code to send an HTTP request to OpenAI and confirm that we can get a response back. So, we begin by adding the following library into our `pom.xml` that we'll use to send our request:

```
<dependency>
    <groupId>dev.langchain4j</groupId>
    <artifactId>langchain4j-open-ai</artifactId>
    <version>0.31.0</version>
</dependency>
```

LangChain4j is a Java implementation of the popular LangChain toolset that's written in Python. It offers a collection of tools that can be used to integrate with different LLMs. For our example test, we'll be relying on OpenAI's GPT models to generate our test data. So, we'll use the OpenAI specific version of LangChain to get basic access to sending a prompt. However, if we wanted more control or options, we could use the full AI services version of LangChain.

> **gpt-3.5-turbo and other models**
>
> One of the features offered by the OpenAI API platform is the ability to send prompts to different LLM models. gpt-3.5-turbo is the model that is, at the time of writing, used to power the free version of ChatGPT. As we'll learn, we can swap this out to call other models such as gpt-4o. Different models offer different features at different price points. For example, gpt-4o is a more effective LLM compared to gpt-3.5-turbo. However, the price point to use gpt-4o is much higher. More details on other models can be found in the OpenAI platform documentation at https://platform.openai.com/docs/models/overview.

With the necessary libraries installed, our next step is to build a prompt that will request an LLM to generate our required test data. The initial instructions use the structured output and delimiter tactics:

 You are a data generator. Create me random data in a JSON format based on the criteria delimited by three hashes. Additional data requirements are shared between back ticks.

Data to be processed is added with additional instructions:

 ###
name
email
phone `UK format`

```
    subject `Over 20 characters in length`
    description `Over 50 characters in length`
    ###
```

We can test this prompt by adding it and the necessary code to send the prompt into a new automated check:

```
@Test
public void exampleContactUsFormTestWithGPT() {
```

We create a new OpenAIChat model and provide an API key:

```
OpenAiChatModel model = OpenAiChatModel.withApiKey("Enter API key");
```

Then we add our prompt to a string:

```
String prompt = """
        You are a data generator. Create me random data in a
        JSON format based on the criteria delimited by three hashes.
        Additional data requirements are shared between back ticks.
        ###
        name
        email
        phone `UK format`
        subject `Over 20 characters in length`
        description `Over 50 characters in length`
        ###
        """;
```

Finally, we send the prompt to a GPT model and store the response in a string:

```
String testData = model.generate(prompt);

System.out.println(testData);
}
```

Running the check again, we'll see the LLM returns something similar to

```
    {
        "name": "John Doe",
        "email": "johndoe@example.com",
        "phone": "+44 1234 567890",
        "subject": "Lorem ipsum dolor sit amet consectetur",
        "description": "Lorem ipsum dolor sit amet, consectetur adipiscing
          elit. Suspendisse aliquet, tortor eu aliquet tincidunt, erat mi.»
    }
```

Next, we'll need to parse this into a Java object, so we create a new class `ContactForm-Details` that can convert the JSON into an object:

```
public class ContactFormDetails {

    private String name;
```

```
        private String email;
        private String phone;
        private String subject;
        private String description;

        public ContactFormDetails(String name, String email,
        String phone, String subject, String description) {
            this.name = name;
            this.email = email;
            this.phone = phone;
            this.subject = subject;
            this.description = description;
        }

        public String getName() {
            return name;
        }

        public String getEmail() {
            return email;
        }

        public String getPhone() {
            return phone;
        }

        public String getSubject() {
            return subject;
        }

        public String getDescription() {
            return description;
        }
}
```

With our `ContactFormDetails` class created, we can now convert the prompt response, which is currently a string, into a POJO for further use:

```
OpenAiChatModel model = OpenAiChatModel.withApiKey("Enter API key");
String prompt = """
        You are a data generator. Create me random data in a
        JSON format based on the criteria delimited by three hashes.
        Additional data requirements are shared between back ticks.
        ###
        name
        email
        phone `UK format`
        subject `Over 20 characters in length`
        description `Over 50 characters in length`
        ###
        """;

String testData = model.generate(prompt);

ContactFormDetails contactFormDetails =
    new Gson().fromJson(testData, ContactFormDetails.class);
```

We now have the necessary test data to use in our automated check:

```
@Test
public void exampleContactUsFormTestWithGPT() {
```

The following block of code sends a prompt to OpenAI to generate test data:

```
OpenAiChatModel model = OpenAiChatModel.withApiKey("Enter API key");
String prompt = """
        You are a data generator. Create me random data in a
        JSON format based on the criteria delimited by three hashes.
        Additional data requirements are shared between back ticks.
        ###
        name
        email
        phone `UK format`
        subject `Over 20 characters in length`
        description `Over 50 characters in length`
        ###
        """;

String testData = model.generate(prompt);
```

Next, we extract the test data from the responses and convert it into an object:

```
ContactFormDetails contactFormDetails =
    new Gson().fromJson(testData, ContactFormDetails.class);

driver.get("https://automationintesting.online/#/");
```

Then we use the test data to complete the Contact Us form and assert success:

```
ContactFormPage contactFormPage = new ContactFormPage(driver);
contactFormPage.enterName(contactFormDetails.getName());
contactFormPage.enterEmail(contactFormDetails.getEmail());
contactFormPage.enterPhone(contactFormDetails.getPhone());
contactFormPage.enterSubject(contactFormDetails.getSubject());
contactFormPage.enterDescription(contactFormDetails.getDescription());
contactFormPage.clickSubmitButton();

assert contactFormPage.getSuccessMessage()
        .contains("Thanks for getting in touch");
```

This completes the integration of the OpenAI API platform into our automated check. Upon executing the check, we should see it pass and that test data has been successfully used to create a contact message, as shown in figure 6.3.

We could improve the code further by perhaps storing prompts in external files and importing them into our checks when required. This may be beneficial when prompts are used on multiple occasions. It would also mean that when changes are required for test data, we would simply update our prompts with new details in a way that anyone, regardless of the experience of working with test data, could do.

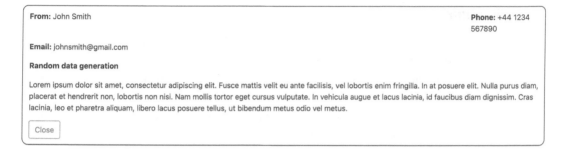

From: John Smith   **Phone:** +44 1234
                                                                                         567890

Email: johnsmith@gmail.com

Random data generation

Lorem ipsum dolor sit amet, consectetur adipiscing elit. Fusce mattis velit eu ante facilisis, vel lobortis enim fringilla. In at posuere elit. Nulla purus diam, placerat et hendrerit non, lobortis non nisi. Nam mollis tortor eget cursus vulputate. In vehicula augue et lacus lacinia, id faucibus diam dignissim. Cras lacinia, leo et pharetra aliquam, libero lacus posuere tellus, ut bibendum metus odio vel metus.

Close

Figure 6.3   A message created using LLM test data

Activity 6.5

Create a new automated check that requires inputting test data. Using the prompt method, create a new prompt to generate test data and then pass it through your automated check.

6.4   *Benefiting from generated test data*

This chapter demonstrated that LLMs can be quite adept at generating test data. It can help us quickly create data for various testing activities from automation to exploratory testing, support managing complex data sets, and simplify the process of managing test data using natural language prompts. However, for this, we need to create prompts that provide clear instructions about the format we want data in and what examples to draw from, ensuring that what we're sending to an LLM doesn't impact personal and organizational privacy. Going back to our area of effect model, we can see the roles of humans and AI in test data generation described in figure 6.4.

By using the tactics we've learned with prompt engineering in a creative manner, we can create test data for a wide range of situations, from simple to complex, to help us save time in test data management.

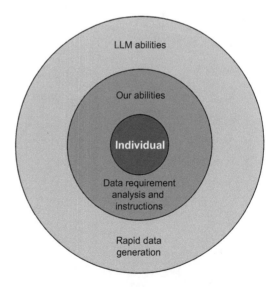

Figure 6.4   The area of effect model describing the roles of humans and AI in test data generation

Summary

- Prompts can be built to rapidly generate data in any common format (JSON, XML, or SQL, for example).

- The relationship between data can sometimes be incorrect if not explicitly set in a prompt.

- Prompts can also be built to transform data from one format into another, while ensuring the raw data from an original format is copied over.

- We can use data specification formats such as OpenAPI and XSD in prompts to set our expectations of how data is structured.

- Using SQL statements that create the initial structure of a database can be used to prompt LLMs when working with distributed data structures.

- OpenAI offers an API platform that can be used to interact with different AI models, including gpt-3.5 and gpt-4o.

- We can programmatically build HTTP requests to send prompts to OpenAI LLMs to generate test data.

- Prompting LLMs for test data requires building clear prompts with explicit expectations and useful examples.

7
Accelerating and improving UI automation using AI

This chapter covers

- How to create UI automation rapidly using GitHub Copilot and ChatGPT
- How to improve UI automation rapidly using GitHub Copilot and ChatGPT

If there is one area in the software testing industry that has garnered the most attention regarding the use of AI tools, it's UI automation. As large language models (LLMs) began capturing attention, people in the testing world quickly focused on how UI automated checks could be easily generated through tools such as Copilot and ChatGPT. The possibilities and ideas around using AI tools for UI automation have been expanding rapidly. But although the enthusiasm for these tools is significant, and tool vendors and automators alike rush to use AI, we must be mindful of where and how AI can be of use.

Success with AI in creating automation is as much about knowing *when* to use AI tooling as it is about knowing *how* to use it. For this reason, this chapter focuses on how to break down the process of creating and maintaining automated checks and discover where AI tools can speed up our processes, while ensuring that we still deliver valuable automation.

7.1   *Rapidly creating UI automation*

Head to ChatGPT and ask it to generate a Selenium test in Java that automates a login page, and it will happily oblige. This might seem like an effective path to take, but let's take a look at a brief example of this process and see what happens. For the prompt, we can use

 Assuming the role of a test automator, create an automated test using Selenium and Java that automates and validates the log in process for an application

It will return a code example such as

```java
import org.openqa.selenium.By;
import org.openqa.selenium.WebDriver;
import org.openqa.selenium.WebElement;
import org.openqa.selenium.chrome.ChromeDriver;

public class LoginTest {
    public static void main(String[] args) {
        // Set the path to the chromedriver executable
        System.setProperty("webdriver.chrome.driver", "path/to/
        ➥ chromedriver");

        // Create an instance of ChromeDriver
        WebDriver driver = new ChromeDriver();

        // Open the application login page
        driver.get("https://example.com/login");

        // Find the username and password input fields
        WebElement usernameField =
        ➥ driver.findElement(By.id("username"));
        WebElement passwordField =
        ➥ driver.findElement(By.id("password"));

        // Enter the username and password
        usernameField.sendKeys("your-username");
        passwordField.sendKeys("your-password");

        // Submit the login form
        driver.findElement(By.id("login-button")).click();

        // Wait for the page to load
        // You can use an explicit wait here to ensure the page is
        ➥ fully loaded

        // Verify the login success by checking for a specific
        ➥ element on the next page
        WebElement welcomeMessage = driver.findElement(By.xpath("//
        ➥ h1[contains(text(), 'Welcome')]"));
        if (welcomeMessage.isDisplayed()) {
```

```
            System.out.println("Login successful!");
        } else {
            System.out.println("Login failed!");
        }

        // Close the browser
        driver.quit();
    }
}
```

The code looks correct and would likely compile. But if we were to bring this code into our automation framework, we should ask ourselves, "How much of this would we need to change to make it work with our product under test?" Chances are we would need to

- Remove the `Driver` instantiation to use our own driver factory.
- Point the check to the correct application by updating `driver.get`.
- Move the `findElements` methods to relevant Page objects.
- Update the selectors so that they are using the ones that align with our product.
- Update the assertion to meet our assumptions.

Before we know it, we've ended up replacing nearly all the code suggested by ChatGPT, which doesn't feel like an efficient use of our time. This is because although tools such as ChatGPT and Copilot can rapidly generate code on demand, they lack the context of our systems. That is, if we ask these tools to create our automated checks with little input provided, the result will be code that requires extensive rework. Instead, we want to take a more symbiotic approach, using AI tools in targeted ways to help us with specific tasks in creating automated UI checks.

Consider the visualization in figure 7.1, which breaks down the various components included in a common automated check that works on the UI layer.

As we can see, there are many moving parts—from the framework itself, which handles the dependencies and reporting of automated checks, to the various activities that an automated check carries out to create state, interact with a UI, and assert against expectations. Each of these parts can be guided using AI, so, rather than attempting to rely on an AI to create everything at once, we focus on specific tasks throughout building and maintaining of our automated check and use LLMs to speed up the process.

AI compared to record and playback tools

A valid question to ask is how the use of AI differs from record and playback tools and their ability to record our actions and convert them into code. If we were to use LLMs to generate automated checks, then the difference wouldn't be great. In fact, record and playback tools would likely be better because they are interacting with the system and implicitly learning about the product's context and rules during recording.

However, one limitation of record and playback is when they encounter more complex frameworks that will be arranged using approaches such as Page Object and Screenplay patterns to make them more maintainable. Record and playback tools tend to output

(continued)
resulting code as a script run by itself, separate from others. When that script needs to be integrated into the framework, we will likely need to rework and reorganize our initial script dramatically, which brings us back to the initial problem—slow progress in creating automated UI checks.

What this chapter proposes is that we use LLMs in very specific situations, targeting specific actions. If we want to rapidly create Page objects, then an LLM can help us with that task—its output can be quickly plugged into a wider framework with minimum rework.

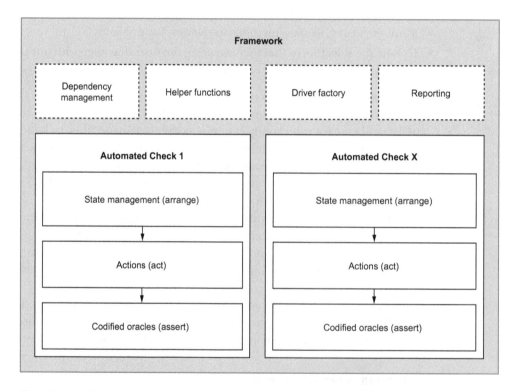

Figure 7.1   A visual representation of the component parts of an automated UI check

To demonstrate this process, let's take a look at how we can use tools such as Copilot and ChatGPT in our automation workflow, selecting specific actions that AI tools can assist with, by building an automated check for the website https://automationintesting .online, which is a mock bed-and-breakfast booking site that can be used to practice various testing and automation activities.

In this example, we check whether a message is shown in the admin section of the website. To do this, we'll need to codify the following steps:

1 Launch a browser.
2 Head to automationintesting.online.
3 Complete the Contact Us form on the home page.
4 Head to the Admin section of the site and log in.
5 Load the Message section and confirm that the created message appears.

This process is summarized in figure 7.2.

1. Complete contact us form   2. Log in as admin   3. Validate message appears

Figure 7.2   Visual representation of the automated UI check that will be created

Although the example itself is nothing spectacular, what we'll learn is that we can accelerate our work using AI tools as we complete each step—so let's begin. For reference, you can review the code that was generated for this example on GitHub (https://mng .bz/4pXB).

> **Setting up Copilot**
>
> This chapter assumes that you have installed and configured the Copilot plugin within your IDE. If you haven't already completed the setup process, you can find installation instructions in appendix B.

> **Activity 7.1**
>
> Follow the steps in this chapter to see whether you can generate a similar automated check. As always, remember that the output that comes from ChatGPT and Copilot may differ from what has been captured in the following example.

7.1.1   Setting up a project

We'll carry out the example in this section in Java. This is a useful language to demonstrate the value of using AI tools, because Java is known for its reliance on boilerplate code (a great place in which LLMs can help build for us). For our first step, we need to create a new Maven project and, once the project is created, add the following dependencies into our `pom.xml` file:

```
<dependencies>
    <dependency>
        <groupId>org.junit.jupiter</groupId>
        <artifactId>junit-jupiter-engine</artifactId>
        <version>5.9.2</version>
        <scope>test</scope>
    </dependency>
    <dependency>
        <groupId>org.seleniumhq.selenium</groupId>
        <artifactId>selenium-java</artifactId>
        <version>4.9.1</version>
        <scope>test</scope>
    </dependency>
    <dependency>
        <groupId>io.github.bonigarcia</groupId>
        <artifactId>webdrivermanager</artifactId>
        <version>5.5.3</version>
        <scope>test</scope>
    </dependency>
</dependencies>
```

Now we have everything we need to start developing our automated check.

With our dependencies in place, we can create the necessary packages—`com.example` and our `Test` class—which we'll name `MessageTest`. From here, we can begin to use Copilot to build our automated check, but we need to prompt Copilot with some information to begin the process. So first we add in a `WebDriver` variable inside our `MessageTest` class

```
private static WebDriver driver;
```

followed by the code comment:

```
// Use WebDriverManager to download the driver binaries
// and start the browser server for us.
```

The combination of code and comment acts sufficiently as a prompt to trigger the following response from Copilot:

```
public static void setupClass() {
    WebDriverManager.chromedriver().setup();
}
```

This is a good start, but it's missing the driver instantiation and `BeforeAll` hook, which we can add to the next line below the `WebDriverManager` call:

```
driver = new ChromeDriver();
```

which gives us the following Before hook:

```
@BeforeAll
public static void setupClass() {
    WebDriverManager.chromedriver().setup();

    driver = new ChromeDriver();
}
```

To tweak or not to tweak prompts: Making the efficient choice

Another observation about working with prompts to generate desired output is that it can be tempting to want to tweak a prompt multiple times to produce the right output, which can be time consuming. In the previous example, the code comment was likely not clear enough for Copilot to produce the complete code snippet we required. The options then are to improve the prompt or add the missing sections of code that are required. In this context, adding the required code made sense. I knew what I required, and spending time tweaking the prompt would have been wasteful. However, if my knowledge of what I wanted was shallower, then I might have chosen to tweak the prompt further. Efficiency is created by being aware of what is the right choice to make at a given time.

We have our `BeforeAll` hook in place, so next we want to create a teardown hook, which we can do by adding the annotation

```
@AfterAll
```

prompting Copilot to return

```
public static void teardown() {
    driver.quit();
}
```

Our second prompt is arguably more accurate than the first one because we are beginning to flesh out the context in which Copilot can be prompted. The more we add to our codebase, the more potential Copilot has to accurately add in what we want. Finally, to verify that everything is working, let's add in a bare-bones `@Test` to ensure that everything is running:

```
@Test
public void testMessageIsCreated() {
    driver.get("https://automationintesting.online");
}
```

So far, so good. We've set up our project and our initial test with the support of Copilot. We've also observed that, initially, Copilot is lacking details to help recommend the correct lines of code. But as we develop, we'll start to observe its accuracy improve. This is a great start—now let's see how tools such as ChatGPT can help speed up our work even more.

7.1.2   *Creating our initial check with ChatGPT support*

With the framework in place, we can turn our attention to completing the Contact Us form on the home page. To help contextualize what we'll be working with, see figure 7.3.

The figure shows multiple form fields to complete and a Submit button, all of which we will need to codify in our automated check. To do this, we'll need to create a Page object that captures each of the elements, which we'll use in our check to populate and submit the form. This process is a laborious one (and one that I personally find to be time consuming and boring, which are the types of emotional triggers explored in chapter 1). So, how can we speed up the process of creating Page objects? We could use Copilot to help us author our classes, but the process of identifying each CSS selector for each element has the potential to take up a lot of time. Instead, let's take a look at how we could use a prompt in ChatGPT to rapidly create our Page object for us.

Figure 7.3   The Contact Us form on the website under test

First, let's take a look at a prompt that can be used to trigger ChatGPT to generate our Page object (you can copy and paste the prompt into ChatGPT: https://mng.bz/QVpm). We set out instructions with the delimiter tactic:

 You are an expert Java Developer. Convert the HTML delimited by three hashes into a Java Selenium Page object using the `PageFactory` library and `@FindBy` annotations.

We provide HTML in the delimited section:

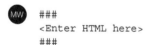
```
###
<Enter HTML here>
###
```

Breaking down the prompt, we can observe that it takes this form:

- Clear instructions at the start, informing ChatGPT of what we want to achieve
- A list of constraints that specifies clear instructions for what we expect from ChatGPT, stating which libraries and methods we'd like to explicitly use when creating our Page object

To create the Page object, we take the prompt we have just explored and add the HTML from our Contact form to the bottom before pasting it into ChatGPT. Again, feel free to use the already created prompt available on GitHub at https://mng.bz/QVpm:

```
<form>
    <div class="input-group mb-3">
      <div class="input-group-prepend">
        <span class="input-group-text" id="basic-addon1">
          <span class="fa fa-id-card"></span>
        </span>
      </div>
      <input type="text" data-testid="ContactName"
      class="form-control" placeholder="Name" aria-label="Name"
      id="name" aria-describedby="basic-addon1">
    </div>
    <div class="input-group mb-3">
      <div class="input-group-prepend">
        <span class="input-group-text" id="basic-addon1">
          <span class="fa fa-envelope"></span>
        </span>
      </div>
      <input type="text" data-testid="ContactEmail"
      class="form-control" placeholder="Email" aria-label="Email"
      id="email" aria-describedby="basic-addon1">
    </div>
    <div class="input-group mb-3">
      <div class="input-group-prepend">
        <span class="input-group-text" id="basic-addon1">
          <span class="fa fa-phone"></span>
        </span>
      </div>
      <input type="text" data-testid="ContactPhone"
      class="form-control" placeholder="Phone" aria-label="Phone"
      id="phone" aria-describedby="basic-addon1">
    </div>
    <div class="input-group mb-3">
      <div class="input-group-prepend">
        <span class="input-group-text" id="basic-addon1">
          <span class="fa fa-envelope"></span>
        </span>
      </div>
      <input type="text" data-testid="ContactSubject"
      class="form-control" placeholder="Subject" aria-label="Subject"
      id="subject" aria-describedby="basic-addon1">
    </div>
    <div class="input-group">
      <div class="input-group-prepend">
        <span class="input-group-text">Message</span>
      </div>
      <textarea data-testid="ContactDescription" class="form-control"
      aria-label="Description" id="description" rows="5"></textarea>
    </div>
    <br>
    <button type="button" class="btn btn-outline-primary float-right"
    id="submitContact">Submit</button>
</form>
```

Entering this prompt into ChatGPT yields the following code for our Page object:

```java
import org.openqa.selenium.WebDriver;
import org.openqa.selenium.WebElement;
import org.openqa.selenium.support.FindBy;
import org.openqa.selenium.support.PageFactory;

public class ContactFormPage {

    // WebDriver instance
    private WebDriver driver;

    // Constructor to initialize the PageFactory
    public ContactFormPage(WebDriver driver) {
        this.driver = driver;
        PageFactory.initElements(driver, this);
    }

    // WebElements for the form fields
    @FindBy(id = "name")
    private WebElement nameInput;

    @FindBy(id = "email")
    private WebElement emailInput;

    @FindBy(id = "phone")
    private WebElement phoneInput;

    @FindBy(id = "subject")
    private WebElement subjectInput;

    @FindBy(id = "description")
    private WebElement descriptionTextarea;

    @FindBy(id = "submitContact")
    private WebElement submitButton;

    // Methods to interact with the form
    public void enterName(String name) {
        nameInput.sendKeys(name);
    }

    public void enterEmail(String email) {
        emailInput.sendKeys(email);
    }

    public void enterPhone(String phone) {
        phoneInput.sendKeys(phone);
    }

    public void enterSubject(String subject) {
        subjectInput.sendKeys(subject);
    }

    public void enterDescription(String description) {
```

```
            descriptionTextarea.sendKeys(description);
    }

    public void clickSubmitButton() {
        submitButton.click();
    }
}
```

ChatGPT has not only successfully created a class that includes all the necessary methods required to complete and submit the contact form, but this was also done rapidly after a single prompt. In this example, the class was quite small, but regular Page objects can be pretty large. The time taken to write and maintain Page objects is compounded by the amount we require. So, by using ChatGPT to rapidly generate our code for us, we can continue developing our automated check faster.

Testability and AI tools

Even with AI tools, the testability of a product influences a tool's effectiveness. The way in which the HTML for the Contact Us form has been created can be said to have a high *testability*. The HTML is semantically correct, and it contains clear, stable HTML attributes in the `input` and `textarea` elements that ChatGPT can predict to put into the created class. If, however, the HTML we are working with requires us to identify more complex selectors, perhaps due to autogenerated IDs or a lack of HTML elements, then the performance of our prompt may not be as effective, requiring us to update and tweak our Page object to better suit our needs.

With our Page object created, we can head back to `MessageTest` and tab through Copilot's suggestions to create our necessary Contact Us form-filling code:

```
ContactFormPage contactFormPage = new ContactFormPage(driver);
contactFormPage.enterName("John Smith");
contactFormPage.enterEmail("test@email.com");
contactFormPage.enterPhone("0123456789");
contactFormPage.enterSubject("Testing");
contactFormPage.enterDescription("This is a test message");
contactFormPage.clickSubmitButton();
```

Copilot has read our object and helped us map out filling in the form. But although it can read the methods that exist in `ContactFormPage` and predict what's next, it lacks context on validation rules for each form field, which affects the test data it creates. Unlike in the previous chapter, in which test data was accurately set based on expectations, the data returned is generic and will cause problems. For example, the validation rule set for the Phone Number field requires 11 or more digits to be entered, so our predicted test data would cause our automated test to fail. Therefore, let's update the `enterPhone` parameter with data that will pass the phone number validation:

```
contactFormPage.enterPhone("07123456789");
```

With our message created, we now want to log in, which can be achieved by following a pattern similar to the one we have just followed. First, we create the necessary code to head to the Admin page:

```
driver.get("https://automationintesting.online/#/admin/");
```

Then, returning to our current chat with ChatGPT, we can reuse our earlier prompt to create a Page object for the admin login page, this time simply referring to the original prompt and providing it with new HTML to generate our class:

 Follow the previous prompt again, but this time use the following HTML:

```
<div class="col-sm-4">
    <div class="form-group">
        <input data-testid="username" type="text"
        style="border: 1px solid grey;" class="form-control"
        id="username"
        placeholder="Username">
    </div>
    <div class="form-group">
        <input data-testid="password" type="password"
        style="border: 1px solid grey;" class="form-control"
        id="password"
        placeholder="Password">
    </div>
    <button type="submit" data-testid="submit" id="doLogin"
    class="btn btn-primary float-right">Login</button>
</div>
```

This yields the following `LoginPage` code to add to our project:

```java
import org.openqa.selenium.WebDriver;
import org.openqa.selenium.WebElement;
import org.openqa.selenium.support.FindBy;
import org.openqa.selenium.support.PageFactory;

public class LoginPage {

    // WebDriver instance
    private WebDriver driver;

    // Constructor to initialize the PageFactory
    public LoginPage(WebDriver driver) {
        this.driver = driver;
        PageFactory.initElements(driver, this);
    }

    // WebElements for the form fields
    @FindBy(id = "username")
    private WebElement usernameInput;

    @FindBy(id = "password")
    private WebElement passwordInput;
```

```
@FindBy(id = "doLogin")
private WebElement loginButton;

// Methods to interact with the form
public void enterUsername(String username) {
    usernameInput.sendKeys(username);
}

public void enterPassword(String password) {
    passwordInput.sendKeys(password);
}

public void clickLoginButton() {
    loginButton.click();
}
}
```

Next, we create the `LoginPage` class in our code, fixing our missing imports, and then return to `MessageTest` and use Copilot to create our login step by tabbing through suggestions to produce the following:

```
LoginPage loginPage = new LoginPage(driver);
loginPage.enterUsername("admin");
loginPage.enterPassword("password");
loginPage.clickLoginButton();
```

Finally, we can execute one more loop of using ChatGPT and Copilot to complete our automated test by first adding the necessary code to navigate to the message page:

```
driver.get("https://automationintesting.online/#/admin/messages");
```

Then we create our final Page object, this time tweaking our prompt to ChatGPT to create a method that returns a count of messages:

 Follow the prompt again, this time I require a method that returns me the count of messages:

```
<div class="messages">
    <div class="row">
        <div class="col-sm-2 rowHeader">
            <p>Name</p>
        </div>
        <div class="col-sm-9 rowHeader">
            <p>Subject</p>
        </div>
        <div class="col-sm-1"></div>
    </div>
    <div class="row detail read-false" id="message0">
        <div class="col-sm-2" data-testid="message0">
            <p>James Dean</p>
        </div>
        <div class="col-sm-9" data-testid="messageDescription0">
            <p>Booking enquiry</p>
        </div>
```

```
        <div class="col-sm-1">
            <span data-testid="DeleteMessage0" class="fa fa-remove
roomDelete"></span>
        </div>
    </div>
</div>
```

It returns the following `MessagePage` class:

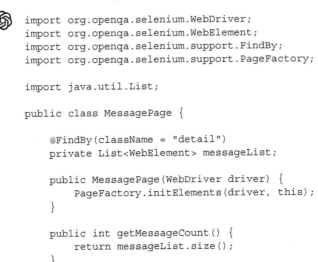

```
import org.openqa.selenium.WebDriver;
import org.openqa.selenium.WebElement;
import org.openqa.selenium.support.FindBy;
import org.openqa.selenium.support.PageFactory;

import java.util.List;

public class MessagePage {

    @FindBy(className = "detail")
    private List<WebElement> messageList;

    public MessagePage(WebDriver driver) {
        PageFactory.initElements(driver, this);
    }

    public int getMessageCount() {
        return messageList.size();
    }
}
```

Like before, we create a `MessagePage` class in our codebase, fix our imports, and return to `MessageTest` to let Copilot predict the following code to complete our automated check:

```
MessagePage messagePage = new MessagePage(driver);
assert messagePage.getMessageCount() == 1;
```

7.1.3   *Filling in gaps from generated code*

This completes our automated check, but if we were to run this code, it would likely result in the failure of the automated check. The failure occurs because, to get the message count, we must wait for the count to load, which is missing from our automated check. Although this failure differs from the incorrect test data being added by Copilot we experienced earlier, the reason for our current problem is similar. ChatGPT predicts the code we require based on what the prompt is asking and the HTML provided. It lacks the ability to understand what parts of our system may require waits in place to prevent an automated check from failing. However, we can resolve this problem by returning to ChatGPT and submitting the prompt:

 Can you improve the `MessagePage` class and have it wait for the message list to load

ChatGPT responds with an updated version of `MessagePage`:

```
private WebDriver driver;
private WebDriverWait wait;

@FindBy(className = "detail")
private List<WebElement> messageList;

public MessagePage(WebDriver driver) {
    this.driver = driver;
    // Adjust the timeout as needed
    this.wait = new WebDriverWait(driver, 10);
    PageFactory.initElements(driver, this);
}

public int getMessageCount() {
    wait.until(ExpectedConditions.visibilityOfElementLocated(
      By.className("detail")));

    return messageList.size();
}
```

This is a step forward in improving our automated check, but it also demonstrates again how ChatGPT is trained on older versions of libraries and APIs. If we copy this code over to our check, we'll see that `WebDriverWait` makes errors because it no longer takes integers—a change that came in after ChatGPT was trained on Selenium material. So, we need to update `WebDriverWait` to take a `Duration` parameter instead:

```
this.wait = new WebDriverWait(driver, Duration.ofSeconds(10));
```

Finally, to improve the feedback we get from our automated test, we update the assertion suggested by Copilot to a more informative one:

```
assertEquals(1, messagePage.getMessageCount());
```

With all this in place, assuming there are no extra messages on the platform, we can run the check and see it pass. The key behavior to observe is how we used Copilot and ChatGPT to rapidly build our automated check. Instead of sending a prompt to ChatGPT such as

 Create an automated test for a contact us form and check if the message has been created

which would result in quite a generic output requiring a lot of modification, we worked through each step of our automated check using Copilot and ChatGPT to rapidly create parts of the check, switching between tools to help us solve specific problems. If we return to our area-of-effect model, this approach is summarized in figure 7.4.

The model shows us that if we are able to identify the specific actions that occur in an automated check—like determining what state a check requires or what assertions to make—then we can use an LLM effectively with said actions. As demonstrated in the example, ChatGPT and Copilot (and other LLM tools) are incredibly fast at predicting and generating code for our automation. However, they lack access to the context of the product we're automating. Problems such as incorrect test data and missing waits require us to lead the creation of automation, with AI tools offering support where we need it most.

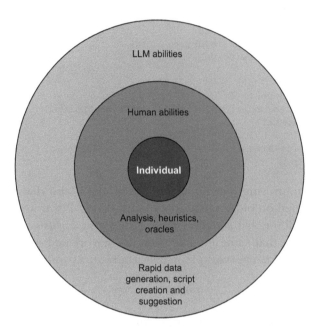

Figure 7.4   Area-of-effect model showing the skills an individual and tooling bring to the development of automated checks

Activity 7.2

Use Copilot and ChatGPT to create your own automated check with https://automationintesting.online. This time, create an automated check that does the following:

- Logs in to the admin section of the site
- Creates a new room
- Asserts that the room appears on the home page

Use the prompts shared in the example to generate your own Page objects, or build your own prompts that might be more effective.

7.2   *Improving existing UI automation*

Our initial example demonstrated how we can work with LLM tools to rapidly create new automated checks, but what about existing checks? Working with automation means handling automated checks that fail due to flakiness or rapid changes within the product under test. How can LLM tools help us improve our automation rapidly, while ensuring they still deliver value? Let's go back to the automated check we have just created and see how the patterns of use for LLMs can help us make more robust automated checks.

7.2.1 *Updating state management to use an appropriate layer*

If we assess what our automated check is focused on, we can see that the goal is to check whether messages can be seen in the Admin panel. What this means for our state management is that we don't need to create our message through the UI. It's slow and potentially brittle. So, let's instead take a look at how we can create the message with an API call so that we can improve our automated check and learn how to use LLMs to build API calls.

Our goal is to capture the HTTP request sent when creating a message via the Contact Us page and codify that into our automated test. So, our first step is to capture the HTTP request as a `curl` command by following these steps:

1 Open up Dev Tools within our browser.
2 Select the Network tab.
3 Manually send a message via the Contact Us form in the UI.
4 Locate the HTTP request on the Network tab and then copy the request to a `curl` command (right-click the request in Dev Tools).

With our command located, we can once again build a prompt that will convert our `curl` request into the required Java code using the following prompt. We first set out instructions for prompt and use delimiter tactic:

 Convert the following `curl` request delimited by triple hashes into Java using the following rules:

1 The request is encapsulated in a method
2 The method will use spring framework to send the HTTP request
3 The HTTP response doesn't need parsing
4 The method will take a POJO that represents the HTTP payload as a parameter

We provide the `curl` request in the delimited section:

```
###
curl 'https://automationintesting.online/message/' -X POST -H
  'Accept: application/json' -H 'Content-Type: application/json'
  --data-raw '{"name":"Mark","email":"test@test.com",
  "phone":"071234567890","subject":"This is a test message",
  "description":"This allows me to create a message rapidly"}'
###
```

Similar to the prompt we used to create Page objects, this prompt sets out what we want ChatGPT to do in the initial sentence before adding specific instructions to help ChatGPT predict the correct code we require—for example, stating that the method wants the body payload parameter to come in the format of a POJO (Plain Old Java Object), ensuring that ChatGPT generates a solution that utilizes Java classes to construct our payload, rather than a JSON object stored within a large String that would be hard to parse and maintain. Passing the prompt in with the `curl` request added to the bottom of the prompt will yield the following code:

```java
import org.springframework.http.HttpHeaders;
import org.springframework.http.HttpMethod;
import org.springframework.http.MediaType;
import org.springframework.http.RequestEntity;
import org.springframework.web.client.RestTemplate;

public class HttpRequestSender {
    public void sendRequest(MessagePayload payload) {
        // Create a RestTemplate instance
        RestTemplate restTemplate = new RestTemplate();

        // Set the request URL
        String url = "https://automationintesting.online/message/";

        // Set the request headers
        HttpHeaders headers = new HttpHeaders();
        headers.set(HttpHeaders.ACCEPT,
        MediaType.APPLICATION_JSON_VALUE);
        headers.set(HttpHeaders.CONTENT_TYPE,
        MediaType.APPLICATION_JSON_VALUE);

        // Create the request entity with the payload and headers
        RequestEntity<MessagePayload> requestEntity = new
        RequestEntity<>(
                payload,
                headers,
                HttpMethod.POST,
                URI.create(url)
        );

        // Send the HTTP request
        restTemplate.exchange(requestEntity, Void.class);
    }
}
```

This predicted code requires new dependencies to be added to our project, which we can request from ChatGPT with the following prompt:

 What dependencies are required for this method?

which results in ChatGPT returning

```xml
<dependency>
    <groupId>org.springframework.boot</groupId>
    <artifactId>spring-boot-starter-web</artifactId>
    <version>2.5.0</version>
</dependency>
```

We can then add the dependency into our pom.xml, ensuring that we are using the latest versions, followed by copying the HTTP request code into our framework in a new package named requests. I opted to rename the class from HttpRequestSender to MessageRequest.

This gives us the required code to send a request, but because we informed ChatGPT that sendRequest would take a POJO parameter for the body of our request, we next need ChatGPT to create the code to build our POJO. To do this, we return to our existing chat with ChatGPT and add the following prompt:

 Create me a POJO for MessagePayload including constructors and getter and setter methods

The prompt makes it clear that we require constructors and getter/setter methods because these will be necessary for creating and sending our HTTP request. Sending the prompt to ChatGPT yields the following code:

```java
public class MessagePayload {
    private String name;
    private String email;
    private String phone;
    private String subject;
    private String description;

    public MessagePayload() {
    }

    public MessagePayload(String name, String email, String phone,
String subject, String description) {
        this.name = name;
        this.email = email;
        this.phone = phone;
        this.subject = subject;
        this.description = description;
    }

    public String getName() {
        return name;
    }

    public void setName(String name) {
        this.name = name;
    }

    public String getEmail() {
        return email;
    }

    public void setEmail(String email) {
        this.email = email;
    }

    public String getPhone() {
```

```
        return phone;
    }

    public void setPhone(String phone) {
        this.phone = phone;
    }

    public String getSubject() {
        return subject;
    }

    public void setSubject(String subject) {
        this.subject = subject;
    }

    public String getDescription() {
        return description;
    }

    public void setDescription(String description) {
        this.description = description;
    }
}
```

Because we provided the `curl` request in the initial prompt, ChatGPT can predict what the code for our POJO should look like to create a message to send via HTTP, which can then be copied over to a `MessagePayload` class in the `requests` package of our project.

With our classes in place to create a message payload and send a request to the `POST` `/message/` endpoint, we can then return to our `MessageTest` and use Copilot to improve our check. First, we remove the following section of our check:

```
driver.get("https://automationintesting.online");

ContactFormPage contactFormPage = new ContactFormPage(driver);
contactFormPage.enterName("John Smith");
contactFormPage.enterEmail("test@email.com");
contactFormPage.enterPhone("07123456789");
contactFormPage.enterSubject("Testing");
contactFormPage.enterDescription("This is a test message");
contactFormPage.clickSubmitButton();
```

and start typing `MessagePayload` to trigger Copilot to add the following code as a replacement:

```
MessagePayload messagePayload = new MessagePayload();
messagePayload.setName("Test User");
messagePayload.setEmail("test@email.com");
messagePayload.setPhone("0123456789");
messagePayload.setSubject("Test Subject");
messagePayload.setDescription("Test Description");

MessageRequest messageRequest = new MessageRequest();
messageRequest.sendRequest(messagePayload);
```

Similar to when we used Copilot to generate code for creating a message in the UI, running the automated check for the first time will result in a failure. The check will run and then receive a 400-status code because the predicted test data didn't match the validation rules again. Therefore, to ensure that our message matches the necessary validation rules, we need to update the following methods with correct test data:

```
messagePayload.setPhone("074123456789");
messagePayload.setDescription("Test Description that is larger");
```

Once these test data parameters are updated, we should now see the automated check pass again.

This example demonstrates that we can use LLM tools to help us update specific aspects of our automated checks to make them more robust, but it requires us to have a good analytical eye for which areas of our checks require improvement. This is because we have knowledge of both our automated checks and our system under test, which is lacking in the tools we've used so far. For example, if we were to give ChatGPT the prompt

 Suggest ways in which this automated test can be improved to make it less flakey

and then add our automated check code to the prompt, these would be the returned suggestions (in summary):

- Add explicit waits
- Use stable locators
- Handle asynchronous operations
- Isolate the test
- Retry failed actions
- Check for error conditions
- Review and update the test environment

These are all legitimate considerations, but they are generic problems and don't necessarily give us enough information to solve specific problems. So instead, we frame the process of improvement, looking to tools to help us rapidly generate the necessary code.

Activity 7.3

Using ChatGPT and Copilot, try turning the login process into an API call as well. For this exercise, you will need to create the code to

- Send credentials to `POST /auth/login`
- Extract the `token` value from the HTTP response
- Store the `token` value as a cookie in the browser before heading to the message page

7.2.2   *Getting into the groove with AI tools*

This chapter demonstrated that regardless of whether we are building UI automation, API automation, or something entirely different, the pattern of success with AI is always the same. Our deep understanding of the design and structure of automated checks informs us when and where to use AI tools to help us with specific tasks to create and maintain valuable automation. The marketing around AI automation would have us believe that our role in creating automated checks is limited when AI is involved. But if we want automation that helps us create high-quality products, then our best course of action is to build a relationship with AI tools that places our skillset at the core of the work.

Summary

- Attempting to generate a whole automated UI test using only a tool such as ChatGPT will likely require a lot of rework. Instead, we want to use AI tools selectively at specific points of the UI automation process.
- Starting a new project with a tool such as Copilot can yield varying results.
- The more detail we add to our project, the more accurate Copilot will be.
- With the right type of prompt, we can rapidly generate Page objects in ChatGPT by providing it with HTML and instructions to convert it.
- We can rapidly generate automated checks by combining ChatGPT and Copilot (or similar tools).
- The output of AI tools is not 100% accurate, because it lacks context—for example, with test data or using up-to-date methods from libraries.
- Success with AI tools when creating automated checks comes from using AI tools to complete specific tasks within the creation process.
- We lead the creation process, identifying when AI tools can help us speed it up.
- If we are able to identify improvements to specific elements of an automated check, we can employ AI tools to make the improvements faster.
- If we ask LLMs to evaluate our checks and offer improvements, we get generic answers in return.
- We can use the same process of using AI tools on specific tasks within our automated checks to maintain them.

Assisting exploratory testing with artificial intelligence

This chapter covers

- Enhancing exploratory testing charter creation using LLMs
- Identifying opportunities for using LLMs in exploratory testing sessions
- Using LLMs to support various activities during exploratory testing sessions
- Summarizing exploratory testing session reports with LLMs

So far, we've explored how large language models (LLMs) can help us with a range of testing activities and artifacts that are algorithmic. Activities such as code and data generation have distinct syntax and formatting rules, and come with a certain degree of repeatability that works well with LLMs. But what about the more heuristic-based testing activities, such as exploratory testing? How can LLMs support us when we are executing testing ourselves? It's important to repeat that LLMs cannot replace testing or testers, but by carefully observing what we're doing during exploratory testing and knowledge of prompt engineering, we can selectively enhance our exploring in a way that doesn't undermine the core value of exploratory testing. To do this, we'll examine the following three aspects of exploratory testing and how LLMs can help: organizing exploratory testing with charters, performing exploratory testing, and reporting what we've discovered.

Algorithmic and heuristic-based activities

When we refer to an activity as being heuristic-based, we're specifying that the activity doesn't have clear steps to carry out or is difficult to define explicitly, whereas algorithmic activities are more procedural in nature and can be defined in explicit terms. In the context of testing, test cases and scripts can be seen as algorithmic in nature, whereas exploratory testing is more heuristic because it relies on human ability to observe and analyze situations to determine next actions.

8.1   *Organizing exploratory testing with LLMs*

Let's begin by focusing on how LLMs can help us identify charters for exploratory testing. Normally, when performing exploratory testing sessions, they are guided by a test charter such as:

 Explore flights booking with various providers to discover if all providers are shown in results

In this charter example, we're following the charter template proposed by Elisabeth Hendrickson in her book *Explore It* (from Pragmatic Bookshelf):

```
Explore <target>
With <resource>
To discover <information>
```

It's from these charters that we can frame what we want to focus our exploratory testing on and what to ignore. The idea is to have many different charters exploring features and products from different perspectives, or more specifically, different risks. When generating charters, we ideally want to be deriving them from risks, so that when we run exploratory testing based on charters, we know the following:

- What priority we should put our charters in (the higher the risk, the higher the priority)
- What risks have been explored and what haven't
- What value we are getting from each exploratory testing session

To put this into a visual model, figure 8.1 demonstrates the relationship between risks, charters, and exploratory testing sessions.

The model shows that we first identify risks, which are then codified into charters, and it's those charters that we can run multiple exploratory testing sessions on to see what we can learn.

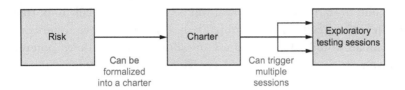

Figure 8.1 A visual model showing the relationship between risks, charters, and exploratory testing

Identifying risks and charters is predominantly a heuristic-based activity, as there is no clear pattern or procedure that can be followed to identify risks. It's based on a tester and their team's critical and lateral thinking skills. However, the structured nature of how we format risks into charters means there are times when LLMs can help augment our existing skills and increase our coverage.

8.1.1 Augmenting identified risks with LLMs

Because identifying risks is a heuristic-based activity, it is subject to bias. This means that, at times, we can miss potential risks requiring our attention (for example, functional fixedness cognitive bias in which we are so focused on observing one event that we completely miss another). So, how do we prevent these gaps from appearing? Testers work hard to develop their skills to embrace and handle such biases and utilize testing heuristics to help us change our perspectives when identifying risks. But we can also use LLMs as an additional tool to help us consider different avenues and perhaps highlight potential risks we hadn't considered.

To help demonstrate how they can help, let's explore a sample user story that has been created by a team:

- In order to manage my bookings as an administrator I want to be able to view a report of all my bookings
- Acceptance Criteria:
  - Given I am logged in as an administrator, and I have multiple bookings made, when I load a report page then I am presented with my bookings in a monthly calendar view and the month selected is the current month
  - Given I am on the report page when I click on the navigation controls then I am able to move to different months in a year
  - Given I am on the report page when I click and drag across multiple dates then I am presented with a new booking form with the following fields | firstname | lastname | room | deposit paid |
  - Given I have admin booking popup loaded when I complete the rest of the booking form then the report is reloaded and the new booking appears

Using examples, the user story details how we would expect the feature to work from a user perspective. It's this type of user story that we would typically come across in a planning session (with perhaps more or less detail), and it would be used as a jumping-off point to start discussing how it will be built and, equally important, what risks could affect the quality of our feature. Typically, this is where testers or quality-minded individuals would take time to ask questions and note down potential risks for further investigation. For example, a basic list of risks might contain the following items:

- Bookings are not shown in the report view.
- Report view is hard to parse.
- Navigation controls don't work correctly.
- Admin bookings can't be submitted.

This is a great start, but it feels insufficient. This list emulates situations in which we may find ourselves struggling to identify further risks, so at this time, we can opt to use a prompt like the following to help expand our analysis. We use delimiter tactic in instructions to distinguish different data sets being sent:

 You are a professional software tester. You will be provided with a user story delimited by three hashes and a list of identified risks delimited by three back ticks. Review the user story and expand the list of risks.

Next, we instruct the model to work out solutions before outputting them:

 Check that all generated risks are not duplicates of original risks and that they relate to the following quality characteristics: Usability and Accuracy.

Finally, we provide data sets in delimited sections:

 ###
<User story added here>
###
```

- Bookings are not shown in the report view
- Report view is hard to parse
- Navigation controls don't work correctly
- Admin bookings can't be submitted
```

In this prompt, we're providing three different sets of data to help guide the LLM:

- *Quality characteristics*—Quality characteristics help us define what quality means to our end users. For example, the quality characteristic of a trading platform might be quite different from the characteristics of a personal assistant app. Adding these to our prompt helps us make explicit which areas of risks we're interested in and prevents an LLM from hallucinating risks that are irrelevant or not of interest.

- *User story*—We provide the user story to give the prompt context. Once again, the more description we can provide around what a feature is expected to do, the more we will maximize the relevance of the risks that the LLM will output.
- *Current risks*—Finally, providing existing risks prevents the LLM from simply outputting information we already have. By asking the LLM to work out solutions before outputting risks, we ensure that the risks being output are new for consideration. That doesn't mean that its output is more useful but that it helps frame what we've been thinking about.

The goal of this prompt is to have an LLM provide additional risks that could be added to our existing list. For example, sending the prompt to ChatGPT returned the following output:

 Usability Risks:

User Confusion: Users may not easily understand how to access the report page, resulting in frustration and poor user experience.

Complex Calendar View: The monthly calendar view may be overwhelming or confusing for administrators if it's not designed intuitively, impacting usability.

Navigation Controls: If the navigation controls for moving between months are not user-friendly or responsive, administrators might struggle to navigate, affecting usability.

Booking Form Usability: The new booking form generated by clicking and dragging across dates should be user-friendly and intuitive. If it's not, administrators might make mistakes while filling it out.

Lack of Feedback: If there's no feedback or confirmation message after submitting a new booking, administrators may be uncertain whether the booking was successful or not, affecting usability.

Error Handling: Poor error handling, such as not handling edge cases or invalid input in the booking form, could lead to confusion and frustration for administrators.

Accuracy Risks:

Missing Bookings: Bookings not being displayed in the report view may result in incomplete or inaccurate reporting, impacting data accuracy.

Data Integrity: If the system doesn't properly validate and save the booking data entered by administrators, it may lead to inaccurate data in the reports.

Incorrect Month Selection: If the default month displayed in the report is not the current month as specified, it would be an accuracy issue.

Incorrect Navigation: If the navigation controls don't function as expected, administrators may not be able to accurately navigate to the desired month.

Missing Bookings in Report Refresh: If new bookings don't appear in the report after completing the booking form, it would affect the accuracy of the displayed data.

Failed Booking Submission: If admin bookings cannot be submitted correctly, it would result in incomplete or missing data in the system, affecting data accuracy.

The first thing to observe is that ChatGPT has effectively categorized the proposed risks by quality characteristics. The second observation is how each risk comes with a short sentence to explain it further. This can help us contextualize the risks it has output or spark ideas around further risks.

Looking at the list of proposed risks, some stand out as useful and relevant to our user story, such as:

- User confusion
- Error handling
- Missing bookings in report refresh
- Data integrity

Further analysis shows that some risks displayed are almost a repetition of one another: for example, `Navigation controls` in the `usability` category and `Incorrect Navigation` in the `accuracy` category (note that these are not duplicates of our original risks). Although they are worded differently, the focus appears to be the same: navigation controls not working properly. The combination of new risks and repetition demonstrates that LLMs can be a useful tool for expanding our risk analysis, but they do not serve as a replacement for our ability to identify risks. So, after reading the list of risks from ChatGPT, we may choose to expand our list of risks to include

- Bookings are not shown in the report view.
- Report view is hard to parse.
- Navigation controls don't work correctly.
- Admin bookings can't be submitted.
- Confusion over how to use the report controls and admin booking.
- Errors are not handled correctly.

In our final list, we have chosen to adopt and reframe some of the risks received from ChatGPT and have ignored others. If we are not satisfied, we can ask ChatGPT to return more risks to review. However, there is a tradeoff that if we request more risks, we face an increased chance of repetition creeping into ChatGPT's responses. Once we're happy with our list, we can begin to convert these into charters and return to an LLM for further assistance for ideas.

Activity 8.1

Pick a user story or list of requirements from the backlog of a project you are working on. Identify some initial risks and then compile a prompt that will suggest additional risks to consider. If you are unaware which quality characteristics to use in your prompt, pick one or two from this comprehensive list of characteristics from *The Test Eye*, available at https://mng.bz/XV9Y.

8.1.2 Augmenting charter lists with LLMs

Once we have our risks identified, we can now convert them into test charters to guide our exploratory testing. For example, the following risk:

 Bookings are not shown in the report view

can be translated into:

 Explore how bookings are rendered in the report view

With a collection of bookings

To discover if all bookings are shown correctly

This charter gives us a bit more detail about what we want to focus on, what tools we are going to use, and what we're hoping to discover. As mentioned before, the way charters are formed follows a clear structure that, just like with risks, we can feed into an LLM to expand the list of charters we could consider for future testing.

So once again, we create a prompt similar to our previous risk-focused prompts. First, we provide initial instructions and delimiter tactic to clarify where charters will be found:

 You are a professional software tester. Review the exploratory testing charters delimited by three hashes and suggest additional charters.

Then we instruct the model to work out solutions before outputting them:

 Check that all generated charters are not duplicates of original charters and that they relate to the following quality characteristics Usability and Accuracy, before outputting the additional charters.

The following prompt provides data sets in delimited sections:

 ###

Explore how bookings are rendered in the report view

With a collection of bookings

To discover if all bookings are shown correctly

Explore how bookings are rendered in the report view

With a very large collection of bookings

To discover if large amounts of bookings are easy to read

Explore navigating report view

With a collection of bookings

To discover that the navigation controls work as expected

Explore submitting booking

With the admin booking form

To discover if bookings can be submitted by an admin

Explore using core features of the report view

Using different personas

To discover if the report features are easy to understand

Explore different error outputs in the admin form

Using malformed data and proxy tools

To discover if errors are handled correctly

###

The prompt is structured in a similar fashion to the one where we provided context to the prompt in the form of quality characteristics and the current list of identified charters. There is also an element of few-shot prompting occurring as each charter follows the same template. This means that when I send the prompt to ChatGPT, I get the following suggested charters:

 Explore the responsiveness of the report view

With varying screen sizes and devices

To discover if the report view adapts well to different screen sizes

Explore search functionality in the report view

With a variety of search criteria

To discover if users can accurately find specific bookings

Explore the accuracy of date filtering in the report view

With different date ranges and time zones

To ensure that bookings within the specified date range are displayed correctly

Explore user permissions in the admin booking form

With different user roles (admin, regular user)

To ensure that only admins can access and submit bookings in the admin form

Explore the accuracy of booking data storage

By submitting bookings with various data formats and inputs

To verify that all data is stored accurately in the system

Just as with other LLM outputs, there is a range in quality in what has been returned. Some charters stand out as suitable candidates for additional charters, for example:

- Explore the responsiveness of the report view

- With varying screen sizes and devices
- To discover if the report view adapts well to different screen sizes

Others, like the following one, which is beyond the scope of adding a booking to a report, could be discarded:

- Explore search functionality in the report view
- With a variety of search criteria
- To discover if users can accurately find specific bookings

Again, what this demonstrates is that LLMs can help us expand our options and identify new avenues to explore. But they are by no means perfect. And while tweaking prompts to make them more reliable can certainly help, we should always be selective in what to take from an LLM and what to ignore, which once again can be summarized using the area of effect model, as shown in figure 8.2.

Our ability to think creatively and use lateral and critical thinking skills to identify and organize our exploratory testing is essential. In this example, LLMs give us a way to shake things up when we're out of ideas.

Activity 8.2

Take the risks from the previous activity and convert some of them into charters using the Explore, With, Using template. Add those into the prompt we've just explored to see what suggested prompts are returned.

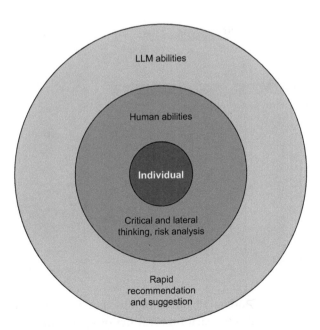

Figure 8.2 Area of effect model demonstrating how LLMs can expand our analysis

8.2   *Using LLMs during exploratory testing*

We've seen how we can work with LLMs to organize exploratory testing. Now let's take a look at how to use LLMs as we perform exploratory testing.

What makes the use of LLMs in exploratory testing so interesting is the mix of activities that might occur during an exploratory testing session. There are technical elements to a session in which we need to rely on tools to manipulate a system in a specific way, and there are heuristic human-driven elements where we employ mental heuristics and oracles to make sense of what we've learned and use it to inspire further testing. Both aspects can be supported with the use of LLMs, so to help us better appreciate where to get the most value, let's explore a use case of an exploratory testing session in which the following charter was used:

 Explore how bookings are rendered in the report view

With a very large collection of bookings

To discover if large amounts of bookings are easy to read

To help contextualize the session further, the goal of the session was to test the rendering of the report page, as shown in figure 8.3.

Today	Back	Next			November 2023		
Sun	**Mon**	**Tue**	**Wed**	**Thu**	**Fri**	**Sat**	
29	30	31	01	02	03	04	
			James Dean - Room: 101				
05	06	07	08	09	10	11	
	Janet Jones - Room: 101						
12	13	14	15	16	17	18	
		Sally Brookes - Room: 101					
19	20	21	22	23	24	25	
26	27	28	29	30	01	02	

Figure 8.3   The report page under test

The calendar in the report page renders all the bookings that exist for each room within the application, and our goal is to learn how it functions when there are many bookings, specifically learning how it might affect the rendering and usability of the calendar. This means there were challenges to overcome around understanding how data is sent to the calendar, how to create it quickly, and what types of testing aligned with the charter we might carry out.

8.2.1 Establishing an understanding

The first challenge is to understand how the report data arrived into the calendar, which means analyzing the `Report` API code to better understand it. To do this, I created the following prompt. We first set out the instruction to add code comments and give the system time to think:

 You are a Java Developer. Create code comments for the code delimited by three hashes. Check that the code has not been modified and that comments match each section of the code provided before outputting the created code.

Next, we provide the code to comment using the delimiter tactic:

```
###
public Report getAllRoomsReport(String token) {
        List<Room> rooms = roomRequests.searchForRooms().getRooms();
        List<Entry> parsedRooms = new ArrayList<>();

        for(Room r : rooms){
            Bookings roomBookings = bookingRequests.getBookings
            ⇒ (r.getRoomid(), token);

            for(Booking b : roomBookings.getBookings()){
                Entry entry = new Entry(
                ⇒b.getBookingDates().getCheckin(),
                ⇒b.getBookingDates().getCheckout(),
                ⇒b.getFirstname() + " " + b.getLastname() + " - Room: " +
                ⇒r.getRoomName());
                parsedRooms.add(entry);
            }
        }

        return new Report(parsedRooms);
    }
###
```

The prompt is designed to take the service layer code that existed in the `Report` API and code comment it for me. Through the use of code comments, I could learn more about how it worked and how it built the necessary report data sent to the calendar (something I discovered by using tools to monitor HTTP traffic being sent to the calendar). This type of prompt is helpful when we want to quickly build up an understanding of how a part of a system works, and it can be extremely useful for those who might not be confident coders.

So, I built the prompt and then sent it to ChatGPT, which returned the following code that was code commented:

```
/**
 * Method: getAllRoomsReport
 * Description: Retrieves a report containing booking details for all
 * rooms.
 *
 * @param token The authentication token for accessing room and
 * booking information.
 * @return Report object containing parsed room booking entries.
 */
public Report getAllRoomsReport(String token) {
    // Retrieve a list of rooms
    List<Room> rooms = roomRequests.searchForRooms().getRooms();
    // Initialize a list to store parsed room entries
    List<Entry> parsedRooms = new ArrayList<>();

    // Iterate through each room
    for(Room r : rooms){
        // Retrieve bookings for the current room
        Bookings roomBookings =
            bookingRequests.getBookings(r.getRoomid(), token);

        // Iterate through each booking in the room
        for(Booking b : roomBookings.getBookings()){
            // Create an entry for each booking with relevant details
            Entry entry = new Entry(
                b.getBookingDates().getCheckin(),
                b.getBookingDates().getCheckout(),
                b.getFirstname() + " " + b.getLastname() + " - Room: " +
                r.getRoomName());
            // Add the entry to the list of parsed rooms
            parsedRooms.add(entry);
        }
    }

    // Return a new report containing parsed room entries
    return new Report(parsedRooms);
}
```

Due to the instruction Check that the code has not been modified inside the initial prompt, the original code that was provided is the same (although it's important to check just in case hallucinations slip in and modify the code). In addition to code, we now have code comments, which gave me a bit more context and detail about how the code works. This in turn allowed me to model the data-retrieval process into a visualization similar to the one in figure 8.4.

The model is based on the information from the prompt to determine how the data is created and helped clarify how I needed to go about creating the required data. This is a great way to rapidly build understanding, but as always, it's important to ratify that understanding and mitigate risks of LLM hallucinations. That's why I visually modeled the process afterward so that the visualization can be easily shared with others to confirm whether my assumptions were correct or needed updating.

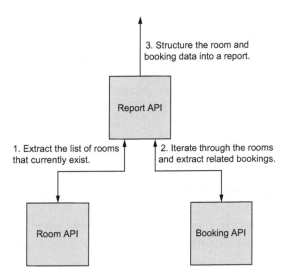

Figure 8.4 A model representing how the report data was created

8.2.2 Creating data requirements for a session

With a deeper understanding of how the report data was built, I could move on to the next challenge in the exploratory testing session—creating test data. I required a lot of bookings (thousands, in fact), which meant

- Creating test rooms to add bookings to
- Creating at least 1000 test bookings to assign to each test room

To do this, I once again used an LLM to help me generate SQL data I could add to seed.sql files that existed as part of the room and booking API projects. If I could get the correct SQL data in these seed files, then I could start the product up with all the data necessary for my testing.

We've already explored data creation in chapter 6, so the first prompt for the Room API will feel familiar. To create the necessary room data, I built the following prompt. First, we use the initial instructions and the delimiter tactic to provide SQL data:

> 🔵 You are a MySQL generator. Create a MySQL script to insert 10 new records that follow the structure of the MySQL statement delimited by three hashes.

Then we provide additional details to handle the creation of array data:

> 🔵 * If the keyword ARRAY is used, use the MySQL ARRAY function to create related data type

The instruction concludes with the time-to-think tactic:

> 🔵 Check that each new entry matches the correct data types and uses valid MySQL before outputting it.

Finally, we provide the SQL data that will be expanded into further test data:

```
###
INSERT INTO ROOMS (room_name, type, beds, accessible, image,
description, features, roomPrice) VALUES ('101', 'single', 1,
true, 'https://www.mwtestconsultancy.co.uk/img/testim/room2.jpg',
'Aenean porttitor mauris sit amet lacinia molestie. In posuere
accumsan aliquet. Maecenas sit amet nisl massa. Interdum et
malesuada fames ac ante.', ARRAY['TV', 'WiFi', 'Safe'], 100);
###
```

The prompt is designed to take an existing INSERT statement and expand it into multiple INSERT statements that can be added to my seed.sql file. One specific instruction that was needed was the handling of String arrays within the INSERT statements. Before it was added, the ARRAY data type wasn't created correctly, which led to odd data being created for features. However, with the addition of the following rule to the prompt

```
If the keyword ARRAY is used, use the MySQL ARRAY function to create
related data type
```

the LLM was able to create the necessary data. This is a good demonstration of a moment where an existing prompt (like the original data creation prompt from chapter 6) needs tweaking to suit specific requirements.

With the prompt created, I sent it to ChatGPT which returned the following data (I've shortened it, but the original response gave me my ten required records):

```
-- Record 1
INSERT INTO ROOMS (room_name, type, beds, accessible, image,
description, features, roomPrice) VALUES ('101', 'single', 1, true,
'https://www.mwtestconsultancy.co.uk/img/testim/room2.jpg', 'Aenean
porttitor mauris sit amet lacinia molestie. In posuere accumsan
aliquet. Maecenas sit amet nisl massa. Interdum et malesuada fames
 ac ante.', ARRAY['TV', 'WiFi', 'Safe'], 100);

-- Record 2
INSERT INTO ROOMS (room_name, type, beds, accessible, image,
description, features, roomPrice) VALUES ('102', 'double', 2, false,
'https://www.example.com/image2.jpg', 'Lorem ipsum dolor sit amet,
consectetur adipiscing elit. Nullam eget odio nec urna consequat
placerat.', ARRAY['WiFi', 'Mini Fridge'], 150);

-- Record 3
INSERT INTO ROOMS (room_name, type, beds, accessible, image,
description, features, roomPrice)VALUES ('103', 'suite', 3, true,
'https://www.example.com/image3.jpg', 'Sed et fermentum lectus.
Proin feugiat tortor sed elit feugiat, vel laoreet ante fermentum.',
ARRAY['TV', 'WiFi', 'Kitchen', 'Balcony'], 250);
```

The data generated isn't the most inspiring, but given that my focus was on simply having some rooms added to the API, it was enough. Adding this information to the `seed.sql` file, with the comments stripped, I was able to rebuild the `Room` API with the necessary data.

Next, I turned my attention to creating 1,000 bookings to be added to the booking API's `seed.sql` file. However, this posed a new challenge. Asking an LLM to respond with 1,000 `INSERT` statements is a taxing activity for any LLM to do. Some LLMs are restricted to a certain size of response, and some are simply unable to respond with a token count size that I required. So, I had to approach the problem differently. Instead of prompting an LLM to create the necessary data, I asked it to create a script that would generate the `INSERT` statements for me. The initial instructions that use the delimiter tactic were

 You are a NodeJS creator. Create a script to insert 1000 new records into a SQL file named `seed.sql` that follows the structure of the MySQL statement delimited by three hashes.

These are additional instructions to ensure correct data is generated:

 * RoomId must be between 1 and 10

* Checkin and Checkout dates must be between 2023-11-01 and 2023-11-30

The following code provides an SQL statement that the script will ultimately generate:

```
###
INSERT INTO BOOKINGS (roomid, firstname, lastname, depositpaid,
  checkin, checkout) VALUES (1, 'James', 'Dean', true, '2022-02-01',
  '2011 03 05');
###
```

In this prompt, I asked an LLM to transform a SQL statement into a NodeJS script that would output a `seed.sql` file with all the necessary data I need. That way, I could run the script once and then move the newly created `seed.sql` file into my booking API. The choice of language was purely a personal preference, but using the format tactic, we could quickly update this to have the LLM produce a script in a different language.

Sending this prompt to ChatGPT triggered the LLM to return the following script to use:

```
const fs = require('fs');

// Function to generate a random date between two dates
const randomDate = (startDate, endDate) => {
  return new Date(startDate.getTime() + Math.random() *
(endDate.getTime() - startDate.getTime()));
}

// Function to generate a random boolean value
const randomBoolean = () => {
  return Math.random() < 0.5;
}

// Function to generate a random integer between min and max
```

```
// (inclusive)
const randomInt = (min, max) => {
  return Math.floor(Math.random() * (max - min + 1)) + min;
}

const generateSeedData = () => {
  const startDate = new Date('2023-11-01');
  const endDate = new Date('2023-11-30');
  const bookings = [];

  for (let i = 0; i < 1000; i++) {
    const roomId = randomInt(1, 10);
    const firstName = `First${i}`;
    const lastName = `Last${i}`;
    const depositPaid = randomBoolean();
    const checkinDate = randomDate(startDate,
    endDate).toISOString().slice(0, 10);
    const checkoutDate = randomDate(new Date(checkinDate),
    endDate).toISOString().slice(0, 10);

    const booking = `INSERT INTO BOOKINGS (roomid, firstname, lastname,
    depositpaid, checkin, checkout) VALUES (${roomId}, '${firstName}',
    '${lastName}', ${depositPaid}, '${checkinDate}',
    '${checkoutDate}');\n`;

    bookings.push(booking);
  }

  return bookings.join('\n');
}

const seedData = generateSeedData();

fs.appendFile('seed.sql', seedData, (err) => {
  if (err) {
    console.error('Error appending data to seed.sql:', err);
  } else {
    console.log('Data appended to seed.sql successfully!');
  }
});
```

Copying this script into a file and then running it, I got the `seed.sql` file that I needed. This approach meant I was still able to get the test data I required, but the prompt and response were much smaller than the large response I would have gotten back if I had directly asked for the SQL.

Once again, with the necessary data now in my booking `seed.sql` file, I was able to rebuild the `booking` API, start the application with all my required data, and begin exploring how it coped with such a massive data set.

8.2.3   *Exploring and investigating bugs*

With the test data in place, I was able to try out a collection of test ideas inspired by the charter for this session, including the following:

- *What happens when I load the page?* I discovered that I could see bookings in the calendar view and that additional bookings needed to be viewed by clicking the "View more" text for a specific day. I also learned that the page was very slow to load data when lots of bookings were in place.

- *What happens when I work with navigation controls?* Similar to previous observations, the calendar was slow to load when navigating between months. But I was able to navigate through the calendar despite the page slowness.

- *What if I wanted to view more bookings?* I discovered a bug around the pop-up that shows additional bookings for the day flow off the top of the page, so certain bookings could not be read. It was also slow to load the pop-up for days with considerable bookings.

- *Can I access the calendar using a keyboard?* I found that I was able to tab through the main view of the calendar successfully and that hitting Enter on a "View more" link opens up the pop-up with additional bookings. I also found bugs around tabbing into a pop-up in which I was unable to focus on bookings that overflowed out of the bounds of the page.

What each of these ideas has in common is they were identified using mental heuristics I have developed after years of exploratory testing. This concept of the use of unconscious heuristics, ones that have been internalized through experience, is explored in the article "Mind the Gap," by Richard Bradshaw and Sarah Deery: https://mng.bz/yoRJ. It talks about how we use both conscious and subconscious heuristics to guide our exploratory testing. In the context of my exploratory testing so far, I have relied on unconscious heuristics. However, as I came to the point in which my ideas were running dry, I turned to more explicit conscious heuristics to generate further test ideas—for example, using the test mnemonic PAOLO.

PAOLO is a mnemonic, created by Maik Nog, that serves as a tool to trigger test ideas around the screen orientation and rendering. Each letter stands for a different aspect of orientation and rendering to consider, specifically:

- *Portrait*— How does it look in Portrait view?
- *Audio*— Are there audio artifacts to consider?
- *Objects*— What other objects are in view that need considering?
- *Landscape*—How does it look in the Landscape view?
- *Overlay*—Are there overlays to consider?

The value of mnemonics is that they help trigger different ideas for different individuals—which is a blessing and a curse as we are still somewhat reliant on our personal experiences and biases to generate new ideas. So, to help break out of my thinking, I created a new prompt using the PAOLO mnemonic to see what ideas I might get from an LLM. In the first prompt, we set instructions, use the delimiter tactic, and provide context:

You are an exploratory tester. Using the list of criteria delimited by three hashes, suggest different test ideas for each list item to try out a report calendar that has many bookings. Format them by mentioning the list item first, followed by the suggestions.

Then I use few-shot tactics to set out the format I want the responses in:

 For example:

Navigation - Can the keyboard be used to navigate the report calendar.

Next, I provide the mnemonic in the delimited section:

 ###

* Portrait

* Audio

* Objects

* Landscape

* Overlay

###

In this prompt, I need to provide some context around what I want test ideas generated for. Omitting these details would likely result in a fairly generic response or risk hallucinations. So, I provided details to improve the ideas I might receive. Then I provided the written-out mnemonic to frame the response and, if I wanted to, I could change the mnemonic to see what other ideas an LLM might return. Sending this prompt to ChatGPT returned a large collection of ideas, such as these notable ones:

 Portrait

- UI Responsiveness: Verify how the report calendar displays in portrait mode across different screen sizes and resolutions.

- Interaction Testing: Test the functionality of adding/editing/deleting bookings while in portrait mode.

- Scrolling Behavior: Check if scrolling through the calendar in portrait mode is smooth and doesn't cause any glitches or overlaps between bookings.

- Portrait-Specific Features: Explore if there are any unique features or options specific to portrait mode and validate their functionality.

- Text Legibility: Ensure that text and labels within the calendar remain clear and legible when the device is switched to portrait orientation.

Landscape

- Orientation Switch: Test the transition between portrait and landscape modes and ensure the calendar adjusts smoothly without losing data or causing display issues.

- Bookings Layout: Verify the layout and arrangement of bookings in landscape mode, ensuring they remain organized and easily readable.
- Multi-Day Bookings: Check how multi-day bookings display and behave when the device is in landscape orientation.
- UI Consistency: Ensure that all features and functionalities available in portrait mode are also accessible and functional in landscape mode.
- Rotation Speed: Test if the calendar responds quickly to changes in device orientation without lagging or delays.

From this list, I hand-picked some of the ideas that stood out to me, specifically:

 How the report calendar displays in portrait mode across different screen sizes and resolutions.

This triggered the idea of zooming in and out of the calendar to observe what would happen, resulting in the discovery of performance problems when zooming out and the calendar hiding the Show More Buttons link when zoomed in. The next prompt idea was:

 Test if the calendar responds quickly to changes in device orientation without lagging or delays.

This triggered the question: What if I try out different screen sizes? Attempting to view the calendar with different mobile screen sizes found yet more performance problems as the page attempted to organize itself for the new view. However, the calendar ultimately did handle different views nicely. Finally, I chose the prompt idea:

 Ensure that text and labels within the calendar remain clear and legible when the device is switched to portrait orientation.

I followed this suggestion more explicitly and discovered that, on mobile screen sizes, text is tiny and hard to read.

There were more ideas I used and more that I could potentially explore, but as this was a session to demonstrate the value of LLMs in exploratory testing, I chose to end the session and collate my notes for future reporting.

8.2.4 *Using LLMs to assist exploratory testing*

This use case demonstrates again how LLMs can be employed to fast-track us through specific technical needs, such as data generation, and act as a suggestion engine when we need new ideas. At no point was the LLM in charge of the exploratory testing. It was utilized to help me as I progressed—all of which can be defined, once again, using the area of effect model shown in figure 8.5.

The key skill is to be able to identify when an LLM could be of use to us in a way that doesn't disrupt the flow of exploratory testing. This is where creating a library of prompts can become useful. By building a library of prompts, we begin to identify the

pain points at which LLMs can help solidify our appreciation of when to use them. Then, once we're in a session, we can quickly copy in a prompt of our choosing, generate the required response, and move on rapidly.

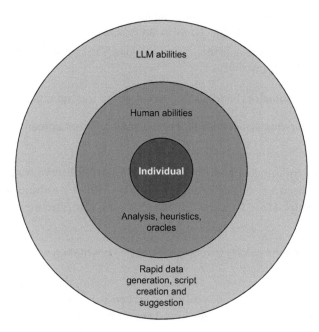

Figure 8.5   The area of effect model covering the roles in exploratory testing

The key skill is to be able to identify when an LLM could be of use to us in a way that doesn't disrupt the flow of exploratory testing. This is where creating a library of prompts can become useful. By building a library of prompts, we begin to identify the pain points at which LLMs can help solidify our appreciation of when to use them. Then, once we're in a session, we can quickly copy in a prompt of our choosing, generate the required response, and move on rapidly.

Activity 8.3

Consider an exploratory testing session you have carried out in the past, or a situation in which you had to debug a complex problem. Write down different ways in which an LLM might have been of benefit in performing your exploratory testing or problem solving.

8.3   *Summarizing testing notes with LLMs*

Once an exploratory testing session is concluded, the results need to be reported to relevant individuals, which can be challenging, unlike the reporting of other testing activities. Given that our goal is to share what we've learned, it can be difficult to distill all the details of a session into a succinct report that shares details such as

- How we approached our exploratory testing sessions
- What setup was required
- What testing we did
- What we learned from our testing
- What bugs were discovered

Ideally, we create notes as we explore to capture the aforementioned details. But to ensure that our note-taking doesn't overwhelm or distract us from our exploring, we tend not to add too much detail. This works well if we are debriefing after a session. We can share what we've learned by using our notes as a trigger to discuss certain aspects of our testing. The problem is that if we are asked to share details about a session that was run in the past, our notes can go only so far as to prompt our memory.

So, as an alternative, we can turn to LLMs to have them create a *testing story,* a type of report that tells the story of how some testing was carried out and what was learned during it. To do this, we can create the following prompt:

 You are an exploratory tester. Convert the exploratory testing notes delimited by three hashes and convert them into a test story that details what happened in the exploratory testing sessions.

* Ensure that all bugs identified are listed at the end of the story for quick reference.

###
<Enter original testing notes>
###

In this prompt, we're asking the LLM to convert our testing notes into a testing story. In the case of my exploratory testing session, the notes were written in Markdown (see appendix C for the full notes) and would be copied into the delimited section found in the prompt (again, see appendix C for the full notes). The prompt also contains additional instructions to list the bugs found as a separate list, which might be useful when discussing them with our team. Copying my testing notes from Appendix C into the delimited section and sending the results to ChatGPT returned the following response.

 Test Story: Exploring Bookings Rendering in Report View

In a recent exploratory testing session, I delved into the rendering of bookings within the report view interface, focusing on the display of a large volume of bookings. The primary goal was to assess the readability and functionality when dealing with extensive booking data.

Session Overview

I commenced the session by analyzing the code structures in the APIs associated with rooms and bookings to comprehend data generation for the report page. Here's a breakdown of my exploration:

Data Setup:

* Explored generating test data for the report page, resulting in creating test data for both the room and booking APIs.
* Encountered challenges in rebuilding the booking API due to test data integration issues, necessitating direct manipulation via the IDE.

Investigation:

* Loading Page Performance:
    * Observed significant slowness in loading the page when a substantial number of bookings were present.
* Navigation Controls:
    * Noted slowness in the calendar view when navigating between busy and quiet months, although navigation remained functional.
* Viewing Bookings:
    * Discovered issues with the popup displaying bookings, causing overflow and making certain bookings unreadable.
    * Encountered delays in loading the popup for days with numerous bookings.
* Creating New Bookings:
    * Identified a delay issue when canceling the creation of a new booking, impacting the calendar component's rendering time.
* Keyboard Accessibility:
    * Successful tab navigation through the calendar but faced challenges with tabbing into and navigating within popups.

Further Explorations:

* Tested the calendar's behavior under different scenarios, such as resizing, zooming, and device orientation changes, revealing multiple rendering and display issues across various screen sizes and orientations.

Bugs Identified:

1 Page loading significantly slows down with a high volume of bookings.
2 Calendar navigation experiences slowness when transitioning between busy and quiet months.
3 Popup for viewing bookings overflows and obstructs readability for certain bookings.
4 Delay issue when canceling the creation of a new booking affects calendar rendering.
5 Accessibility issues with keyboard navigation within popups.
6 Slow rendering and content disappearance when resizing and zooming the calendar.
7 Text readability problems on mobile devices due to small font size.
8 Inability to perform click-and-drag actions for admin booking on mobile devices.

These findings indicate several areas that require attention to enhance the performance, usability, and display of the booking system within the report view.

The LLM has managed to successfully convert my exploratory testing notes, which are a mix of headers and short sentences and are somewhat structureless in form (the raw notes can be found in appendix C for comparison), into a much richer report. It starts with a summary of the exploratory testing as a whole and what my intention was before going into the session details.

Reviewing this report demonstrates a choice that can be made when using LLMs. The report shows heavy use of bullet points and numbered lists, a pattern that is quite common for ChatGPT. However, we could fix this by applying additional instructions or specific template structures to the prompt. For example, if we updated our prompt to use the Cornell method (https://mng.bz/M1M2):

 You are an exploratory tester. Convert the exploratory testing notes delimited by three hashes into a report using the Cornell method of note taking.

<Enter original testing notes>

We get a different type of report which has the title, cues, notes, and summary structure that can be found using the Cornell method:

 Report on Exploratory Testing: Bookings Rendering in Report View

Summary:

The exploratory testing aimed to assess the rendering of bookings in the report view, particularly focusing on handling large volumes of bookings. The examination involved investigating page loading times, navigation controls, creating new bookings, keyboard accessibility, responsiveness to screen size changes, device orientations, and text legibility in both portrait and landscape modes.

Cue Column:

Charter: Explore bookings' rendering in the report view with a vast collection of bookings to determine readability.

Session Notes:

- Data Creation for APIs:
  - Analyzed code in APIs (room and booking) to understand data generation.
  - Strategies devised to generate test data for the room and booking APIs using SQL and scripts.
- Investigations:
  - Loaded page: Noticed slow loading times for pages with numerous bookings.
  - Navigation Controls: Page sluggishness observed when transitioning from busy to quiet months.

- Viewing More Bookings: Popup issues detected - overflow and slow loading.
- Creating New Bookings: Lag experienced after canceling the booking action.
- Keyboard Accessibility: Successful tab navigation, issues with tabbing into popups.

- PAOLO Mnemonic:
  - Portrait Mode: Calendar responsiveness on different screen sizes and resolutions assessed.
  - Zooming In/Out: Issues identified with slow resizing and content hiding.
  - Device Orientation: Handling of screen resizing and orientation changes examined.
  - Text Legibility: Problems noted with tiny text on mobile screens.

Notes Column:
- Issues/Bugs:
  - Slow page loading with numerous bookings.
  - Sluggishness navigating between busy and quiet months.
  - Popup display issues - overflow, slow loading.
  - Lag after canceling a booking action.
  - Tabbing issues with popups, especially on overflowed content.
  - Slow resizing, content hiding on zooming in/out.
  - Messy initial layout on screen resizing.
  - Tiny text on mobile screens affecting readability.
  - Inability to click and drag on calendar for admin bookings in mobile view.

Summary Column:
- Key Findings:
  - Performance issues with page loading and navigation controls.
  - Popup display problems affecting user interaction.
  - Resizing and text legibility concerns on mobile devices.
  - Limited functionality for admin bookings on mobile view.

Evaluation Column:
- Implications:
  - Performance optimizations needed for smoother page loading.
  - Popup display improvements for better user experience.
  - Responsive design adjustments required for various screen sizes and orientations.
  - Text size adjustments for better readability on smaller screens.

Action Column:

- Action Items:
  - Optimize page loading times for better performance.
  - Prioritize fixing popup display issues for enhanced usability.
  - Implement responsive design enhancements for different screen sizes.
  - Adjust text sizes for improved readability on mobile devices.

Reflection:

The exploratory testing revealed critical issues related to performance, usability, and responsiveness in rendering bookings within the report view. Addressing these findings would significantly improve the overall user experience and functionality of the system.

Experimentation is key here, but what this demonstrates is that LLMs have the potential to support us in ways that other, more traditional tools are unable to. Reporting sometimes gets short shrift in testing because rapidly sharing a wealth of knowledge can be difficult, which encourages teams to rely on more quantitative, test script-based reports that we normally see. However, with the use of LLMs, we can now structure and present reports that give a fuller picture of what we've learned during exploratory testing, sharing the rich information that hides behind the numbers of how many test scripts or sessions have been run.

Activity 8.4

Create a testing report based on notes you have captured in the past. Copy the notes into one of the prompts we've explored in this part of the chapter to see what sort of report is produced. Reflect on whether it's of use to you or if the prompt needs tweaking to improve the reporting.

Summary

- LLMs can be used in the process of identifying risks and charters for exploratory testing.
- When identifying risks, biases such as functional fixedness can make us miss potential risks to explore.
- We can use LLMs to analyze risks we've already discovered and then propose additional risks for further consideration.
- Risks generated by an LLM will contain a mix of suggestions that may or may not be useful.
- We can carry out a similar process of requesting LLMs to suggest additional test charters.

- In the context of exploratory testing and LLMs, the goal is to use LLMs to shake up our thinking and offer new perspectives, not to accept them blindly as additional risks and charters.
- LLMs can be used to help support activities in exploratory testing sessions.
- We can use LLMs to transform code and add code comments, which can help improve our understanding.
- We can also use LLMs to create required test data by asking them to output test data for us or create scripts that we can use to generate our data.
- Combining prompts with testing heuristics can generate suggested test ideas.
- We can determine which of the suggested test ideas are of use and discard the rest.
- LLMs can be used to convert testing notes into richer test reports, such as testing stories.

AI agents as testing assistants

Over the previous few chapters, we saw how large language models (LLMs) can assist us in testing. We also learned how to employ various prompt techniques to get the most out of LLMs and curate different prompts that can be utilized when required. This is a great position to be in, but what if we could take our new understanding one step further to create custom-made AI testing assistants?

As LLMs have advanced, so have the opportunities to create AI agents, applications that can take a goal and autonomously interact with other systems, collect data, analyze information, and adapt a suitable response to achieve said goal. In the field of AI, an agent can be implemented in many ways, but the goal tends to be the same—to create something that we can give a task to be solved. The scope of designing and building AI agents is large, but in this chapter, we'll learn a bit more about their potential and how they work in the context of generative AI. We'll also create our own basic test data AI agent to demonstrate the power and potential of this technology.

9.1   Understanding AI agents and LLMs

When we discuss AI agents, we need to specify what we mean. AI agents can be implemented in different ways, depending on the field of AI we are working in. But that's not to say that there aren't expected behaviors of an agent regardless of how it works. So, before we begin to implement our agents, let's first define what these expected behaviors might look like and then how agents might be built in the context of generative AI.

9.1.1   What defines an AI agent?

To comprehend what defines an agent, we have to focus more on the characteristics that are imbued within it than on its implementation. There is no explicit list of characteristics an agent is expected to meet, but the following attributes are usually found:

- *Being goal-driven*—An agent must be able to receive a goal that it can ultimately achieve. The goal itself can be something that is either specific, such as "Make me a hotel booking for X," or more abstract, such as "Determine the most successful stock to buy next month based on current trends." Regardless of the scope of the goal, some sort of direction is required to help us evaluate whether the actions an agent is taking are bringing it closer to completing its task.

- *Being perceptive*—An agent must also be able to interact with the wider world. This might mean extracting information, or interacting with a system to produce results. Examples might include making an HTTP request to a web API to get data for processing or running web automation code to complete a booking form. Whatever we want our agent to achieve, we have to give it the ability to interact with the world outside so that it can solve problems for us.

- *Have autonomy*—Perhaps most crucially, an agent must be able to autonomously decide how a problem is solved. Instead of following a clear, algorithmic path that we set out, it can pick and choose what tasks to do and in what order. This is where the core element of an agent is usually found. By evaluating the goal it has been given, it can interact with the world, carry out tasks, and evaluate whether said tasks align with the goal it's been set.

- *Being adaptive*—Finally, agents must also be able to learn from actions. For example, agents that can complete video games do so by learning from the mistakes they make. But it can just mean reacting to specific information that is retrieved at a given point in time. Much like in autonomy, the goal that has been set plays a role in determining if an agent has been successful when carrying out a specific task. If it has not, we want our agent to be able to react to that failure not to repeat it or to work around it to achieve its set goal.

This is not an exhaustive list of characteristics. Depending on the problem an agent is being asked to solve will determine which characteristics matter more. However, the examples provided give us a sense of what an AI agent might look like and how it behaves. Thus, an agent is an autonomous piece of software thar can be given a relatively complex task and solve it for us.

9.1.2   *How an agent works with LLMs*

So, how are these characteristics created when using LLMs to drive an agent? The answer is, "through the use of an LLM feature called *function calling*," which allows us to encapsulate code into functions that an LLM can trigger for us when it is prompted to complete a task. To help us better understand this process, figure 9.1 outlines the general process of how function calling works.

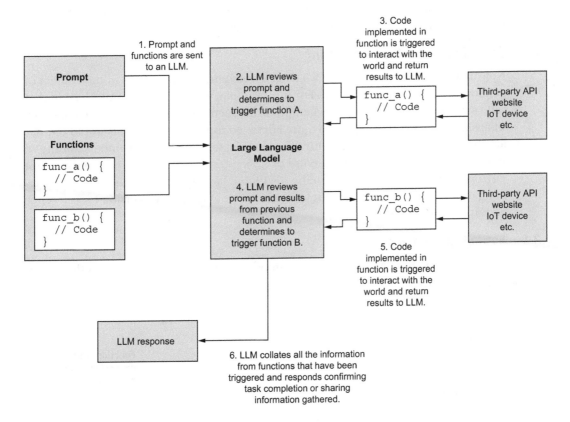

Figure 9.1   An outline of an LLM agent using function calling

As described in the figure, function calling works by providing both a prompt and encapsulated code to an LLM. The LLM can then determine which function to run to achieve the goal set within our prompt. Inside each function, there will be code built by us that will process information or interact with the outside world in some shape, form, or manner. For example, a function might extract data from a web API, scrape a web page, or gather information from a sensor. A function may also be sent parameters from the LLM to apply further processing on received data before sending it back to the LLM for future use.

What gives our agents their autonomous characteristic is an LLM's ability to determine which functions are called when and with what data. Each function we create is provided with some additional instructions to help the LLM determine what our code within the function does. When given a task to complete, the LLM can process the initial prompt, select the right function to call first, and store any information that is returned by a function into the prompt itself.

This autonomy is what distinguishes an agent from a tool that executes an ordered list of functions that interacts with different APIs or services. An agent may be given a large collection of various functions that process information and interact with the world in different ways, utilizing only the necessary functions to solve a problem.

9.2   *Creating an AI Test Assistant*

Now that we have a grounding in what agents are and how they work in the context of generative AI, let's build our own. For this example, we'll be building an AI agent that will read and create data for us when given instructions. This might feel like a somewhat simple agent, but to get into more advanced topics around agents would require another whole book. However, with this example, we'll get a better understanding of how an agent can be built with the use of LLMs so that we can take both our prompt engineering and agent building to the next level. We'll go through the process of creating our AI agent step by step, but you can check our completed version for reference at: https://mng.bz/aVlJ.

9.2.1   *Setting up our dummy AI agent*

We begin by creating a Maven project, and within our `pom.xml` file, we add the following dependencies:

```
<dependencies>

    <dependency>
        <groupId>dev.langchain4j</groupId>
        <artifactId>langchain4j-open-ai</artifactId>
        <version>0.31.0</version>
    </dependency>

    <dependency>
        <groupId>dev.langchain4j</groupId>
        <artifactId>langchain4j</artifactId>
        <version>0.31.0</version>
    </dependency>

    <dependency>
        <groupId>com.h2database</groupId>
        <artifactId>h2</artifactId>
        <version>2.2.224</version>
    </dependency>
</dependencies>
```

Functions to quickly connect to OpenAI platform

AI services to create our AI agent

Database to manipulate with our agent

We'll be using LangChain4J (https://docs.langchain4j.dev) to manage both the communication with our LLM and the necessary functions we want our agent to execute. This will become clearer when we implement said functions, but first, let's establish our connection to LLM by creating a new class called `DataAssistant` with a `main` function:

```java
public class DataAssistant {

    public static void main(String[] args) {

    }

}
```

Now we can update the class with the necessary code to send a basic prompt to a gpt-3.5-turbo model:

```java
public class DataAssistant {

    static interface DataAssistantService {
        String sendPrompt(String userPrompt);
    }

    public static void main(String[] args) {

        OpenAiChatModel model = OpenAiChatModel
                .builder()
                .apiKey("API-KEY-HERE")
                .modelName(OpenAiChatModelName.GPT_3_5_TURBO)
                .build();

        DataAssistantService dataAssistantChat =
        ⇒ AiServices.builder(DataAssistantService.class)
                .chatLanguageModel(model)
                .build();

        String response = dataAssistantChat.sendPrompt("Hi, can you
        ⇒ introduce yourself?");
        System.out.printf(response);
    }

}
```

Creates an interface to add our AI services into

Sets up access to our OpenAI model and model preference

Uses AiServices.builder to add our model to our DataAssistantService

Sends a basic prompt to OpenAI, stores the response, and outputs it

The `OpenAiChatModel` portion of the code establishes which model we want to connect and our authorization method. Within the `.apiKey` method, we provide an API key from OpenAI that can be generated via their API keys page found at https://platform.openai.com/api-keys. We then provide the model as a parameter when setting up our `DataAssistantService` using the `AiServices` library. This lets us keep our model choice and our AI services separate, allowing us to easily change the model we want to use. The `DataAssistantService` interface helps to configure the method we want to use to send our prompt, as well as add other advanced features if we desire, such as system prompts that contextualize the user prompts that we want to send once our service is established. We'll start to see how `AiServices` comes into its own shortly, but for now, we can test our implemented code out by running it and getting a response similar to the following:

 Hello, I am a language model AI assistant created by OpenAI. I am here to help answer your questions and assist you with any information you may need. How can I help you today?

Now that we are connected to our LLM, we can begin to build out the tasks we want our agent to trigger to give our assistant some agency. To do this, we create a new class called `DataAssistantTools` and add the following code:

```java
public class DataAssistantTools {

    @Tool("Create room records")
    public void createRooms(@P("Amount of room records to create")
    int count) {
        System.out.println("You want me to create " + count + "
        rooms.");
    }

    @Tool("Create booking records")
    public void createBookings(@P("Amount of booking records to
    create") int count) {
        System.out.println("You want me to create " + count + "
        bookings.");
    }

    @Tool("Show results of database")
    public void displayDatabase() {
        System.out.println("I'll then share current database
        details");
    }

}
```

We've now created three functions that our LLM can choose to trigger when prompted. But how does the LLM determine which function to trigger at a given time? This is achieved by using the `@Tool` annotation provided by `LangChain4J`. The `@Tool` annotation not only identifies what method to trigger, but also indicates to the LLM in natural language what the code does, so that the LLM can determine if it's a function that is worth calling. For example, our first tool has the annotation `@Tool("Create room records")`. If we send a prompt to our LLM, along with our tool, asking it to create some rooms, then the LLM will determine that our tool should be executed. If we were to send a prompt with an entirely different message, then the tool might not be used. We'll see this in action shortly, but first, let's update our `AiServices` builder so that it incorporates our newly created `DataAssistantTools`:

```
DataAssistantService dataAssistantChat =
  AiServices.builder(DataAssistantService.class)
              .chatLanguageModel(model)

              .tools(new DataAssistantTools())    Adds our tools via the tools()
              .build();                           method within the builder

     while(true){                                              Sets up a
         Scanner scanner = new Scanner(System.in);            Scanner to
         System.out.println("What do you need?");             keep the app
                                                              running and
         String query = scanner.nextLine();                  receive
         String response = dataAssistantChat.sendPrompt(query);  prompts
         System.out.println(response);
     }
```

As we can see, the `AiServices` builder begins to demonstrate its value by allowing us to set both the model we want to use and the tools we want the agent to use. We've also updated our means of inputting prompts so that the application stays up and running continuously and we can test out our new agent with different instructions. So, when we run the agent and are asked

 What do you need?

we can submit our prompt:

 Can you create me 4 rooms and 2 bookings and tell me what's in the db

to be returned the following response:

 You want me to create 4 rooms.

You want me to create 2 bookings.

I'll then share current database details

Let's break down how this output has been generated. First, we've sent our prompt and tools to gpt-3.5-turbo to process. The model then evaluates the details of the prompts and looks through the list of tools we've tagged using the `@Tool` annotation to find which tools are relevant to our instructions. At the start of the prompt, we requested "Can you create me 4 rooms," and the LLM has determined that our `createRooms` tool should be run because of its relevance to the annotation `@Tool("Create room records")`. Next, we can see that the output correctly stated that we want to create four rooms. This is because we passed a parameter into our `createRooms` method using LangChain's `@P` annotation in the form of `@P("Amount of room records to create")` `int count`. Notice how we provide natural language context again to the `@P` annotation in a similar fashion to the `@Tool` annotation. This allows the LLM to do a similar relevancy match, extract what it believes is the necessary data from our prompt, and provide it as a parameter to be output.

We can now also test our agent's ability to determine which tool to use autonomously by giving it different instructions. This time, when asked for a prompt, we sent

 Can you tell me what's in the database currently

Running this would return the response:

 I'll then share current database details

In this case, the LLM has triggered only one of our tools, specifically `displayDatabase` annotated as `@Tool("Show results of database")`. Since we've not mentioned creating rooms or bookings in our prompt, the related tools are deemed not relevant to our instructions and are therefore ignored. This demonstrates the power of agents. Imagine if we had not just 3 tools, but 10, 20, or more. The more we add, the more ways we give an agent the ability to react to our instructions and solve our requested problems.

9.2.2   *Giving our AI agent functions to execute*

We have the decision-making process wired up, so now let's complete our agent and give it the ability to carry out some database queries for us. For this, we're going to create a dummy database using h2 with some basic tables to demonstrate how we can have our LLM execute actions for us. To do this, we'll start by creating a new class `QueryTools` and adding the following code:

```
public class QueryTools {

    private final Connection connection;

    public QueryTools() throws SQLException {
        connection = DriverManager.getConnection("jdbc:h2:mem:testdb");
        Statement st = connection.createStatement();
        st.executeUpdate("""
            CREATE TABLE BOOKINGS (
                bookingid int NOT NULL AUTO_INCREMENT,
                roomid int,
                firstname varchar(255),
                lastname varchar(255),
                depositpaid boolean,
                checkin date,
                checkout date,
                primary key (bookingid)
            );
            CREATE TABLE ROOMS (
                roomid int NOT NULL AUTO_INCREMENT,
                room_name varchar(255),
                type varchar(255),
                beds int,
                accessible boolean,
                image varchar(2000),
                description varchar(2000),
                features varchar(100) ARRAY,
```

On startup, creates a database with the necessary tables

```
            roomPrice int,
            primary key (roomid)
        );
    """);
}


public void createRoom() throws SQLException {
    Statement st = connection.createStatement();
    st.executeUpdate("""
        INSERT INTO ROOMS (room_name, type, beds, accessible,
        ⇒image, description, features, roomPrice)
        VALUES (
            '101',
            'single',
            1,
            true,
            '/images/room2.jpg',
            'A generated description',
            ARRAY['TV', 'WiFi', 'Safe'],
            100);
    """);
}


public void createBooking() throws SQLException {
    Statement st = connection.createStatement();
    st.executeUpdate("""
        INSERT INTO BOOKINGS (roomid, firstname, lastname,
        ⇒depositpaid, checkin, checkout)
        VALUES (
            1,
            'James',
            'Dean',
            true,
            '2022-02-01',
            '2022-02-05'
        );
    """);
}


public void outputTables(String query) throws SQLException {
    Statement st = connection.createStatement();
    ResultSet rs = st.executeQuery(query);
    ResultSetMetaData rsmd = rs.getMetaData();

    int columnsNumber = rsmd.getColumnCount();
    while (rs.next()) {
        for(int i = 1 ; i <= columnsNumber; i++){
            System.out.print(rs.getString(i) + " ");

        }
        System.out.println();
    }
}
}
```

On startup, creates a database with the necessary tables

A basic method to create rooms

A basic method to create bookings

A basic method to output the contents of each table

With our `QueryTools` class created, we can then expand our tools to interact with the database how we like by updating `DataAssistantTools`:

```java
public class DataAssistantTools [

    QueryTools queryTools = new QueryTools();

    public DataAssistantTools() throws SQLException {
    }

    @Tool("Create room records")
    public void createRooms(@P("Amount of room records to create")
    int count) throws SQLException {

        for(int i = 1; i <= count; i++){
            queryTools.createRoom();
        }
    }

    @Tool("Create booking records")
    public void createBookings(@P("Amount of booking records to
    create") int count) throws SQLException {

        for(int i = 1; i <= count; i++){
            queryTools.createBooking();
        }
    }

    @Tool("Show results of database")
    public void displayDatabase() throws SQLException {

        System.out.println("Current ROOM database state:");
        queryTools.outputTables("SELECT * FROM ROOMS");

        System.out.println("Current BOOKING database state:");
        queryTools.outputTables("SELECT * FROM BOOKINGS");
    }

}
```

> Creates a new instance of our database on startup

> Creates rooms by looping through the number of rooms requested

> Creates bookings by looping through the amount of bookings requested

> Outputs the contents of each table

Finally, we update our `main` method within our `DataAssistant` class to handle `SQLException`, resulting in the following completed code:

```java
public static void main(String[] args) throws SQLException

        OpenAiChatModel model = OpenAiChatModel
                .builder()
                .apiKey("API-KEY-HERE")
                .modelName(OpenAiChatModelName.GPT_3_5_TURBO)
                .build();

        DataAssistantService dataAssistantChat =
        AiServices.builder(DataAssistantService.class)
                .chatLanguageModel(model)
```

```
        .tools(new DataAssistantTools())
        .build();

while(true) {
    Scanner scanner = new Scanner(System.in);
    System.out.println("What do you need?");

    String query = scanner.nextLine();
    String response = dataAssistantChat.sendPrompt(query);
    System.out.println(response);
    }
}
```

With everything in place, we can now test the agent by first requesting it create our desired data:

 Create me 2 rooms and 3 bookings

It then results in a response such as:

 Two rooms and three bookings have been successfully created.

We can then confirm that our data has been created by sending additional instructions to the agent

 List me the database contents

resulting in an output that looks similar to

 Current ROOM database state:

101 single 1 TRUE /images/room2.jpg A generated description [TV, WiFi, Safe] 100
101 single 1 TRUE /images/room2.jpg A generated description [TV, WiFi, Safe] 100

Current BOOKING database state:

1 James Dean TRUE 2022-02-01 2022-02-05
1 James Dean TRUE 2022-02-01 2022-02-05
1 James Dean TRUE 2022-02-01 2022-02-05

With our database queries now wired into our tools, we can interact with our agents and have them carry out our tasks. However, let's go one step further with our agent and give it the capability to run multiple tools in a chain, utilizing data created in one tool in another.

9.2.3   *Chaining tools together*

Currently, our tools are independent of one another. The room tool creates rooms that generate unique `roomid` keys for each row, but we're not using them when we create new bookings. We're simply hardcoding our values. So, to make our agent more dynamic, and to give it a more complex problem, let's look at how we could pass the `roomid` of the most recently created room to the booking tool.

To begin, we need to create an additional method in our `QueryTools` class that will either return the `roomid` of the most recently created room or an `id` of `0` if there are no rooms currently in the database:

```
public int getRoomId() throws SQLException
    Statement st = connection.createStatement();
    ResultSet rs = st.executeQuery("SELECT roomid FROM ROOMS
    ➥ORDER BY roomid DESC");

    if(rs.next()){
        return rs.getInt("roomid");
    } else {
        return 0;
    }
}
```

With our new method in place, we next create a new tool with `DataAssistantTools`:

```
@Tool("Get most recent roomid from database after
➥rooms have been created")
public int getRoomId() throws SQLException {
        return queryTools.getRoomId();
}
```

Notice how we have set out within the `@Tool` annotation that we expect this prompt to be run after rooms have been created. Although this doesn't guarantee the order in which tools are run by our LLM, it acts as a guardrail if we want rooms and bookings to be created in a specific order. Additionally, we are returning the `roomid` integer to the LLM. This is then stored in the context of our original prompt for future use, which we'll establish by updating our `createBookings` method to the following:

```
@Tool("Create booking records")
public void createBookings(@P("Amount of booking records to create")
➥int count, @P("Most recent roomid") int roomid) throws SQLException {
    System.out.println("I will create the bookings for room: " +
    ➥roomid);
    for(int i = 1; i <= count; i++){
        queryTools.createBooking(roomid);
    }
}
```

In this updated method, we've added a new parameter in the form of `@P("Most recent roomid") int roomid`. To see the `roomid` extraction in action, we `System.out` the `roomid` before passing it `createBooking` for use in our `INSERT` statement. To use the `roomid`, we return to `QueryTools` and update the `createBooking` method to take `roomid` as a parameter and add it to our SQL statement:

```
public void createBooking(int roomid) throws SQLException
    Statement st = connection.createStatement();
    st.executeUpdate("""
            INSERT INTO BOOKINGS (roomid, firstname, lastname,
            ➥depositpaid, checkin, checkout)
            VALUES (
                ?,
                'James',
                'Dean',
                true,
                '2022-02-01',
                '2022-02-05'
            );
        """.replace("?", Integer.toString(roomid)));
}
```

Now we have the code in place for our agent to extract the `roomid` from our database using one tool and then use that value within a second tool, which we can see in action in this example chat I had with my version of our agent:

What do you need?

Create three rooms

Three rooms have been successfully created.

What do you need?

List database

Current ROOM database state:
101 single 1 TRUE /images/room2.jpg A generated description [TV, WiFi, Safe] 100
101 single 1 TRUE /images/room2.jpg A generated description [TV, WiFi, Safe] 100
101 single 1 TRUE /images/room2.jpg A generated description [TV, WiFi, Safe] 100

Current BOOKING database state:
The database has been successfully displayed.

What do you need?

Create three bookings

I will create the bookings for room: 3

Current ROOM database state:

```
101 single 1 TRUE /images/room2.jpg A generated description [TV, WiFi,
Safe] 100
101 single 1 TRUE /images/room2.jpg A generated description [TV, WiFi,
Safe] 100
101 single 1 TRUE /images/room2.jpg A generated description [TV, WiFi,
Safe] 100
```

Current BOOKING database state:

```
3 James Dean TRUE 2022-02-01 2022-02-05
3 James Dean TRUE 2022-02-01 2022-02-05
3 James Dean TRUE 2022-02-01 2022-02-05
```

Three bookings have been successfully created.

Breaking down the output, we can see that three rooms were created, which we confirm by asking the agent to list the current rooms. Then the agent was asked to create three bookings, which it did successfully. Notice the second integer on each row underneath `Current BOOKING database state:`. See how they are now using the `roomid: 3`. The agent has successfully utilized both tools to query the most recent `roomid` before passing the retrieved `id` to the second tool that creates our bookings for us. We can confirm this isn't a coincidence by creating further rooms to confirm that a newer, more recent `roomid` is added to the additional bookings we create (in this example, `roomid` ticks up to `6`).

 What do you need?

 Create three more rooms

 Three rooms have been created successfully. Here is the updated database:

 What do you need?

 Create three more bookings

 I will create the bookings for room: 6
Three bookings have been successfully created.

 What do you need?

 List database

Current ROOM database state:

101 single 1 TRUE /images/room2.jpg A generated description [TV, WiFi, Safe] 100

101 single 1 TRUE /images/room2.jpg A generated description [TV, WiFi, Safe] 100

101 single 1 TRUE /images/room2.jpg A generated description [TV, WiFi, Safe] 100

101 single 1 TRUE /images/room2.jpg A generated description [TV, WiFi, Safe] 100

101 single 1 TRUE /images/room2.jpg A generated description [TV, WiFi, Safe] 100

101 single 1 TRUE /images/room2.jpg A generated description [TV, WiFi, Safe] 100

Current BOOKING database state:

3 James Dean TRUE 2022-02-01 2022-02-05

3 James Dean TRUE 2022-02-01 2022-02-05

3 James Dean TRUE 2022-02-01 2022-02-05

6 James Dean TRUE 2022-02-01 2022-02-05

6 James Dean TRUE 2022-02-01 2022-02-05

6 James Dean TRUE 2022-02-01 2022-02-05

This completes our basic data creator agent. We've looked at how we can create multiple tools for an agent to use and solve specific requests for us. These tools allow us to give an agent the ability to interact with the world around us. For example, we could create code to extract relevant data from a data source, connect to sensors or IoT (Internet of Things) devices, or interact with external websites. We've also seen how the results of those interactions with third parties can be fed back into our LLM for it to determine what next steps to take, as well as utilize extracted information for further use.

> **Activity 9.1**
> Consider different ways in which this agent could be expanded to do further data assistant tasks. Perhaps it could delete or update data or carry further analysis on what exists with the example database. Alternatively, consider building an agent that carries out other tasks.

9.3   *Moving forward with AI test assistants*

Our test data assistant demonstrates the potential of AI agents as tools that can help support testing activities. We can see AI agents as an approach to use when we reach a point where our prompts become too complicated, or we want to extend them to interface with third-party systems. It's important, however, to have a clear sense of both the opportunities and the challenges of developing AI agents. So, let's reflect on the various areas of testing we've used LLMs to support us in, the way AI agents could be designed to take our prompts further, and what problems might await us.

9.3.1   *Examples of AI test assistants*

We've already seen how an AI agent could help extend the use of LLMs in the test data space. But to help tie it all together, here are some examples of other types of AI agents that would take our prompts and LLM work further.

ANALYSIS AI AGENTS

We've learned how LLMs can help us expand our thinking, suggesting ideas and risks that we might not have considered. As AI agents can be connected to a range of data sources, an AI agent that enhances our suggestion prompts could be built into an assistant that offers suggestions based on collated information across a business domain. For example, we might have an agent like the one shown in figure 9.2.

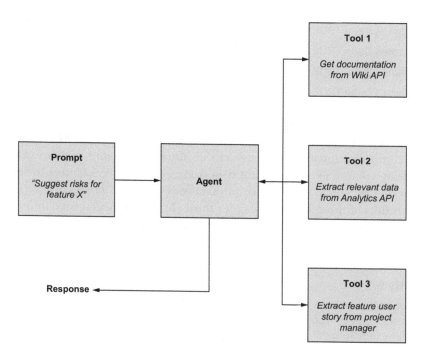

Figure 9.2   An AI agent connected to multiple data sources

An AI agent such as this one would be able to determine what data sources to access based on the instructions given. It might be able to pull in relevant documentation from knowledge bases and project management tools or raw data from monitoring and analytics tools. All this collated data can then be used to improve responses from the LLM when asked a question, a topic we'll explore more in the following chapters.

AUTOMATION ASSISTANT AI AGENTS

We also looked at how LLMs are most effective in the test automation space if we create prompts that focus on specific tasks when building automation. That said, an AI agent's potential to interact, parse, and share information across tools means that we could create an agent like the one in figure 9.3.

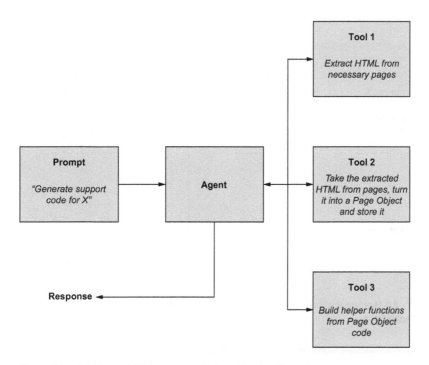

Figure 9.3   An AI agent that processes information in different ways

An AI agent such as this one would be able to build the parts of automated tests in sections. The built sections could then be passed to other tools to be utilized in various ways. This doesn't mean that these types of agents could still fully create valuable automation in one shot. Context, again, is an important factor that would need to be fed into these types of AI agents to enable them to embed rules and expectations into our automation that align with how our product works.

EXPLORATORY TESTING AI AGENTS

Finally, in this example, we're not suggesting that the AI agent could do the exploratory testing for us, but an AI agent might prove useful as an assistant to the person testing, as shown in figure 9.4.

Notice how, in the AI agent, we're creating an assistant that takes an initial prompt and then fires off further prompts to an LLM to help develop valuable suggestions. Since AI agents can interact with any system via its tools, there's no reason an AI agent couldn't interact with an LLM as well. The agent in this example helps to parse initial instructions and then use them to determine which further prompts could be utilized,

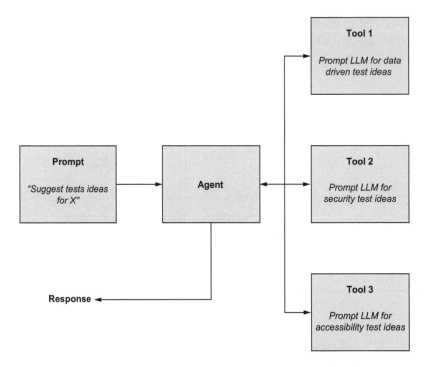

Figure 9.4   An AI agent that takes relevant information and uses additional prompts to build suggestions

creating a cascade of different prompts being triggered to create some interesting outputs.

These are, of course, just hypothetical AI agents, but each example demonstrates that their success is rooted in the types of prompts created for the instructions an agent receives and the prompts assigned to each tool. Our data agent example had only rudimentary prompts, but it is in those spaces where we can provide the expectations, parameters, and context to each tool to help an AI agent react in a way that proves valuable to us.

9.3.2 Handling the challenges of working with agents

However, it's not to say that building, using, and maintaining agents comes without its challenges. Here are a few challenges that need to be kept in mind.

EXAMINING AN LLM'S DECISION-MAKING PROCESS

Unsurprisingly, one of the biggest challenges with developing agents is their indeterministic nature. There's a good chance that, as you worked through the example agent in this chapter, you experienced the agent either not executing tools when expected or creating more or fewer data than required. The LLM component of an agent that determines what to run and what data to share between tools is opaque to us. In our example agent, we are using a third-party LLM, meaning we have no insight into its decision-making process. Nor do we have any ability to monitor its behavior or control how the LLM is tuned and operates. This lack of control and observability can become a major risk in developing agents. As they grow in complexity, not only can they become more brittle, but we also have little insight into what went wrong.

Some steps can be taken to mitigate this risk. We could host models on our platforms and increase observability. But while this might give us more insights into what decisions were made and when by an LLM, it still doesn't mean we can guarantee the outcome of an agent's responses.

NAVIGATING GUARD RAILS AND SECURITY CONCERNS

This brings us to the second problem when using agents: ensuring that we have the necessary prompts and code in place to handle situations in which an agent may hit an edge case, as well as preventing bad actors from using our agents to negatively affect our business or others. Utilizing good prompting techniques in outlining the purpose of each tool and adding checks and balances to help our agent reject invalid or undesirable requests is a must, but that means identifying those potential scenarios and implementing guard rails for them. The upshot is that agents require extensive testing and evaluation, which can come at a cost that outweighs the initial value of using them in the first place.

MANAGING WHEN THINGS GO WRONG

That said, despite our best efforts, there will be times when an agent does something wrong. Either tools are run in an incorrect order, data isn't passed between tools successfully, or the code within our tools has bugs. In the context of our example agent, these potential errors will be swallowed up by the OpenAI platform. When I first developed the example agent, it was throwing exceptions as the JDBC library failed, and the exceptions were consumed by the agent, which triggered all sorts of unusual behavior. In one example, the JDBC code failed in a way that caused the agent to continue attempting to create new records, repeatedly firing the broken function, to the point at which the whole agent crashed as it hit a limit in the amount of function calls it could carry out. The problem was that this exception wasn't shared with me, making the debugging of the problem difficult.

Again, observability and monitoring are essential, as well as ensuring our code is written defensively against potential exceptions or errors. If we don't catch and report them, then they are hidden, leading to wasted time trying to debug what was wrong in the first place.

Ultimately, agents promise the potential of making us, the individual, more efficient by supporting us in task completion. Given the autonomous abilities of agents, it can be easy to buy into the hype of their potential. But just like any software we seek to utilize, its creation, use, and maintenance come with a cost. Similarly, like all software, it's not a silver bullet for all our problems. To use agents successfully, we need to take the time to consider the problem we are attempting to solve. At times, agents may be of use to us, but other options such as a well-crafted prompt might do the work just as well, or we might have better success with other non-AI-based tools. In the end, agents are just another addition to our tool belt to employ when the time is right.

Summary

- AI agents exist in many different fields of artificial intelligence.
- AI agents are expected to be goal-driven, able to perceive the wider world, autonomous, and adaptable.
- Agents within the context of LLMs are created using function calling.
- Function calling is achieved by providing a prompt and code grouped into functions that an LLM can call to achieve a goal within a prompt.
- Function calling can be used to interact with other sites and services, feeding information back to the LLM for further processing.
- LangChain4J is a useful library for easily connecting to LLM platforms and managing AI services such as tools.
- We can create tools using the `@Tool` annotation, which helps the LLM match up our instructions to which method to run and when.
- We pass extracted values from our prompt into methods as parameters using the `@P` annotation, which works similarly to the `@Tool` annotation.
- Agents can also send data between tools by returning data out of a method and using the `@P` annotation to pull the data in as a parameter.
- When agents fail to carry out tasks or an error occurs, it can be hard to detect what went wrong.
- LLMs are opaque when it comes to decision-making, which can also make debugging problems challenging.
- Exposing agents to a wider user base means they require guard rails in place to prevent agents from either not fulfilling tasks or being vulnerable to bad actors.

Part 3

Context: Customizing LLMs for testing contexts

Throughout the previous chapters, we've seen how generalized prompts that are lacking in hints toward how our products work or what rules and expectations are in place return less valuable prompts. Although slicing our tasks down to a sensible size is key, providing that vital information to set clear boundaries on an LLM's output can make or break a response. That's why we'll conclude the final part of the book with an exploration on embedding context into our work.

In the following chapters, we'll depart a little from the techniques we've learned so far and explore different ways in which context can be retrieved and added to LLMs and prompts alike. This means dipping our toes into more advanced topics such as retrieval-augmented generation and fine-tuning, not to make us experts in these fields, but rather to appreciate how they work and how they can be utilized to get the most out of LLMs. So, let's dive in and see what exciting options await us to take LLMs to the next level as testing assistants.

Introducing customized LLMs

10

This chapter covers

- How a lack of context affects an LLM's performance
- How RAG works and its value
- How the fine-tuning of LLMs works and its value
- Comparing RAG and fine-tuning approaches

Over the past few chapters, we saw how to hone our skills to identify distinct, focused tasks that large language models (LLMs) can support. Combined with a range of prompt-engineering techniques, we've been successful in getting LLMs to return responses that are valuable for our testing activities. However, despite the lessons we learned, the responses we receive might still not be completely aligned with our needs and context. Although it would be foolish to think that we can completely align an LLM with our context, there are more advanced options that can be utilized along with prompt engineering to further maximize the output of an LLM in support of our testing. So, in this final part, we're going to examine ways in which we can enhance LLMs so that they can become more embedded in our context, specifically focusing on retrieval-augmented generation (RAG) and fine-tuning. But before we dig into the specific details and actions of how these approaches work, we'll first examine why more commonly used LLMs such as ChatGPT, Claude, and Gemini may struggle to tune to our context and then slowly familiarize ourselves with the more advanced topics of RAG and fine-tuning, comparing them to determine which one is more suitable in a given situation.

10.1   *The challenge with LLMs and context*

We learned that the key challenge of working with LLMs is getting them to respond with an output that

- Is relevant to our context
- Follows the rules of our prompt
- Contains no hallucinations

The prompt-engineering techniques we've used have helped us achieve these goals so far. For example, if we return to our example prompt from chapter 5, we can see a weak prompt such as

 Create tests for a file upload feature

which returns a weak response with quite generalized results:

 1 Test for File Upload Functionality:
- Test Case 1.1: Upload a Valid File
  - Input: Choose a file with a valid format (e.g., .jpg, .pdf).
  - Expected Outcome: The file is successfully uploaded, and a confirmation message is displayed.
- Test Case 1.2: Attempt to Upload an Invalid File
  - Input: Choose a file with an invalid format (e.g., .exe, .html).
  - Expected Outcome: An error message is displayed, indicating that the file format is not supported.

2 Test for File Size Limit:
- Test Case 2.1: Upload a File Below the Size Limit
  - Input: Choose a file smaller than the maximum allowed size.
  - Expected Outcome: The file is successfully uploaded, and a confirmation message is displayed.
- Test Case 2.2: Attempt to Upload a File Exceeding the Size Limit
  - Input: Choose a file larger than the maximum allowed size.
  - Expected Outcome: An error message is displayed, indicating that the file exceeds the maximum size limit.

However, a prompt with more detail and the right prompt-engineering tactics can result in a more optimal response. A prompt such as

 You are an expert software tester. Generate as many test cases as possible for the behavior delimited by three hashes.

An Authorization API that will take a token from a different API and check to see if the token is valid and in date before either responding positively or negatively depending on the result.

returns more specific results, such as

 1. Valid Token Check:

- Test with a valid token that is within the expiration date. Expected result: API responds positively.

2. Expired Token Check:

- Test with a valid token that has expired. Expected result: API responds negatively.

3. Invalid Token Check:

- Test with an invalid token format (e.g., incorrect characters, wrong length). Expected result: API responds negatively.

4. Empty Token Check:

- Test with an empty token input. Expected result: API responds negatively or returns an appropriate error message.

5. Null Token Check:

- Test with a null token input. Expected result: API responds negatively or returns an appropriate error message.

Our second prompt is more successful because we've shared more of our context within as well as used specific prompt engineering tactics. Therefore, if we want to get the most out of an LLM, we not only need to rely on good prompt-engineering techniques, but also provide the most relevant context possible. The reasons for this are twofold:

- It is more than likely that an LLM has not been trained on our context. Therefore, an LLM has no increased weighting or bias toward our context.
- An LLM is trained on such a massive amount of generalized data that when asked a generic question, it will rely on stronger, more generalized patterns it has identified from the training process.

So, if we want to get the best out of an LLM, on the surface, the answer seems simple enough: provide it with as much context detail as possible (which we have been doing to some degree already). However, if we were to do this, we'd quickly run into some limitations around the amount we can send in a prompt.

10.1.1 *Tokens, context windows, and limitations*

Before we talk about this prompting limitation, there are some other concepts around LLMs that we need to be aware of—namely, tokens and context windows. Understanding these two aspects of LLMs will help us appreciate why current LLMs have an upper limit on how much context can be provided and how that affects our strategies of use.

TOKENS

Imagine we are sending the following prompt to an LLM:

 List me five of the most populated cities in the world.

How does an LLM, which can only interpret information using machine code, parse this prompt and return a response? This is done through a process known as *tokenization,* in which natural language text is converted into matching integers that can be read by an LLM. To understand how this works, let's consider our populated cities prompt. If we were to put this through the tokenization process, the sentence would be sliced into smaller, discrete parts. For example, our prompt could be broken into 12 sections:

```
List
 me
 five
 of
 the
 most
 populated
 cities
 in
 the
 world
.
```

As we can see, each word in the sentence and the period at the end have been sliced into their own smaller sections, known as *tokens.* Notice how they also include the whitespace to the left of each word. It's a general rule of thumb that each word in a sentence is split into its token; however, some tokenizers (the tools used for making this conversion) can sometimes break up larger words into individual tokens or group smaller words together.

Once a sentence has been sliced into tokens, each one is converted into an integer with a unique number being used as an identifier for each word. For example, completing the tokenization of our prompt would result in a list of numbers (the commas and whitespace have been added to help readability):

 861, 757, 4330, 315, 279, 1455, 35459, 9919, 304, 279, 1917, 13

Each number in this list correlates to a specific slice taken from our prompt. For example, the token the has an id of 279 and we can see that it appears twice in the list for each instance when the was used in the sentence. Once the prompt has completed the tokenization process, the model we use is then able to process the list of integers and start determining how to respond. Then the process of tokenization is used again to create the response text we receive from a model, so our model might respond with a series of integers:

```
53954, 16417, 11, 6457, 198, 16939, 6151, 11, 6890, 198, 2059, 31170,
11, 5734, 198, 50, 3496, 38026, 11, 16327, 198, 44, 30955, 11, 6890
```

When converted back into text, it would result in the following response (line breaks are also included in the integer list, and each mention of iteration of 11 is a line break):

Tokyo, Japan

Delhi, India

Shanghai, China

São Paulo, Brazil

Mumbai, India

Experimenting with tokenizers

To better understand how the tokenization process works and how words, numbers, and symbols are sliced, we can experiment with preview tools for tokenizing such as the one at https://gpt-tokenizer.dev/.

So, tokens are an important aspect of LLMs because they inform us not just of how a model can parse a prompt and form a response, but also of how large a prompt can be sent to said model before we run into problems. This brings us to context windows and the crux of our context challenge.

CONTEXT WINDOWS

Given that the tokenization process takes natural language and turns it into a series of numbers for an LLM to process, the longer a prompt is, the more tokens there are to process. The problem with prompts that have larger sets of tokens is that it affects how effectively an LLM processes our prompt and the resources it consumes. The larger a prompt, the more complex it becomes to generate a response, which means more hardware usage. All of this will come at a cost, either in hosting fees if utilizing a private LLM or API costs for sending prompts (platforms such as OpenAI charge based on the number of sent and received tokens).

Add to this that a larger context window doesn't necessarily mean a better-performing LLM, and we start to see that providers of LLMs have a tradeoff to make. As a result, LLMs will likely have some sort of limitation built into the model on the number of tokens it can receive at a given time. This is known as a model's context window. Different models contain different-sized context windows, which are sometimes also referred to as the context length. All of this depends on the type of model that has been trained, the hardware it is running on, and how it has been deployed with other supporting applications. For example, OpenAI's ChatGPT 4 is estimated to have a context window of 128k tokens, whereas that for Meta's Llama-2 is 4k (before modifications are made). Therefore, when it comes to determining which LLM to use in a given situation, we must be aware of the context length. Choosing a model that is limited in size to save cost might limit what context we can add to a prompt.

> **Not all context windows are the same**
>
> One thing to note when discussing context windows is that just because a model is able to take, for example, a 128k token request, it doesn't mean that the response will have the same limitations. In fact, it may be that the response has a much smaller window to help keep costs down. This won't necessarily affect our learning in the following chapters, but it's a useful detail to keep in mind when expecting a model to return a large response.

10.1.2 *Embedding context as a solution*

Now that we understand that LLMs interpret our requests through tokenization and that the size of tokens we can send to an LLM is limited, we can start to see the problem we face when adding further context to our prompts. Although LLMs are developing rapidly, becoming more efficient and offering larger context windows, it's simply not cost-effective to, for example, add a complete code base of an application with prompt's instructions. We'd either end up hitting the upper limits of a model's capabilities or burning our budget at a rapid pace. Instead, to maximize accuracy, we need to consider how we embed context into our prompts and our LLMs in an intelligent way. Fortunately, there has been a lot of work in the AI community that we can use to embed our context further in a way that improves accuracy and doesn't break the bank (or the model) in the process.

10.2 *Embedding context further into prompts and LLMs*

To improve the ability to increase an LLM's exposure to our context, we can utilize one of two techniques. The first is RAG, and the second, fine-tuning. Throughout the remaining chapters, we'll explore how these two approaches work, how they differ from one another, and how we can determine which is a more suitable approach to improving an LLM's responses. Although both approaches are different in application, the end goal of both is similar: to help us improve a model's performance by allowing us to add more context to an LLM's workflow. Retrieval-augmented generation looks to solve the problem by focusing on ways in which we can enhance our prompting, whereas fine-tuning looks to bake our context directly into the model itself. Let's take a look at both briefly so that we can become more familiar with them and determine which approach is more suitable in a given situation.

10.2.1 RAG

As we learned earlier, if an LLM has limitations in the size of a prompt it can receive due to a context window, it's inadvisable to attempt to throw all our context into a single prompt hoping that it will improve an LLM's response. However, that doesn't mean we can't be selective with the type of context we provide in a prompt. What this means is that accuracy can be improved in an LLM not by brute-forcing our context onto an LLM, but by crafting our prompts so that they contain all the relevant information about our context to support our instructions. In more concrete terms, this means that if we wanted an LLM to generate boilerplate page objects for an automated check, it would be better to provide the specific HTML for a page and any relevant code for said page than add the entire code base to a prompt.

On the surface, this seems like an effective and simple approach: write our prompt, find the relevant supporting information, combine the two into a final prompt, and send it to an LLM. The problem though is that this can be a labor-intensive activity, researching and determining what information to add and what to ignore. Fortunately, this is where RAG can help us. As shown in figure 10.1, RAG works by automating the process of embedding relevant information into our prompts through using our prompt's initial instructions to determine what information to add to our prompt.

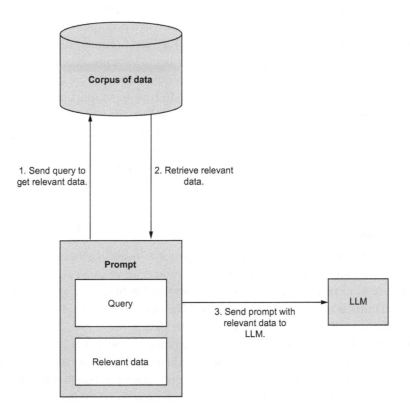

Figure 10.1 A high-level workflow diagram for RAG

To help us better understand the process, let's return to our Page-object-generation prompt example. With a RAG framework, the approach would work like this:

1 A corpus of information will have been created. In our example, it may contain labeled HTML documents for each page of our application.

2 A prompt is created in which we ask for an LLM to generate a Page object for our booking listing page.

3 Our RAG framework analyzes our prompt and programmatically finds the most relevant document in our corpus of HTML documents. If the RAG framework is working correctly, it will determine that the HTML document that contains the booking listing is the most relevant.

4 The most relevant HTML document is added to the prompt that we initially created, and the prompt is then sent to an LLM to return a response.

The RAG helps us contextualize our prompts further by analyzing what we're asking and then automatically identifying the right type of context. What makes this useful is that it helps us create a prompt with the information that is of most use for an LLM to create a more accurate response than if the information didn't exist. It's also a useful approach because RAG allows us to embed any type of data that is easy to parse and search for relevancy, whether it's code, documentation, database entries, or raw metrics. We also can control how relevancy is determined, meaning that we still have control over the type of information that might be added to a prompt.

For these reasons and its relative ease of setup, RAG has become a popular approach to enhancing our interaction with LLMs. Once we begin to appreciate how RAG works, we can begin to see how it might be useful in a testing context. We've already explored the idea of using RAG to extract sections of a code base to support prompts that are looking to create automation, but it can also be used to support queries around risk analysis, understanding how our products work and generating test ideas. There is also the potential to use testing artifacts in RAG frameworks, such as exploratory testing notes, test scripts, or automation code, to bolster the prompting ideas we explored in the previous chapters. At its core, if the data we want to use can be stored in a consistent format and easily queried, then it has the potential to be used in a RAG framework.

10.2.2 *Fine-tuning LLMs*

Although RAG focuses on ways to enhance a prompt by adding targeted contextual material, fine-tuning focuses on enhancing the model we're using itself. Fine-tuning utilizes a collection of tools and techniques used to further train a model that has already been initially trained in hope that it will bias the model further toward the data it has been fine-tuned on, as summarized in figure 10.2.

As the figure shows, fine-tuning takes place against a model that has already been trained on a large corpus of data. For example, the free version of ChatGPT is a fine-tuned version of OpenAI's gpt-3.5-turbo model. gpt-3.5 went through a series of training processes to get its core abilities, but when interacted with, it lacks the tone and

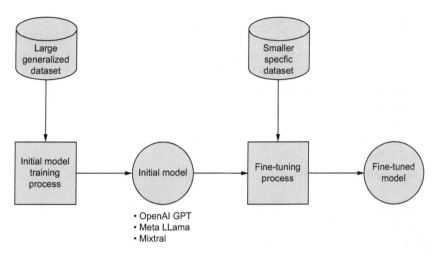

Figure 10.2　A visualization outlining the difference between training and fine-tuning

characteristics of a chatbot. For example, after sending the following prompt to gpt-3.5 (before fine-tuning):

 You are an expert travel agent. Give me a list of the top three places to visit in London.

I received the following response:

　1　The British Museum - This iconic museum houses a vast collection of art and artifacts from all corners of the globe, including the Rosetta Stone and the controversial Elgin Marbles. It is a must-visit for history and culture enthusiasts.

　　　　2　The Tower of London - This historic fortress on the banks of the River Thames has served as a royal palace, prison, and armory. Visitors can explore the Crown Jewels, see the famous ravens, and learn about the Tower's fascinating history.

　　　　3　The West End - London's renowned theater district is home to world-class productions and musicals. Take in a show at one of the many historic venues like the Royal Opera House or the National Theatre, and experience the magic of London's vibrant performing arts scene.

Whereas, upon sending the prompt to ChatGPT (a fine-tuned version of gpt-3.5), I received the following response:

 Absolutely! London offers a plethora of attractions, but here are three must-visit places:

　　　　1　The British Museum: It's a treasure trove of human history and culture, housing millions of artifacts spanning centuries and continents. From the Rosetta Stone to the Egyptian mummies and the Elgin Marbles, the British Museum is a fascinating journey through civilizations.

2   The Tower of London: Steeped in history and legend, the Tower of London is an iconic fortress that has served as a royal palace, prison, and treasury over the centuries. Visitors can explore its ancient walls, marvel at the Crown Jewels, and hear tales of famous prisoners and executions.

3   Westminster Abbey: A masterpiece of Gothic architecture, Westminster Abbey is not only a place of worship but also the site of royal coronations, weddings, and burials. Visitors can admire its stunning stained glass windows, intricate stone carvings, and the tombs of famous figures like Isaac Newton, Charles Darwin, and Elizabeth I.

These attractions offer a rich glimpse into London's history, culture, and heritage.

Factually, they are similar. But looking at the second response, we can see that it has a bit more flavor to it. It has a more casual and friendly tone, all of which comes from the fine-tuning process it has undergone to make it feel more chat-like.

Qualities such as ChatGPT's more casual tone are achieved by training a model with a curated dataset in hope of biasing its internal parameters toward a desired tone, style, or specific context. To recap, a model consists of millions or billions of parameters that determine the probability of which word should come after another word or collection of words. These parameters are in place when a fine-tuning session is started, and the fine-tuning process seeks to influence the parameters further toward an end goal. We'll talk about this more in chapter 11, but we can see how this approach works in figure 10.3.

Fine-tuning takes information from a data set and uses it to form a prompt sent to our model that is being fine-tuned. The response is then evaluated against an expected response. If the responses don't align, the model is tweaked so that its chances of an aligned response the next time are increased. This is then done thousands of, or perhaps millions of, times to slowly tune a model closer to our end goal of how we want the fine-tuned model to respond, which means that a very large corpus of data is required to successfully train a model.

Applying fine-tuning to a model can have a range of benefits. We have already seen them in the fine-tuning of GPT into ChatGPT, but we've also taken advantage of fine-tuned GPT models in the form of GitHub Copilot. These examples demonstrate the range of uses that fine-tuning can provide in a testing context. Thus, we can tune models based on natural language text that might come from documentation or testing artifacts. This could be used to embed domain language into its responses and promote responses that are more tuned to our context. They can also be tuned on our code base to help us with additional risk analysis, comprehension of what our code is doing, or acting as a more aligned code assistant.

When discussing fine-tuning, we need to be careful not to fall into the trap of thinking we're teaching a model about our context. LLMs don't think like humans do. But, as an analogy, teaching a model about our context is a close one. The challenge is that it's not an exact process, meaning that multiple iterations are likely required to get the result we want, and as our context changes, further tuning sessions would likely be required.

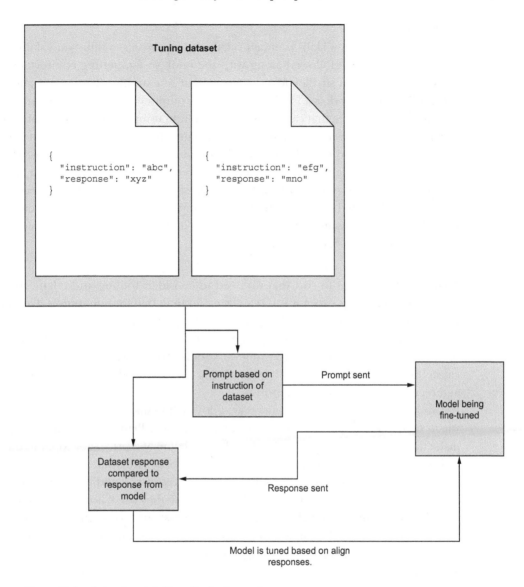

Figure 10.3   A visual model of how fine-tuning works

10.2.3 *Comparing the two approaches*

Knowing which approach to take depends very much on the goals we want to achieve, and the constraints put upon us. The two approaches aren't entirely the same. But if we ever come into a position where we need to decide which approach to take, it can be beneficial to use some general attributes to help us determine the pros and cons of each.

LEARNING CURVE

Although learning new skills is always relative to a person's abilities and skillsets, for those of us who have followed along with the book so far, getting comfortable with RAG frameworks is a smaller learning leap than fine-tuning. It can be argued that using a RAG framework is a form of advanced prompt engineering and many off-the-shelf tools are available that can be used to jump into using RAG with minimum effort.

Fine-tuning, however, has a steeper learning curve because it is a collection of different actions, tools, and considerations that are much larger in scope than using RAG. In the chapter on fine-tuning, you'll learn different steps to take in curating and preparing data for tuning, executing a fine-tuning session, and evaluating success. Each part requires knowledge of tools, frameworks, and approaches to complete each step. Fortunately, the ecosystem around fine-tuning is making the fine-tuning process more accessible and easy to get started with.

COST

There are two aspects to cost that we need to consider: tooling and talent. As we've learned, the learning curve for RAG can be easier than that for fine-tuning. This means that the associated costs around training or hiring talent around implementing RAG are potentially lesser. As for tooling, the cost to get initially set up with RAG can be quite low. However, costs for RAG framework tools and the use of third-party LLMs can cause costs to balloon, especially if we are being charged for the number of tokens sent and received via an LLM API platform.

Unlike the popular RAG frameworks, a lot of fine-tuning tools are open source, which can make initial investment in tooling cheaper. Platforms are appearing that make the fine-tuning process easier, but they do come at a price. For tooling, the cost can be found more in the hardware needed to support fine-tuning. Running tuning sessions requires substantial CPU, GPU, and RAM resources, and if we want to tune at scale, then more investment is required. There is also the cost of hosting a tuned model once it's ready for use. Finally, as fine-tuning consists of a combination of activities, training or hiring can be much more expensive, depending on how much detail we want to go into each part of the tuning process.

SPEED TO PRODUCTION

Given the tools available to support a RAG framework out of the box, getting RAG set up and running can be rather fast. When iterating with RAG, the focus will be on the following two areas: the prompt we want to send to our LLM (that includes the additional data) and the data we want to store and extract relevant information from when required. Although there is a lot of space for improvement, getting these aspects of a RAG framework set up to an initial satisfactory state doesn't take too much time.

Fine-tuning, however, can be relatively slower because there are more activities involved. For example, curating and preparing data sets for fine-tuning can be a complex activity in its own right. Depending on hardware, fine-tuning can also take time to complete with even small tunings taking many hours. Add to this that we would likely need to run multiple tunes because we tweak tuning and model settings, as well as the data set we are using, so it can take a while before we reach a satisfactory tuned model.

CONTROL

Although most of the comparisons so far have been favorable toward RAG frameworks, those benefits do have a tradeoff. When we refer to control as a quality characteristic of using LLMs, this implies how much influence we have on improving the process, what insight we have into how a model is performing, and what control we have over the LLM behavior. Also, there are considerations for privacy controls as well.

Most of the RAG tools available for purchase are hosted on platforms that can be quite opaque. This can mean there is less control over how data is stored for retrieval or how the relevancy algorithms work. For example, one technology that is used in RAG is vector databases. How data is stored and relationships maintained in vector databases can be out of our control but have a big influence on what relevant data is returned. Add to this that a lot of these tools tend to encourage us to use platforms such as OpenAI's API, then we have even less control over which models we want to use and how an LLM will respond.

Fine-tuning is very much about experimentation, which means we must have full control over all aspects of how the tuning is done. Because fine-tuning contains many steps, we have a lot of control over what happens within each part of the process. We have control over what data we want to use and what format it should be in, and we can control which type of model we want to tune and how. Furthermore, because the result is a tuned model that can be deployed elsewhere, we have a lot more control over where a model is deployed and who has access to it, making it more suitable for enterprise-based applications.

These comparisons help us get a flavor of how the two approaches compare, which has been summarized in figure 10.4.

Of course, these comparisons are highly context-dependent, but they do demonstrate that RAG can be a faster, more cost-effective approach to take on first. However, if we want more control over how we want an LLM to respond, then turning to fine-tuning can reward us further if we're willing to invest.

10.2.4 *Combining RAG and fine-tuning*

We've explored how these two approaches differ, but before we conclude the chapter, it's worth stating that these two techniques are not mutually exclusive. Given that RAG focuses on prompts, whereas fine-tuning focuses on changes to a model, both can be combined to further improve responses. The tradeoff is that much more complexity is introduced into building, training, and debugging. It is much more expensive to bring a tuned model inside a RAG framework to production, and if it doesn't work as expected (or desired), how do we determine what needs our attention? This is the challenge of working with indeterministic systems, whether we choose to focus on RAG, fine-tuning, or a combination of both. The approach to evaluating an LLM's use as a testing assistant requires constant, healthy skepticism.

	Learning curve	Cost	Speed to production	Control
Retrieval-augmented generation	Easy enough to pick up if familiar with prompt engineering.	Relatively inexpensive to get started; can get more expensive based on usage.	Can be quick to get a RAG framework setup.	Reliance on other tooling can make control of frameworks hard.
Fine-tuning	Requires experience with multiple tools and processes.	Tooling is low cost, but training hardware costs can be quite expensive.	Can take time to setup a tuning pipeline, and multiple tunes may be required.	Tooling allows low-level control of tuning process and parameters.

Figure 10.4   **A quick comparison of RAG and fine-tuning**

Summary

- One of the key challenges of using LLMs is getting them to return context-sensitive, valuable results.
- To get a well-aligned response, an LLM needs to be given as much relevant context as possible.
- LLMs interpret natural language text by turning text into numbers, known as tokens, through the tokenization process.
- Based on the sophistication of an LLM model and the hardware it is run on, an LLM will only be able to take a certain number of tokens at a given time.
- The number of tokens an LLM can take at a given time is known as the context window.
- Because LLMs have a limited context window, we must come up with different strategies to allow us to embed context in without incurring massive costs.
- Two approaches that can be used to improve context awareness are retrieval-augmented generation (RAG) and fine-tuning.
- RAG is a process in which additional relevant information is added to a prompt to improve an LLM's response.
- RAG works by connecting to a corpus of data and finding the most relevant material based on the provided prompt query. It's then all combined into a single prompt for an LLM.

- Fine-tuning utilizes training techniques to tune an already trained model with additional data.
- Fine-tuning allows us to modify the tone or detail or way in which an LLM responds.
- Fine-tuning can help us promote our context within an LLM's parameters and make it more context-sensitive to our needs.
- Learning how to utilize RAG frameworks tends to be faster and easier than fine-tuning.
- Fine-tuning requires knowledge of different processes and tools to carry out the full fine-tuning process.
- Cost of tooling and talent for RAG is relatively lower than that for fine-tuning.
- Existing RAG platforms make it easy to get set up and running with RAG.
- Fine-tuning requires more investment in time to get a model ready for production.
- Fine-tuning offers much more control than RAG in terms of the model or framework we use at the end.
- RAG and fine-tuning can be used together.

11

Contextualizing prompts with retrieval-augmented generation

This chapter covers

- How RAG works
- Using tooling to create a basic RAG setup
- Integrating vector databases into a RAG setup

As we learned in the previous chapter, one of the challenges of working with large language models (LLMs) is that they lack visibility of our context. In the second part of this book, we saw different ways in which we can arrange our prompts to help provide small insights into our context. However, these types of prompts are only useful before the lack of extra context leads to less valuable responses. Therefore, to increase the value of an LLM's response, we need to place more contextual detail into our prompt. In this chapter, we'll explore how to do this through retrieval-augmented generation, or RAG. We'll learn how RAG works, why it's beneficial, and how it's not a big jump from prompt engineering to building our own RAG framework examples to establish our understanding of how they can help us in a testing context.

218

11.1 Extending prompts with RAG

To recap, RAG is an approach to improving the quality of an LLM's response by combining existing corpus of data with a prompt. Although this broadly explains how RAG works, we need to dig a little deeper to better grasp how this combination of data is achieved. The process of a RAG system is relatively straightforward and can be summarized as shown in figure 11.1.

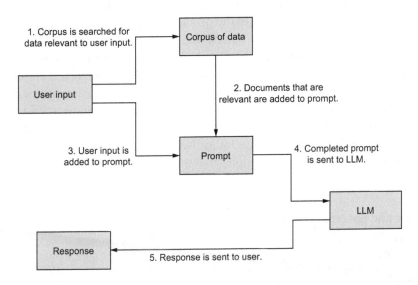

Figure 11.1   A visualization of how a basic RAG system works

We start with a user input, which would be some sort of query. For example, we might send to our RAG system a query such as "I want to test ideas for deleting bookings." This query is then sent to a library or tool that will examine our corpus of data for items within the data relevant to our query. In our example, this might be a collection of user stories that define each feature in the system. The library or tool would determine which user stories are most relevant and then return them to be added to a prompt:

 You are a bot that makes recommendations for testing ideas. You answer with suggested risks to test for, based on the provided user story.

This is the user story: {relevant_document}

The user input is: {user_input}

Compile a list of suggested risks to test for, based on the user story and the user input.

The LLM will then consume both the user query and the relevant documents to return a response that is more accurate than if we sent the query "I want test ideas for deleting bookings" directly to an LLM.

By providing data at the {relevant_document} point within a prompt relevant to the initial query at the {user_input} point, we get a response that has increased accuracy and value. But it does raise a question of why it would go about finding relevant data in the first place. Can't we just send the data we have in each prompt and remove the need to do a relevancy check? Targeting what documents we add to a prompt is important for a few reasons. First, consider the size of the prompt we can create. The size of a prompt we can send to an LLM depends on its maximum sequence length or context window. A context window defines how many words, or tokens, can be processed by an LLM. If we add more tokens than the context window allows, then the LLM will either cut off the excess tokens at the end of the prompt (resulting in a partially completed prompt) or return an error. To put this in real terms, Llama-2, Meta's open-source LLM, has a default context window of 4096 tokens, which is about the average equivalent of 10 pages in a book. This might feel like a lot initially, but it's not unusual for our testing and development artifacts (for example, user stories, test scripts, code) to be much larger.

Tokens and enterprise AI costs

How many tokens we send in a prompt is an important consideration if we're working with models that charge based on the number of tokens that are sent. For example, at the time of writing, the gpt-4 turbo model, which has a context window of 128k, charges $10 per 1 million tokens. So, if we were attempting to max out the context window for each prompt, we would be paying approximately $1.28 per prompt, which would drain our budget fast. Therefore, efficient RAG prompting can be as much about keeping the bills down as it is about getting the most accurate response back from an LLM.

New LLMs appear with much larger context windows that could potentially solve the problem of a prompt size. However, this leads us to our next reason for using relevancy searches—accuracy. If we were to use a larger context window, such as the 128k context window of gpt-4, we might be tempted to add more contextual data. But it runs the risk of diluting the quality of the response from an LLM. The more data we provide, the more potential noise we add to the prompt for the LLM to parse, which may lead to more generalized or unwanted responses. It can also make debugging of prompts and responses harder. As we've explored multiple times in previous chapters, we want to create the right type of prompts that maximize the chances of a desirable response. Therefore, targeting specific information to provide in a prompt can increase that chance, which means striking a balance between not too much context as to water down a response and not too little context as to miss out on important details.

Finally, by storing the corpus of data separately from our prompt generation and LLM, we have better control over said data, which allows us to update the stored data as required. Although vector databases (something we'll explore in detail later in the chapter) have become a tool that is synonymous with RAG platforms, we can use any source of data we like. As long as we can find the relevant data to be added to our prompt, RAG offers a lot of freedom in accessing data for additional context.

11.2 Building a RAG setup

Now that we learned how RAG frameworks work, to better appreciate the parts, let's see how to build a basic RAG setup. We'll do this by creating a framework that will execute the following steps:

1 Ingest a collection of text documents containing user stories.
2 Query the collection of user stories and find the most relevant document based on a user query.
3 Add the relevant document and user query to a prompt and send it to gpt-3.5-turbo via the OpenAI platform.
4 Parse the response and output the details of what the LLM returned.

> **Activity 11.1**
>
> In this part of the chapter, we'll go through the steps required to build a basic example of a RAG system. If you would like to follow along with the example and build your own, download the initial code required for this framework from https://mng.bz/gAIR. All the necessary supporting code can be found in the repository, as well as a completed version of the RAG framework stored in CompletedRAGDemo for reference.

11.2.1 Building our RAG framework

We'll begin with a partially completed project that can also be found in the example framework code on GitHub. The project contains the following info to help us get started:

- A corpus of data that can be found in resources/data
- The necessary dependencies required to build and run our RAG framework in pom.xml
- ActivityRAGDemo, which contains an empty main method where we'll add our framework

Before we begin building our RAG framework, let's review the dependencies stored in our pom.xml file we'll be using. These libraries will help us parse our documents and send our prompt to the OpenAI platform:

```
<dependencies>

    <dependency>
        <groupId>commons-io</groupId>
```
Adds all the user story text files into a string collection

```
        <artifactId>commons-io</artifactId>
        <version>2.16.1</version>
    </dependency>

    <dependency>
        <groupId>org.apache.commons</groupId>
        <artifactId>commons-text</artifactId>
        <version>1.12.0</version>
    </dependency>

<dependency>
    <groupId>dev.langchain4j</groupId>
    <artifactId>langchain4j-open-ai</artifactId>
    <version>0.31.0</version>
</dependency>
```

Provides the functionality to do a similarity check on string collection

Sends our prompt to the OpenAI platform

With our dependencies in place, we now need to import the collection of user stories stored in each text file. Each user story focuses on a specific API endpoint for the sandbox application restful-booker-platform (https://mng.bz/5Oy1). Here's an example:

- As a guest in order to cancel my booking I want to be able to send a DELETE request with the booking ID.
- Acceptance Criteria:
  - The endpoint should accept a booking ID as a parameter in the path.
  - If a valid booking ID is provided, the server should cancel the booking and respond with a status of "OK" (200).
  - If the booking ID is invalid or missing, the server should respond with a "Bad Request" error (400).
  - Optionally, a token can be provided in the cookie for authentication.

These user stories have been synthetically generated for this project's purpose, but we could imagine that this data could have been extracted from a project management platform, a test management tool, or any type of structured data that we feel is relevant, from monitoring metrics to wiki entries.

To pull in our user stories, we first need to add the following method to our ActivityRAGDemo class:

Takes the folder location as a parameter

```
public static List<String> loadFilesFromResources(String folderPath)
    throws IOException {
    List<String> fileContents = new ArrayList<>();

    ClassLoader classLoader = CompletedRAGDemo.class.getClassLoader();
    File folder = new File(classLoader.getResource(folderPath).getFile());

    for (File file : folder.listFiles()) {
        if (file.isFile()) {
```

Locates the folder within resources

Iterates through each file in the folder and its contents to a list

```
        String fileContent = FileUtils.readFileToString(file, "UTF-8");
            fileContents.add(fileContent);
    }
}


    return fileContents;
}
```

Returns the list of file contents for further use

The method `loadFilesFromResources` gives us the ability to load all the user story files into a list of strings that we can later query. To test whether this has worked, we create a `main` method that we can execute to run our RAG setup:

```
public static void main(String[] args) throws Exception {

    List<String> corpus = loadFilesFromResources("data");

    System.out.println(corpus.get(0));
}
```

Loads files from the data folder inside of resources

Prints out the first file in the collection

After running this code within our IDE, we'll see the following result output to confirm that our user stories are indeed being added to a list for future querying:

- As a guest in order to update branding information I want to be able to send a PUT request to /branding/ with necessary parameters.
- Acceptance criteria
    - I should be able to send a PUT request to /branding/ with the necessary parameters including the branding information in the request body and an optional token in the cookie.
    - If the request is successful, the response status should be 200 OK.
    - If the request is unsuccessful due to bad parameters or missing data, the response status should be 400 Bad Request.
    - The request body should contain valid JSON data conforming to the schema defined in the Swagger JSON.

Next, we want to consider the prompt that we'll be sending to gpt3.5-turbo. We'll utilize some of the tactics that should now feel comfortable to us in the following prompt:

 You are an expert software tester that makes recommendations for testing ideas and risks. You answer with suggested risks to test for, based on the provided user story delimited by three hashes and user input that is delimited by three backticks.

Compile a list of suggested risks to test for, based on the user story and the user input.

###
{relevant_document}
###

```
```
```

```
{user_input}
```

```
```
```

Notice how we've parameterized the relevant document and user input sections. Eventually, our code will be replacing these two sections with the relevant documentation and our initial query for processing. We'll come to that shortly, but first, we need to add the prompt to our code base:

```
public static void main(String[] args) throws Exception {

    List<String> corpus = loadFilesFromResources("data");

    String prompt = """
    You are an expert software tester that makes recommendations for
    testing ideas and risks. You answer with suggested risks to test
    for based on the provided user story delimited by three hashes and
    user input that is delimited by three backticks.

    Compile a list of suggested risks to test for, based on the user
    story and the user input.
    ###
    {relevant_document}
    ###
    ```
    {user_input}
    ```
    """;
}
```

Loads files from the
resources folder

Defines the
prompt to
send to
OpenAI

Our next step is to work out which of our user stories is most relevant to the query that we will eventually be inputting. For this, we'll be using the Apache `commons-text` library, which offers a range of different relevancy tools such as Levenshtein distance, Jaccard similarity, and the one we'll be using—Cosine distance. How these different similarity tools work is beyond the scope of this book, but it's worth noting that this area of RAG can influence what data is returned. Various similarity algorithms work in different ways and can become quite complex in production-ready RAG systems. Still, it's worthwhile experimenting with basic approaches to gain a sense of how this part of a RAG system works, so we'll create our similarity-matching method and add it into our class:

```
public static String findClosestMatch(List<String> list, String query) {
    String closestMatch = null;
    double minDistance = Double.MAX_VALUE;
    CosineDistance cosineDistance = new CosineDistance();

    for (String item : list) {
```

Takes the list of user
stories and the user
query as params

```
        double distance = cosineDistance.apply(item, query);
```
Uses cosineDistance to generate a similarity score

```
        if (distance < minDistance) {
            minDistance = distance;
            closestMatch = item;
        }
    }
```
Checks whether the current score is lower than the currently most relevant score

```
    return closestMatch;
}
```
Returns the entry in the list that is the closest match

The method loops through each document and uses `cosineDistance` to work out a similarity score. The lower the score, the more similar the document is to the query. The lowest-scoring document is eventually the one that is returned to us for use in our prompt.

Working with different types of relevancy algorithms

`cosineDistance` is just one of many different tools we can use to determine relevancy, and each has its own pros and cons. We'll look at further tools later in this chapter to improve the relevancy search, but for now, `cosineDistance` will help us build a working prototype that we can iterate on.

Now we can create the necessary code to complete our prompt generation. To do this, we expand our `main` method to first allow a user to enter their query and then do a similarity check before adding it all into a prompt:

```
public static void main(String[] args) throws Exception {

    System.out.println("What would you like help with?");
    Scanner in = new Scanner(System.in);
    String userInput = in.nextLine();
```
Waits for a user to input their query via the command line

```

    List<String> corpus = loadFilesFromResources("data");
```
Loads files from the resources folder
```
    String prompt = """
            You are an expert software tester that makes recommendations
            for testing ideas and risks. You answer with suggested risks to
            test for, based on the provided user story delimited by three
            hashes and user input that is delimited by three backticks.

            Compile a list of suggested risks based on the user story
            provided to test for, based on the user story and the user input.
            Cite which part of the user story the risk is based on. Check
            that the risk matches the part of the user story before
            outputting.

            ###
```

```
        {relevant_document}
        ###


        ```
        {user_input}
        ```
        """;
```

Finds the closest
match to the
user input in the
loaded files

```
String closestMatch = findClosestMatch(corpus, userInput);

prompt = prompt.replace("{relevant_document}", closestMatch)
        .replace("{user_input}", userInput);

System.out.println(prompt);
}
```

Replaces the
placeholder
parameters in
the prompt

We can now run this method, and when asked to add in a query, we can test out the generation of our prompt by submitting a query such as:

 I want test ideas for the GET room endpoint

Sending this results in the following prompt being built:

 You are an expert software tester that makes recommendations for testing ideas and risks. You answer with suggested risks to test for, based on the provided user story delimited by three hashes and user input that is delimited by three backticks.

Compile a list of suggested risks to test for, based on the user story and the user input.

###
As a guest
In order to browse available rooms
I want to be able to retrieve a list of all available rooms

Acceptance Criteria:
* I should receive a response containing a list of available rooms
* If there are no available rooms, I should receive an empty list
* If there's an error retrieving the room list, I should receive a 400 Bad Request error

HTTP Payload Contract
{
  "rooms": [
    {
      "roomid": integer,
      "roomName": "string",
      "type": "Single",
      "accessible": true,
      "image": "string",
      "description": "string",

```
        "features": [
          "string"
        ],
     ,    "roomPrice": integer
        }
    ]
  }
      ###


```

```
I want test ideas for the GET room endpoint
```

As we can see, the user query has been added to the bottom of the prompt, and the user story that has been injected is the one that our `findClosestMatch` method has deemed the most relevant. It's at this point that we'll start to see limitations with our implementation. Trying out different queries will likely result in the selection of a less relevant user story. For example, using this query:

 I want a list of risks to test for the delete booking endpoint

results in the following user story being selected:

 As a guest
In order to retrieve information about a booking
I want to be able to send a GET request with the booking ID

This is because the `cosineDistance` method is limited in how well it can determine relevancy. We'll explore how this can be handled later in the chapter, but it does highlight a limitation or risk of working with RAG frameworks.

Nevertheless, let's complete our RAG framework so that it can send the prompt to OpenAI's GPT model to get a response. For this, we'll be using LangChain again to send our prompt to OpenAI and output a response:

```java
public static void main(String[] args) throws Exception {

    System.out.println("What would you like help with?");
    Scanner in = new Scanner(System.in);
    String userInput = in.nextLine();


    List<String> corpus = loadFilesFromResources("data");


    String prompt = """
        You are an expert software tester that makes recommendations
        for testing ideas and risks. You answer with suggested risks to
        test for, based on the provided user story delimited by three hashes
        and user input that is delimited by three backticks.
```

Receives the user's query for RAG

Loads files from the resources folder

Defines the prompt to be sent to OpenAI

```
    Compile a list of suggested risks based on the user story provided
    to test for, based on the user story and the user input.
    Cite which part of the user story the risk is based on.
    Check that the risk matches the part of the user story before
    outputting.

    ###
    {relevant_document}
    ###
    ```
    {user_input}
    ```
    """;
```

> Finds the closest match to the user query in the loaded files

```
String closestMatch = findClosestMatch(corpus, userInput);

prompt = prompt.replace("{relevant_document}", closestMatch)
            .replace("{user_input}", userInput);

System.out.println("Created prompt");
System.out.println(prompt);
```

> Replaces placeholders in the prompt with the user query and file

> Instantiates a new GPT client using an Open AI key

```
OpenAiChatModel model = OpenAiChatModel.withApiKey("enter-api-key");

String response = model.generate(prompt);
System.out.println("Response received:");
System.out.println(response);
}
```

> Sends the prompt to gpt3.5-turbo and prints the response

Providing an OPEN_AI_KEY

To send a request to OpenAI, a Project API key must be provided, which can be generated at https://platform.openai.com/api-keys. You will need to create either a new account with the OpenAI platform or, depending on whether your credits have expired, add credit to your account, which can be done via https://mng.bz/6YMD. Once it's set up, you will need to either add your Project API key directly in the code, replacing `System.getenv("OPEN_AI_KEY")`, or store your key as an environmental variable under the title `OPEN_AI_KEY`.

With our GPT implementation in place, we should now have a class to run that looks similar to this example:

```
public class CompletedRAGDemo {

    public static List<String> loadFilesFromResources(
        String folderPath) throws IOException {
        List<String> fileContents = new ArrayList<>();
        ClassLoader classLoader = CompletedRAGDemo.class.getClassLoader();
```

```java
        File folder = new
    File(classLoader.getResource(folderPath).getFile());

        for (File file : folder.listFiles()) {
            if (file.isFile()) {
                String fileContent = FileUtils.readFileToString(file, "UTF-8");
                fileContents.add(fileContent);
            }
        }

        return fileContents;
    }

    public static String findClosestMatch(List<String> list, String query) {
        String closestMatch = null;
        double minDistance = Double.MAX_VALUE;
        CosineDistance cosineDistance = new CosineDistance();

        for (String item : list) {
            double distance = cosineDistance.apply(item, query);
            if (distance < minDistance) {
                minDistance = distance;
                closestMatch = item;
            }
        }

        return closestMatch;
    }

    public static void main(String[] args) throws Exception {
        System.out.println("What would you like help with?");
        Scanner in = new Scanner(System.in);
        String userInput = in.nextLine();

        List<String> corpus = loadFilesFromResources("data");

        String prompt = """
            You are an expert software tester that makes
            recommendations for testing ideas and risks. You answer with
            suggested risks to test for, based on the provided user story
            delimited by three hashes and user input that is delimited
            by three backticks.

            Compile a list of suggested risks based on the user story
            provided to test for, based on the user story and the user
            input. Cite which part of the user story the risk is based on.
            Check that the risk matches the part of the user story before
            outputting.

            ###
            {relevant_document}
            ###
            ```
            {user_input}
            ```

            """;
```

```
        String closestMatch = findClosestMatch(corpus, userInput);

        prompt = prompt.replace("{relevant_document}", closestMatch)
                .replace("{user_input}", userInput);

        System.out.println("Created prompt");
        System.out.println(prompt);

        OpenAiChatModel model = OpenAiChatModel.withApiKey("enter-api-key");
        String response = model.generate(prompt);
        System.out.println("Response received:");
        System.out.println(response);
    }
}
```

To recap, we've created the necessary code to:

- Load in a corpus of documents (in this instance, user stories)
- Take in a user query via the command line
- Use the query to find the most relevant document
- Add both the query and the document to our prompt
- Send the prompt to OpenAI and return a response

With everything in place, we're ready to start up our RAG framework and test it out.

11.2.2 *Testing our RAG framework*

Once our RAG framework is up and running, we should be asked what query we would like to input. To test out our RAG framework, we can try inputting the following query:

 What would you like help with?

 I want test ideas for the payload portion of the PUT branding endpoint

Our query retrieves the following user story from our corpus:

 As a guest

In order to update branding information

I want to be able to send a PUT request to /branding/ with necessary parameters

Acceptance criteria

* I should be able to send a PUT request to /branding/ with the necessary parameters including the branding information in the request body and an optional token in the cookie.

* If the request is successful, the response status should be 200 OK.

* If the request is unsuccessful due to bad parameters or missing data, the response status should be 400 Bad Request.

* The request body should contain valid JSON data conforming to the schema defined in the Swagger JSON.

HTTP Payload contract

```json
{
  "name": "string",
  "map": {
    "latitude": 0,
    "longitude": 0
  },
  "logoUrl": "string",
  "description": "string",
  "contact": {
    "name": "string",
    "address": "strings",
    "phone": "string",
    "email": "string"
  }
}
```

The resulting response from gpt3.5-turbo will look something like the response I received:

 Based on the user input, here are some suggested risks to test for:

1 Missing required parameters in the request body, such as name, map (latitude and longitude), logoUrl, description, contact information (name, address, phone, email) - Risk based on the user story mentioning necessary parameters in the request body.

2 Sending invalid data types for parameters in the request body, such as sending a number instead of a string for the name field - Risk based on the HTTP Payload contract defined in the user story.

3 Sending invalid JSON data that does not conform to the defined schema in the Swagger JSON - Risk based on the acceptance criteria specifying valid JSON data conforming to the schema.

4 Not including the optional token in the cookie when sending the PUT request - Risk based on the acceptance criteria mentioning an optional token in the cookie.

5 Sending a PUT request to the wrong endpoint or with incorrect formatting - Risk based on the user story requiring the PUT request to be sent to /branding/ with necessary parameters.

As expected, the response contains the list of risks we asked for, but what is notable is how it has returned context-specific details. For example, for the first risk that is focused on missing required parameters, we can see that it calls out specific parameters that exist in the HTTP payload example within the user story. We can also see that other risks refer to content written in the acceptance criteria, such as the use of an optional token stored within cookies (mentioned in risk 4).

The context-specific information provided in the response exists because of the additional details we provided within the prompt in the form of our user story. To demonstrate how important this additional information is to the quality of an LLM response, here is an example of a response I received using the same prompt without the user story added:

1   Data validation: Test that the payload accepts only the allowed data types and formats as specified in the API documentation. This could help ensure that invalid data does not cause unexpected behavior in the system. (Based on the need to test the payload portion of the PUT branding endpoint)

2   Boundary testing: Test the system's behavior when the payload includes data at the upper and lower limits of allowed values. This could help uncover any edge cases where the system may not handle extreme values correctly. (Based on the need to test the payload portion of the PUT branding endpoint)

3   Performance testing: Test the system's response time and resource usage when handling large payloads. This could reveal any performance bottlenecks or issues with scalability. (Based on the need to test the payload portion of the PUT branding endpoint)

4   Security testing: Test for any vulnerabilities related to the payload input, such as SQL injection or cross-site scripting attacks. This could help ensure that the system is secure against malicious input. (Based on the need to test the payload portion of the PUT branding endpoint)

As we can see, the items returned are more generic and shallow because our prompt lacks that additional context information, thus demonstrating the value of a RAG system in prompting LLMs.

However, RAG frameworks do have limitations, and our basic framework is no different. For example, if we were to send this query:

  What risks should I consider for the Auth API?

we might get a response like the following, which is returning information that is of no use to us:

  1. Risk: Unable to successfully delete a room by providing a valid room ID

- This risk is based on the acceptance criteria of being able to successfully delete a room by providing a valid room ID.

2. Risk: Incorrect error handling for invalid room ID

- This risk is based on the acceptance criteria of receiving a 400 Bad Request error when providing an invalid room ID.

3. Risk: Confirmation message not displayed upon successful deletion

- This risk is based on the acceptance criteria of receiving a confirmation message upon successful deletion.

Although this might feel like our LLM is hallucinating, the problem lies in our relevancy checking. Our query is focused on the Auth API, which includes login, logout, and validate endpoints, but the mention of `room ID` in the response implies that a room-based user story was deemed the most relevant. Once again, we see the challenge of finding the most relevant data to provide in a RAG framework when we start to consider pulling relevant data from multiple data sources at once. Therefore, to progress, we need to consider more advanced tooling to help us improve the performance of our relevancy searches to optimize the LLM's responses.

> **Activity 11.2**
>
> Try out different types of queries based on the user stories found in the project. See which queries returned desired results and which didn't. Consider what tweaks we could make to improve the erroneous queries.

11.3 Enhancing data storage for RAG

Now that we have a deeper understanding of how RAG works, we can begin to explore the types of tools in the market that allow us to quickly implement a framework with our data. The process of finding the right type of data to bolster our prompts can be tricky, but there are some tools and platforms on the market that make setting up RAG frameworks easier through the use of SaaS platforms and vector databases. So, let's conclude our exploration into RAG by discussing briefly what vector databases are, how they help, and how we can use one for our needs.

11.3.1 Working with Vector databases

Unlike a SQL database, in which data is stored as different data types within rows inside tables, *vector* databases store data in the form of mathematical representations. Specifically, they are stored as *vectors,* which is a collection of numbers that represent an entity's location across multiple dimensions.

To give an example of how vectors work and why they are useful, let's consider another area of software development that uses vectors—game development. Let's say we have a character and two other entities in a 2D world and we want to know which of the entities is nearest to our character. We would use a vector that contains an X and Y position to determine the location of both. For example, if our character was in a central position on a map, their vector would be $(0,0)$. Now let's say our entities were in X/Y positions (our vector dimensions) of $(5,5)$ and $(10,10)$, as shown in figure 11.2.

We can see that the later entity with the position of $(10,10)$ is farther away. But we can also calculate the distance of vectors mathematically by comparing them. So $(0,0)$ to $(5,5)$ generates a distance score of 7.071068, and $(0,0)$ to $(10,10)$ has a distance score of 14.14214 (calculated using https://mng.bz/o0lr). This, of course, is a basic example, but with vector databases, an entity may have vectors that contain many different dimensions, which makes the distance calculation much more complex.

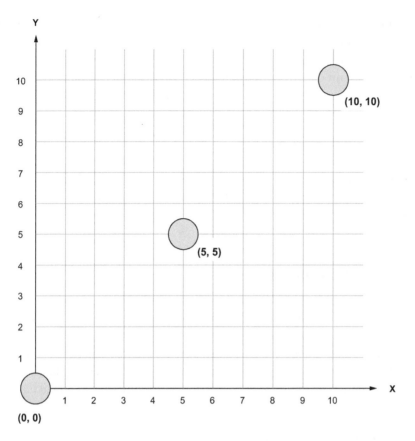

Figure 11.2   Graph showing vectors of a character and entities

How these vectors and the related dimensions for our documents are calculated is beyond the scope of this book, but it is important to recognize that the purpose of using a vector database is to allow us to programmatically work out how close an item of data we're interested in is in relation to our query. In other words, we use vector databases to work out relevancy just like we did in our basic RAG framework. However, instead of doing it across one dimension, we can compare it against many different dimensions at once—meaning in the context of the work we've done so far, increasing the accuracy of which user stories are deemed relevant to our query. Because it also allows support for multiple relevancy, we can extract more than one entity or document to add to our prompt if it is within a range of relevancy.

11.3.2 Setting up a vector-database-backed RAG

There has been massive growth in the vector-database-backed RAG market, with tools such as LlamaIndex (https://www.llamaindex.ai/) and Weviate (https://weaviate .io/). However, to get set up quickly with minimal setup and coding, we'll be looking at a tool called Canopy, which is built by the company Pinecone (https://www

.pinecone.io/). Pinecone offers the ability to create vector databases in the cloud, which are known as indexes on their platform. They have also created Canopy, a RAG framework that integrates with their cloud setup. Canopy is a great choice for a trial RAG framework because, unlike our earlier RAG framework, most of the work is taken care of by the framework. This means we can get started with a vector database-backed RAG framework much faster than if we were to build our own. This of course sacrifices control for convenience, but it will give us what we need to try out a vector-database-backed RAG. You can learn more about the different parts of Canopy in their README (https://github.com/pinecone-io/canopy).

> ### Canopy prerequisites
>
> To run Canopy, you will need Python 3.11 installed on your machine. This is only required to install Canopy. Once installed, we'll exclusively use the Canopy SLI to set up our framework.

To get us started, we'll first need to install Canopy on our machine, which we do by running the `pip3 install canopy-sdk` command.

Once it's installed, we then require a few API keys to get ourselves set up. First, we will need our OpenAI key, which can be found at https://platform.openai.com/api-keys. Next, we'll need to set up an account on Pinecone and extract the API key from it for Canopy to use to create our vector database. To do this, we need to sign up to Pinecone, which can be done here: https://app.pinecone.io/?sessionType=login. During the setup, you will be asked to provide a card for billing details to upgrade the free account to a standard one. We need to upgrade to a standard account to allow Canopy to create the necessary vector database. Failure to do so will cause Canopy to error when we begin to build our index for our RAG framework. At the time of writing the standard account is free, but it is unfortunately necessary to provide our account details to get access to the features we require.

Once we have created our Pinecone account and upgraded it to a standard one, we can start working with Canopy to create our RAG framework. To do this, we need to set some environmental variables:

```
export PINECONE_API_KEY="<PINECONE_API_KEY>"
export OPENAI_API_KEY="<OPENAI_API_KEY>"
export INDEX_NAME="<INDEX_NAME>"
```

Or alternatively, if you are using windows:

```
setx PINECONE_API_KEY "<PINECONE_API_KEY>"
setx OPENAI_API_KEY "<OPENAI_API_KEY>"
setx INDEX_NAME "<INDEX_NAME>"
```

The API keys for Pinecone and OpenAI are straightforward and can be found in the respective admin sections for each platform. The third variable, though, will set the name of the index that will be created on Pinecone's platform, so we need to pick a name for our index, such as `test-index`. Once we have these variables in place, we can start Canopy by running the `canopy new` command.

Assuming our API keys are all correct and our Pinecone account is correctly upgraded, Canopy will set up a new index in Pinecone (see figure 11.3) that we can use to upload our documents when we're ready.

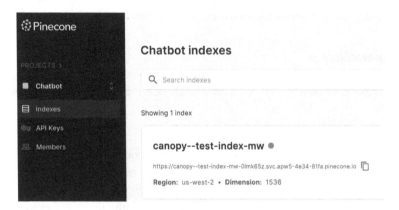

Figure 11.3   Pinecone indexes after a Canopy run

With our index ready, we can begin uploading our user story documents (which can be found in the supporting repository at https://mng.bz/n0dg). We do this by running Canopy's `upsert` command and providing the root folder for our user stories:

```
canopy upsert src/main/resources/data
```

This will kick off a process in which our user stories are uploaded into the index, and once the upload is completed, we can head back into Pinecone and confirm that they are present in our index, as shown in figure 11.4.

We now have everything loaded into our index and are ready to start up our RAG framework by running the `canopy start` command.

This starts the Canopy server, which we can now access to send our queries to. To access it, we open a new terminal/command prompt and run the `canopy chat --no-rag` command. (Be sure to export your `OPENAI_API_KEY` again if you start a new terminal window.)

Notice how we provide a flag of `--no-rag`. This enables Canopy to show, for comparison, both an output that uses RAG and an output that doesn't. Upon starting up the chat feature, we'll receive the following message to confirm that we're ready to begin testing out our RAG framework:

 Let's Chat!

User message: ([Esc] followed by [Enter] to accept input)

canopy--test-index-mw ●

METRIC   DIMENSIONS   HOST
cosine   1536   https://canopy--test-index-mw-0lmk65z.svc.apw5-4e34-81fa.pinecone.io 📋

CLOUD   REGION   VECTOR COUNT
aws AWS   us-west-2 📋   24

BROWSER   METRICS   NAMESPACES (1)

┌ Namespace ────────┐   ┌────────────────┐   ┌ vector ──┐   ┌ Top K * ───┐
│ (Default)   │   │ Query by Vector ▾│   │ 0.15,0.67,0.73,0.72,0.47,0.84,0.83,0.63,0.3,0.58,0.29,0.01,0.81,0.76,0.74,0.3,0.97,(⊗│   │ 10   │   │ Query │
└───────────────────┘   └────────────────┘   └──┘   └────────────┘

⊕ Metadata Filter

Matches: 1-10 of 10   + Upsert Record

        ID   VALUES
  1   get-message-...   -0.00674194889, -0.00745868171, 0.0304174367, 0.0331445187, 0.00511910301, -0.0084725963, -0.0439129882, 0.00183...   🔍 ✏ 🗑

  SCORE
  0.0295   METADATA
                       document_id: "get-message-count"
                       source: "src/main/resources/data/get-message-count.txt"
                       text: "As a user\n\nin order to get the count of messages\nI want to be able to send a GET request to /count endpoint\n\nAcceptance Criteria\n* If successful, the respo...

Figure 11.4   An index uploaded with user stories

11.3.3 *Testing a Vector-database-backed RAG framework*

With Canopy now ready to receive our queries, we can begin testing it out with queries and comparing the performance of our RAG framework. For example, sending the following query:

 List different types of tests for each JSON parameter in the PUT branding endpoint

returned the following response (edited in size to make it easier to read):

The different types of tests for each JSON parameter in the PUT branding endpoint include:

1. **Name**:
- Test for providing a valid string value for the name parameter.

2. **Map (Latitude and Longitude)**:
- Test for providing valid integer values for latitude and longitude parameters.

3. **LogoUrl**:
- Test for providing a valid string URL for the logoUrl parameter.

4. **Description**:
- Test for providing a valid string value for the description parameter.

5. **Contact (Name, Address, Phone, Email)**:

- Test for providing valid string values for name, address, phone, and email parameters in the contact object.

These tests ensure that the JSON data provided in the request body of the PUT request to the branding endpoint conforms to the specified schema defined in the Swagger JSON.

(Source: src/main/resources/data/put-branding.txt)

The response has a few notable points. First, the response has been structured around the different JSON parameters that have been defined within the user story. Second, we can see that Canopy has provided a reference at the bottom of the output (Source: src/main/resources/data/put-branding.txt) to indicate which sources have been deemed most relevant from the vector database. This means that, similar to the basic RAG framework we built earlier, this RAG framework is working as expected, which is even more striking when compared to how our query performed without RAG:

1 Name:
   - Test for presence of name parameter
   - Test for invalid values (e.g. empty string, special characters)

2 Logo:
   - Test for presence of logo parameter
   - Test for valid file format (e.g. PNG, JPEG)
   - Test for size limit (e.g. file size less than 5MB)

3 Color:
   - Test for presence of color parameter
   - Test for valid color code format (e.g. hex code)
   - Test for invalid color values (e.g. 'purple' instead of '#123456')

4 Font:
   - Test for presence of font parameter
   - Test for valid font name or family
   - Test for invalid font values (e.g. empty string, special characters)

5 Description:
   - Test for presence of description parameter
   - Test for valid length limit (e.g. less than 100 characters)
   - Test for invalid values (e.g. special characters, long strings)

6 Website:
   - Test for presence of website parameter

 – Test for valid URL format
 – Test for invalid values (e.g. invalid domain, special characters)

In this response, we can see that there is little connection to the context of our branding JSON payload. Again, this demonstrates the challenge we face when using LLMs and ensuring they have access to our context. But what about our previous problem with the basic RAG framework we created and its inability to bring in multiple user stories into a query? With Canopy backed with a vector database, we can test out how it performs with a query that has the potential to draw on multiple user stories in one single prompt:

 List different types of tests for each Booking endpoint

Sending this to Canopy returned the following response (again, edited in size for readability):

 1 **GET Booking Endpoint:**

 ▪ Functional Tests:

 – Verify that the endpoint returns a list of all bookings.

 – Test the functionality of filtering bookings by providing a room ID as a query parameter.

 2 **POST Booking Endpoint:**

 ▪ Functional Tests:

 – Ensure the endpoint accepts booking details in JSON format and creates a new booking successfully.

 – Test the response and status code when the booking request is invalid.

 3 **GET Booking ID Endpoint:**

 ▪ Functional Tests:

 – Confirm the endpoint retrieves the correct details for a provided booking ID.

 – Test the response when an invalid or missing booking ID is provided.

 4 **PUT Booking ID Endpoint:**

 ▪ Functional Tests:

 – Ensure the endpoint updates the booking information correctly for a given booking ID.

 – Test the response and status code when the booking ID is missing or invalid.

 5 **GET Booking Summary Endpoint:**

 ▪ Functional Tests:

- Verify that the server responds with a summary of bookings for a specified room ID.
- Test the response when the room ID is missing or invalid.

(Source: src/main/resources/data)

Reviewing this response, we can see that the source at the bottom of the prompt is referencing the root folder of our data (Source: src/main/resources/data), indicating that multiple files have been pulled into our query. This is confirmed by how each endpoint has been mentioned in the response as well. We can correlate each entry in the response to a booking-based user story stored within our data set.

> ### Activity 11.3
> Using Canopy and Pinecone, prepare and upload your own custom set of data to an index. Try out different queries with your custom data to see how a RAG framework would perform in your context.

11.3.4 *Going forward with RAG frameworks*

By building our RAG framework before trying out existing platforms for RAG, we've now developed a deeper understanding of how RAG works and how it can be of benefit. However, what we've learned simply serves as an introduction to an area of LLM use that has lots of practical applications. What type of data we can store in RAG frameworks, whether we use vector databases or not, offers a lot of scope. Combined with what we've learned about writing effective prompts, RAG frameworks can be used to provide live analytics, production data, stored user content, and much more to help us create prompts that are more attuned to our context, which ultimately will help increase LLM use in our testing and elsewhere.

Summary

- Retrieval-augmented generation (RAG) is an approach that combines contextual data and user queries in a prompt to an LLM.
- The selection of contextual data is based on its relevancy to the initial user query that has been provided.
- Providing selected data improves accuracy and ensures that errors around context windows are avoided.
- Having contextual data separate from an LLM makes the process of selecting and updating data sources easier.
- For RAG systems to work, we need the ability to upload and store data.
- RAG systems use similarity algorithms and tools to determine which data is most relevant to a query.

- Building prompts that lack contextual data results in responses that are more generic and shallow.

- An LLM can return incorrect responses if the similarity algorithm returns inaccurate data.

- Finding relevant data becomes complex when queries are broad or multiple data sources need to be added to a prompt at once.

- Vector databases store vectors based on multiple dimensions, which are used to determine relevancy to a query.

- Some frameworks and tools offer the ability to quickly set up a RAG framework using vector databases.

- Utilizing vector databases and related tools and platforms makes it easier for us to query them.

- Vector databases allow us to pull multiple relevant files into a query at once.

- RAG frameworks can provide a wide range of types of data that has multiple applications for testing and software development as a whole.

Fine-tuning LLMs with business domain knowledge

This chapter covers

- The fine-tuning process for an LLM
- Preparing a data set to use for fine-tuning
- Using fine-tuning tools to better understand the process

Although the effects of large language models (LLMs) in various industries have been covered extensively in the mainstream media, the ubiquity and popularity of LLMs have contributed to a quiet revolution in the AI open source community. Through the spirit of open collaboration and the support of big technology companies, the ability to fine-tune AI models has become increasingly more accessible to AI enthusiasts. This opportunity has resulted in a vibrant community that is experimenting and sharing a wide range of processes and tools that can be used to better understand how fine-tuning works and how we can tune models ourselves or in teams.

The topic of fine-tuning is vast, and getting into each important detail would require an entire book of its own. However, by taking advantage of the models, data sets, platforms, and tools created by and for the open source community, we can establish an appreciation for the fine-tuning process. These open source resources can prepare us for a future in which we might find ourselves fine-tuning our models within our organizations to help build context-based LLMs. However, fine-tuning is as much about the approach we take as it is about the tools we use. So, in this chapter, we'll go through each important part of the fine-tuning process and learn how to fine-tune our model.

12.1 Exploring the fine-tuning process

Before we learn more about fine-tuning tools, we should first discuss what fine-tuning entails and reflect on what we hope to achieve. As we'll see, fine-tuning involves a series of steps that play an important role in the wider process. Knowing what we hope to achieve helps us not only with the evaluation of a model once it's been tuned, but also guides us in our tuning approach. Each step of the fine-tuning process includes distinct activities and challenges. And although we might not be able to cover all the details, we'll learn enough to understand what happens as we tune models and the challenges that we might face.

12.1.1 A map of the fine-tuning process

As we discovered in chapter 10, fine-tuning is the process of taking an existing model that has already gone through some sort of training, known as a foundational model, and training it further with additional data sets to

- Make a model more attuned to contextual information
- Change the tone of a model
- Help it respond to specific queries or instructions

Just as a foundational model goes through a series of steps to be trained, there is a series of steps to go through during a fine-tuning session. Figure 12.1 summarizes these steps and how they feed into one another.

Figure 12.1 doesn't necessarily cover every nuance of fine-tuning, but it captures the core steps we would typically expect to go through to successfully create a tuned model. Throughout this chapter, we'll examine each step in more detail, but let's first reflect on what might be the most important part of the process, identifying what we hope to achieve from fine-tuning.

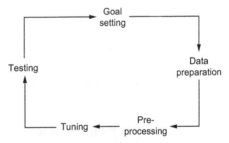

Figure 12.1 **A visual representation of the different steps taken during fine-tuning**

12.1.2 Goal setting

One of the biggest mistakes that we can make when tuning LLMs is not having a clear idea of what we want our tuned LLM to do. Failing to set out clear goals for what problems a tuned model is supposed to help with can affect every part of the fine-tuning process, from data preparation to testing. Given the indeterministic nature of LLMs, this doesn't mean setting goals around specific information we expect to get from an LLM. But we do have to ask ourselves what type of behavior we want and how it fits into our wider context.

To illustrate this, let's consider two different goals. One is to create a code-completion tool that has been fine-tuned on our code base to use an LLM's generative capabilities, without revealing intellectual property to a third party. Another is a Q&A/chat-based LLM that offers support to users, which has been tuned on support documentation and customer data to help answer questions. Depending on which goal we want to pursue, we would need to consider details such as:

- *What datasets to use?* For our code completion scenario, we likely want to create a data set that consists of code broken down into logical sections to tune our model with. We may also be interested in using other data sets that include open source code. This would differ from the Q&A chat scenario in which we would create a corpus of data that includes help guides and documentation.

- *What model to use?* At the time of writing, Hugging Face, an AI open source community site, is currently hosting 500,000+ different models, all of which are designed to serve different purposes such as generation, classification, and translation. When considering our fine-tuning goals, we will need to select models that suit our needs. In our code scenario, we would likely pick a model that has already been trained on a large corpus of code data, making it easier to further tune with our code base. In our Q&A/chat LLM scenario, we would likely want a model that has already been trained to act as a capable chat-based LLM.

- *How big a model to use?* Another question to ask ourselves is how large a model do we need? Depending on the size of the model we want, usually defined by its parameter size, will also determine our hardware requirements. There is a tradeoff that must be considered. If we want our models to be accurate in their responses, then a large amount of hardware needs to be dedicated to the hosting and running of a larger model. If our budget is limited, or the location we have to deploy our model isn't performant, then we may need to consider a smaller model that might not be as accurate or respond as quickly to our requests.

What is Hugging Face?

Hugging Face is a platform for the AI open source community that allows members to host, deploy, and collaborate on their AI work. Notably, Hugging Face offers a place to host data sets and models, as well as the opportunity to let others deploy and interact with AI applications through their space features. There are also other paid-for features such as auto training, which is designed to make fine-tuning easier, as well as increased hardware space to deploy more complex and resource-demanding models. Similar to how GitHub enables teams to collaborate in addition to offering the ability to host code, Hugging Face offers a place to share and learn from AI community members and work together on future AI projects.

This is by no means an exhaustive list of considerations, and as we explore fine-tuning more, we'll learn how there are different options we need to decide on. Fortunately (if you have budget), many tools have been created and put in place to make the experimentation with fine-tuning models easier and faster. Therefore, although it's good to have a goal in mind when setting out on a fine-tuning journey, we are free to switch out models, data sets, and more to learn how to create the most optimal fine-tuned model for a given context.

12.2 Executing a fine-tuning session

Keeping in mind the importance of a goal for a fine-tuned model, in this chapter, we're going to attempt to fine-tune a model using the code base of a project to create a model that can support future analysis. In real terms, this means having a model that, when asked questions about our code base, can give answers that are context-sensitive to our project. To do this, we'll be using the code from the open source project rest-ful-booker-platform (https://mng.bz/vJRJ).

12.2.1 Preparing data for training

Although fine-tuning doesn't require the same volumes of data as a pretrained model, the success of fine-tuning relies heavily on the size and quality of the data we use, which brings us to the question of what sort of data we need. To help us understand the size, scope, and formatting of data sets, we can learn a lot from sites such as Hugging Face, where open source data sets are stored (https://huggingface.co/datasets). Some notable data sets used at the time of writing include:

- *The Stack*—546 million rows of code examples that have been scraped from open source projects on sites such as GitHub (https://huggingface.co/datasets/bigcode/the-stack)
- *Alpaca*—52,000 rows of synthetic data that have been generated using an existing LLM (https://huggingface.co/datasets/tatsu-lab/alpaca)
- *OpenOrca*—2.91 million rows of question and response data (https://huggingface.co/datasets/Open-Orca/OpenOrca)

Looking through each of these data sets, we can see they contain different types of information, from code examples to questions and responses, created in different ways. Data sets such as The Stack are based on real information scraped off the internet, whereas Alpaca has been synthetically generated by an AI. We can also see that Alpaca is a much smaller data set compared with the others in the list, but that doesn't mean it's not useful.

What is synthetic data?

In the context of AI training and fine-tuning, synthetic data is the process of artificially generating data that, while looking like real user data, is not based on real-life data. Using synthetic data is a useful technique for training and fine-tuning AIs because it can

(continued)

provide the necessary data required for carrying out training or fine-tuning. There are side effects to using synthetic data, though. First, there is a cost in generating the test data. Tools such as gretel.ai, mostly.ai, and tonic.ai offer data-generation tools, but they come at a price. Second, and perhaps more important, studies have shown that training models on purely synthetic data can impact the quality of a model's responses. This makes sense because real data will have variances and randomness that are hard to simulate in AI-generated data.

So, when setting out our requirements, we need to consider what we want, what is currently available, and what we might need to build ourselves. Let's return to our code assistant and Q&A model examples. For our code assistant LLM, we are likely going to want a corpus of data that is mostly code based, whereas with our Q&A model, we would need data written in natural language and containing questions and answers in a key–value format (the question being the key and the answer being the value). As we can see, our goals inform our decisions regarding the type of data we require, but with it come additional questions, such as where is the data going to come from and how are we going to format it.

We've already seen that there are lots of publicly available data sets from sites such as Hugging Face (Kaggle available at https://www.kaggle.com/datasets is also a great source of data sets). But if we're attempting to fine-tune a model so it is more aligned with our context, chances are we will want to tune it using data that belongs to our organization. Therefore, an exercise in what data is available, its quality, and how can we access it is required before we decide how we're going to convert it into a format that is suitable for training. Consider the format in which the Alpaca data set has been structured (https://huggingface.co/datasets/tatsu-lab/alpaca). The data set consists of the following four columns: instruction, input, output, and text. As we'll learn in the next step, depending on the way we are fine-tuning a model, we will require different aspects of a data set. For example, if we wanted to fine-tune a Q&A model, we would require, as a minimum, the instruction and output columns to help tune it toward what type of questions to expect and what types of answers to respond with.

The challenge is getting raw data into a structured format like the one we saw in the Alpaca data set. For example, if we consider our Q&A model scenario, we would likely want to train it on our documentation and support documents. Some of this raw data might be in a Q&A format, such as FAQs, but the majority of our data wouldn't be so straightforward. Therefore, we would need to work out a way to parse our data in a way that fits our data set structure. To make matters more complicated, we would also need to do this automatically to generate enough of a corpus of data so that it would be useful. Doing it manually is also an option, but it could be a costly one.

A CASE STUDY IN DATA PREPARATION

The data set we are going to use for our fine-tuning session presents a good example of the challenges we may encounter when building even small data sets. For our fine-tuning session, we'll be using a previously created data set I built that can be found on Hugging Face at https://mng.bz/4pXa. The data set is a JSONL-formatted document that contains parsed sections of the Java portion of restful-booker-platform (RBP), paired with generated instructions, a sample of which is provided here (line breaks have been added for readability):

```
{"instruction": "What is the class declaration for
 BrandingServiceIT","output": "@ExtendWith
 @SpringBootTest
 @ActiveProfiles
public class BrandingServiceIT { }"}
{"instruction": "How does the method setup Restito work for
 BrandingServiceIT?","output": "
 @BeforeEach
 public void setupRestito(){
 whenHttp(server).match(post("/auth/validate"))
 .then(status(HttpStatus.OK_200));
 }"}
```

This snippet will give us everything we need data-wise for tuning, but before we begin, let's explore how it was made. Consider a class like the following and ask yourself how would you break this code up for fine-tuning in a logical fashion?

```
package com.automationintesting.api;

import com.automationintesting.db.BrandingDB;
import com.automationintesting.model.db.Branding;
import com.automationintesting.model.service.BrandingResult;
import com.automationintesting.requests.AuthRequests;
import com.automationintesting.service.BrandingService;
import org.springframework.beans.factory.annotation.Autowired;
import org.springframework.http.HttpStatus;
import org.springframework.http.ResponseEntity;
import org.springframework.web.bind.annotation.*;

import javax.validation.Valid;
import java.sql.SQLException;

@RestController
public class BrandingController {

    @Autowired
    private BrandingService brandingService;

    @RequestMapping(value = "/", method = RequestMethod.GET)
    public ResponseEntity<Branding> getBranding() throws SQLException {
        Branding branding = brandingService.getBrandingDetails();

        return ResponseEntity.ok(branding);
    }

    @RequestMapping(value = "/", method = RequestMethod.PUT)
```

```
public ResponseEntity<?> updateBranding(@Valid @RequestBody
  Branding branding, @CookieValue(value ="token", required = false)
  String token) throws SQLException {
    BrandingResult brandingResult =
      brandingService.updateBrandingDetails(branding, token);

    return ResponseEntity.status(brandingResult.getHttpStatus())
      .body(brandingResult.getBranding());
  }

}
```

Would you fine-tune on a file-by-file basis, a line-by-line basis, or some other way? On a first attempt at testing out fine-tuning of a model on the RBP code base, I opted for the line-by-line approach. It created a script that would iterate through each file in a project and add each line of the file into its row resulting in a table of data that looked similar to the following example table:

```
id, content
1,   @RequestMapping(value = "/", method = RequestMethod.GET)
2,   public ResponseEntity<Branding> getBranding() throws
3,   SQLException {
4,   Branding branding = brandingService.getBrandingDetails();
5,   return ResponseEntity.ok(branding);
6,   }
```

The problem with this approach was that, although it was easy to parse and store the data, I ended up with entries that were lacking context, meaning I was tuning with entries such as } or @Autowired. These don't provide a lot of context or detail about the RBP project, and they raised another question. What type of instruction can be paired with these types of entries? If you recall, during instruction-based fine-tuning, we send an instruction (sometimes with additional input data) and then compare the response with our expected output. The type of instruction we would add to an entry such as } would contain no hints toward our context and potentially contribute to a fine-tuned model that responds in unusual and undesired ways. This is exactly what happened when I attempted to tune a model based on line-by-line material.

Instead, what I opted for (and what can be found in the dataset) is an approach that breaks down the code into logical sections. This means that rather than slicing things line by line, a file would be sliced up based on different attributes within a Java class. For example, a selection of slices from the class I shared earlier would look like the following in an example table:

```
id, content
1,   @RestController
public class BrandingController { }
2,   @Autowired
     private BrandingService brandingService;
3,   @RequestMapping(value = "/", method = RequestMethod.GET)
```

```
public ResponseEntity<Branding> getBranding() throws SQLException {
    Branding branding = brandingService.getBrandingDetails();

    return ResponseEntity.ok(branding);
}
```

Instead of each entry in the data set being a line of code, each entry might contain details of how the class was declared, what variables are being declared in the class, each method in the class, and its containing code. The goal was to keep it detailed enough so the fine-tune would result in a model that had a greater awareness of the code base, but not so granular to lose the context completely. The result was a more successful tune, but the process of parsing became more complex. It required the creation of additional code that would iterate through each file, using JavaParser (https:// javaparser.org/) to ingest the code, build a semantic tree, and then query said tree to extract the information required for the data set (the code of which can be found at https://mng.bz/QVpw).

This example is a very basic one when it comes to preparing a data set for tuning (or training). However, after reflecting on it, it becomes clear that organizing and preparing even a simple data set from scratch has its complexities and challenges. The raw data for this data set was easily parsable with the right tools, but how do we manage data that is diverse in structure or has no discernible structure in the first place? This exploration into data sets highlights that the identification and creation of a data set is a complicated process. How we structure our data and what we put in it is critical for the success of fine-tuned models, and it's where most of the work of fine-tuning and experimenting with LLMs can be found. Therefore, it's important to have the necessary processes and tooling in place so that we can rapidly experiment with different data sets to see how they impact the result of a fine-tuned model.

12.2.2 Preprocessing and setup

With our data set in place, we next need to preprocess our data before tuning and get our tuning tools in place. We'll get to tool setup soon, but first, to understand the preprocessing activities for fine-tuning, we need to skip ahead a little and talk about what happens during a fine-tuning session. Perhaps not surprisingly, given the size of data sets, a fine-tuning session consists of a specific loop, visualized in figure 12.2, which is run multiple times during fine-tuning.

Stepping through the visualization, we start with our data set. Assuming it's structured in a way similar to the _Alpaca_ dataset we looked at earlier (it contains a column of instructions, inputs, and outputs), the data stored in the instruction and input columns are added to a prompt. That prompt is then sent to the model we are fine-tuning and a response is sent back from the model. We then compare the response from the model with the output stored in our data set to determine the *sentiment*. The sentiment indicates how closely aligned the response is to our expected output. The sentiment score is then used to inform what tweaks need to be made to the model's parameters to fine-tune it toward how we want our model to respond. If the sentiment score indicates it's responding desirably, then changes will be minimal. On the other hand, if the sentiment score indicates an undesirable response, then bigger changes will be made.

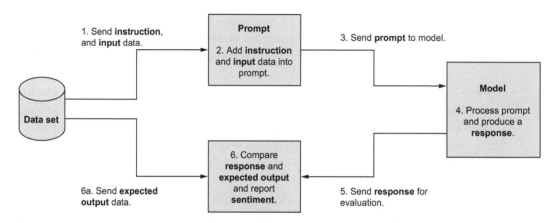

Figure 12.2   A visualization of what happens during fine-tuning

This whole process is done programmatically using different tools and is run multiple times across each entry in a data set. The data set itself is also usually iterated through multiple times known as an *epoch*. It's through iterating across multiple epochs in the fine-tuning process that the model is tuned toward how we want it to respond. This approach to tuning is known as instruction-based fine-tuning, and it's important to understand how it works before we execute our fine-tuning because there are steps we need to take before the tuning can begin. First, we need to design the type of prompt we want to send to our model. Second, we need to determine how we are going to codify our prompt so that our model can read it. Similar to curating our data set, the choices we make for these two steps can also have a dramatic effect on the result of our fine-tuning.

PROMPT DESIGN

Once we know the format of our data set, we need to create an instructional prompt that works with the data within the data set and any additional instructions we want to add. For example, consider these two instruction prompts from the deeplearning .ai course *Finetuning Large Language Models* (https://mng.bz/XV9G). First is a prompt that takes an instruction and an input:

 Below is an instruction that describes a task, paired with an input that provides further context. Write a response that appropriately completes the request.

Instruction:
{instruction}

```
### Input:
{input}

### Response:
```

The second is a prompt that contains just an instruction:

 Below is an instruction that describes a task. Write a response that appropriately completes the request.

```
### Instruction:
{instruction}

### Response:
```

Notice how each prompt contains a combination of static, instructional text that contextualizes what information is being sent, and then tags such as {instruction} to inject data from the data set. Based on the RBP data set we want to use, we could configure our prompt for fine-tuning like this:

 Below is an instruction, delimited by three hashes, that asks a question about the restful booker platform code base. Respond with the necessary code to answer the question. Check that the code compiles correctly before outputting it.

```
###
{instruction}
###
```

The prompt follows some of the prompting tactics we've explored in earlier chapters. We can use those to help us instruct the model clearly in what to expect in our prompt and what we want to see it responds with. To help us better understand the fine-tuning loop, let's imagine we have the following entry in a data set:

```
{
  "instruction" : "How does the method initialiseMocks work for
  BrandingServiceTest?"
  "output" : "@BeforeEach public void initialiseMocks() {
  MockitoAnnotations.openMocks(this); }"
}
```

During fine-tuning, the instruction portion of this data set would be injected into the prompt to create the following prompt

 Below is an instruction, delimited by three hashes, that asks a question about the restful booker platform code base. Respond with the necessary code to answer the question. Check that the code compiles correctly before outputting it.

```
###
How does the method initialiseMocks work for BrandingServiceTest?
###
```

This might result in the model responding with a code example written like this:

```
use Tests\TestCase;
use App\Services\BrandingService;

class BrandingServiceTest extends TestCase {

  protected function setUp(): void { // Initialize mocks

    $this->brandingService = new BrandingService();

  }
```

However, our output in our data set is as follows:

```
@BeforeEach
public void initialiseMocks() {
    MockitoAnnotations.openMocks(this);
}
```

This means that the sentiment score between the two sets of data is a middling one because, although the response is code and it has some similarities to our expected output in solution, the code isn't entirely the same. This sentiment score would then be factored into what tweaks need to be made to the model's parameters so that when this specific row in our data set comes around again, the results are more closely aligned. The prompt template we use affects the results of a fine-tuned model, and the instructions we add make a difference. However, we need to be mindful that what we add to a prompt template doesn't affect just the result of fine-tuning but also has an impact on what is sent to the model in the first place. This brings us to how we turn a text-based prompt into a language that a model understands.

TOKENIZATION

A *token* is a numerical representation of a word, phrase, or character. We covered the topic of tokens in chapter 10. So why do we need to be aware of tokenization as part of the fine-tuning process? First, there are many different tokenizers available that can be utilized during data preprocessing that will tokenize the text in different ways. The type of model we are using will influence the type of tokenizer. Choosing one that doesn't align with the model we're tuning would result in our prompts being converted into token identifiers that don't align with the parameters that exist inside the model we're tuning. Roughly speaking, it would be like being taught a course by a teacher who was speaking in a different or completely made-up language.

The second reason, which relates to our fine-tuning prompt and our data set, is context length. Context length is the total amount of tokens a model can process at once. This is important because if we create a prompt that has a large number of tokens within it or attempt to tune using data containing a large number of tokens within each entry, then our prompts risk breaching the context length, meaning our prompt will be truncated. Every token that is over the context length limit would simply be discarded or ignored, and the result would be a model being fine-tuned on partially complete prompts, which might create unexpected or undesired side effects.

Therefore, we need to keep our context length in mind both when curating our dataset and designing our prompt for tuning. This might mean removing any entries from our data set that have the potential to overflow our context length, writing a prompt that has clear instructions but doesn't overflow the token count, or looking for a new model that contains a larger context length.

TOOLING AND HARDWARE

Given the many steps required for processing data and executing the fine-tuning process, necessary tooling needs to be in place to execute each phase. Fortunately, tooling for fine-tuning has progressed greatly recently. Originally, it would require extensive experience with tools such as Python and libraries such as PyTorch, Tensorflow, or Keras. And though these tools are designed to be as easy to use as possible, the learning curve could be quite steep and require us to build our fine-tuning frameworks from the ground up. If we are comfortable with this type of approach or are working with those who have experience with these types of tools, then it's worthwhile using them. However, as interest has grown around fine-tuning, new tooling built on the aforementioned tools has begun to appear to make fine-tuning more accessible. Frameworks such as Axolotl and platforms such as Hugging Face let us set up fine-tuning quickly in a way that requires minimal tool development. The tradeoff is that these frameworks are either opinionated, for example selecting what tokenizers we should use, or they come at a cost.

It is not only the tooling around AI tuning that has seen growth, but also the infrastructure that supports it. Training models is a hardware-intensive exercise and requires access to graphical processing units (GPUs). This means either purchasing hardware that has a generous amount of CPU, RAM, and GPU for tuning, or provisioning computing from cloud providers. The latter is the popular option for many teams and a massive area of growth as it keeps the costs down for hardware requirements, ensuring access to newer, updated GPUs. Unsurprisingly, the big cloud computing companies such as Google, Microsoft, and Amazon all offer access to dedicated services that are designed specifically for tuning and hosting of LLMs. But some alternatives have begun to appear, such as RunPod, Latitude.sh, and Lambda Labs, which are specialist GPU cloud providers. These are options that can be used in conjunction with the tools we select for fine-tuning, but some services provide both the frameworks for fine-tuning and the computing resources to run the tuning for you.

The market landscape for what we can use for and where we can run our fine-tuning is a fast-growing space. But what it highlights is that research is required to determine what tooling and infrastructure best suits the experience of our team and the type of budget we have available for tuning.

SETTING UP OUR FINE-TUNING TOOLING

There are many tools available for fine-tuning that offer different levels of control of the tuning process, PyTorch being a popular choice. But as mentioned before, there is a learning curve to setting and using these tools. If we were working in a context in which we wanted full control of our prompts, tokenizers, and tuning tools, we might choose these more granular tools. But for new starters, like us, who are happy using tools that trade opinions on approaches for ease of use, we can once again look to the AI open source community. Therefore, for our tuning session, we'll be running our fine-tuning with Axolotl, a tool *designed to streamline the fine-tuning of various AI models, offering support for multiple configurations and architectures.*

We can think of Axolotl as a framework for fine-tuning that contains all the necessary tools and processes to carry out our tuning. That means for our fine-tuning session, the prompting approach and tokenizer have been taken care of for us, allowing us to get into our fine-tuning quickly and without a massive learning curve.

Hardware requirements for using Axolotl

Before we begin, it's important to note that to carry out a fine-tuning session, you will need a system that has access to a GPU. If, however, you don't have access to a GPU, there are cost-effective cloud platforms designed to support AI fine-tuning. Axolotl's ReadMe contains links to two providers: RunPod and Latitude.sh.

As someone who doesn't have access to a GPU, I found RunPod easy to get set up with and reasonably priced to run multiple training sessions for less than $10. If this is the approach you want to take, here are some steps to follow to get set up:

1 Create an account and add credit to it via https://www.runpod.io/console/user/billing. I have found the minimum transaction of $10 to be enough.
2 Head to GPU cloud https://www.runpod.io/console/gpu-cloud, click `Choose Template` at the top of the page, find the `winglian/axolotl-runpod:main -latest` Docker image, and select it.
3 Next, choose a pod to deploy. Depending on the time of day and demand, you will see which ones can be deployed and which can't. At the time of writing, a 1x RTX 4090 will suffice for our tuning exercise. However, if we want the tuning to go faster, we can choose more GPUs or a larger box.
4 Click deploy and go through the setup wizard to fire off the creation of your pod. Head to https://www.runpod.io/console/pods and wait for your pod to deploy.
5 Once the pod is deployed, click on connect to reveal the details to SSH into your pod (This will require you to add an SSH public key before connecting, which can be done here: https://www.runpod.io/console/user/settings.)

Once you are logged into the pod, you'll find Axolotl is installed and ready to use.

We'll start by setting up Axolotl on our machine of choice (if you have chosen the Run-Pod option this can be skipped). The documentation and code for Axolotl can be found at https://mng.bz/yoRG, and it contains comprehensive instructions on how to install the application, offering the option of installing it directly on our machine or via Docker.

12.2.3 *Working with fine-tuning tools*

Once Axolotl is set up, we can begin configuring our session. As mentioned before, we'll be using the RBP data set, which can be found on Hugging Face (https://mng.bz/ M1M7). For our model, we'll also be using a version of Meta's Llama-2 model, which contains 7 billion parameters and a context window of 4k. Much like the prompts and tokenizer, the model settings have been taken care of in an example file that can be found inside the Axolotl project `examples/llama-2/lora.yml`. However, to train the model on our data set, we need to update the `dataset.path` in the YAML file to

```
datasets:
  - path: 2bittester/rbp-data-set
    type: alpaca
```

with `path` dictating where to find the data set on Hugging Face (that is, where it will be downloaded from) and `type` setting out which template prompt we want to use. Looking at the top of the YAML file, we can also see references to the model and the tokenizer that will be used. Again, these can be modified if we want to experiment with other approaches:

```
base_model: NousResearch/Llama-2-7b-hf
---
tokenizer_type: LlamaTokenizer
```

Several other settings can be found in the file and are beyond the scope of this chapter, but there are two we do want to highlight: `sample_packing` and `num_epochs`.

```
sample_packing: false
---
num_epochs: 4
```

As for `sample_packing,` we set it to `false` because the data set isn't large enough for splitting into training and testing sets (more on that later). `num_epochs` determines how many times we want to iterate through our data set. The default is 4, meaning the fine-tuning process will loop through the whole data set four times before it completes. With these changes made to the YAML file, we can save, quit, and begin our fine-tuning.

12.2.4 *Setting off a fine-tuning run*

With our configuration in place, we can begin fine-tuning. To do this, we'll be following the steps found in Axolotl's ReadMe. To start, we trigger a preprocessing step:

```
CUDA_VISIBLE_DEVICES="" python -m axolotl.cli.preprocess
➥ examples/llama-2/lora.yml
```

The preprocessing step downloads the data set and runs it through the tokenizer, translating the data from text to tokens, ready for fine-tuning.

What is LORA?

You may have noticed that the YAML file we've been configuring and are now using to start our fine-tuning session is named lora.yml. LORA is an approach to fine-tuning in which instead of attempting to directly tune the parameters within a model, a smaller subset of parameters that approximate the parameters of the model are created and fine-tuned, creating a LORA adapter. This means that when we deploy the model once it's fine-tuned, the model is loaded with the LORA adapter inside it to give us the tuned behaviors we are looking for. It has become popular because it speeds up the fine-tuning process and allows communities and teams to share their adapters.

Once the preprocessing is complete, we are ready to start the fine-tuning process. Keep in mind that depending on the hardware being used, this process can take anywhere from 30 minutes to 4 hours or more, so pick a time in which the fine-tune can be left to run while you work on other tasks. To trigger the fine-tuning, we run the following command:

```
accelerate launch -m axolotl.cli.train examples/llama-2/lora.yml
```

This will pull in the YAML file that we've edited and kick-start the fine-tuning process. As the tuning begins, we'll start to see details on its progress of the tune like the following example:

```
{'loss': 1.0936, 'learning_rate': 0.00019999154711147226, 'epoch': 0.02}
{'loss': 1.3172, 'learning_rate': 0.00019999135609452385, 'epoch': 0.02}
{'loss': 1.0351, 'learning_rate': 0.0001999911629434316, 'epoch': 0.02}
```

Each entry in the console details the following:

- *Loss*—This score indicates the alignment between the expected output in our data set and the output of the model. The lower the score, the better aligned the expected and actual responses. In this example, the loss score is relatively high because it was taken at the start of a tuning. As the tuning progresses, we would hope to see the loss score reduce.
- *Learning rate*—This is a numerical representation of the step change made to the parameters in the model. Smaller steps mean more gradual changes in tuning. How big a step is made is determined by the sentiment score, as well as the learning rate hyper-parameter. In the context of AI training, a hyper-parameter is a configuration option that we can set before the tuning begins, which impacts the outcome of training or tuning. So, in the case of learning rate, we can increase the step range, which can result in more dramatic tunes to a model. This again may or may not result in a more optimal tune.
- *Epoch*—Earlier, we learned how we can iterate through a data set multiple times during fine-tuning and that each iteration is known as an epoch. The epoch

value shown in the console output simply informs us how far through a given epoch we are.

These metrics are useful to give us an indication of the quality and the progress of a fine-tuning session. Depending on the size of the data set, the model and hardware supporting the tune will determine how long a tune might take. However, it's not uncommon for a tune to take multiple hours, given the volume of work required for tuning. This is why more experienced model tuners will set up processes and tooling so that multiple models can be tuned at once for comparison once the tuning is complete.

12.2.5 *Testing the results of a fine-tune*

Once our fine-tuning has been completed, we'll want to check whether the changes we've made align with the goal that we set at the start of the fine-tuning process. If you recall, during the fine-tuning process, an instruction is sent to a model, and it returns an output. Sentiment analysis then determines how closely aligned the model's output and our expected output are, which informs what tuning to the model's parameters takes place. Consequently, the parameters within a model should now be more biased toward our context. Therefore, to test whether a model has been successfully tuned, we want to check what happens when we ask the model for new instructions that differ from the ones it was tuned on. We can do this in one of the two ways: inference and/or human validation.

INFERENCE

Given the numerous parameters within a model and the options in instructions to send and outputs to receive, inference employs an automated approach to testing the output of a model. Inference works very similar to fine-tuning. We either take a slice out of a larger data set or employ a new data set that follows the same structure as the data set we used for fine-tuning that contains instructions and outputs that are different to the ones in our original tuning data. Then we send each of these sets of instructions to a model, capture the response, and then use sentiment analysis to compare what we expect the model to respond against what it responded. (The key difference between tuning and inference comes after the sentiment analysis. Tuning will make changes to the model, whereas in case of inference, the model is left alone). If the returned sentiment score is high, we can assume the model has been tuned in a way that meets our goals. If it doesn't, then we can start to consider what our next steps are for a future fine-tuning session.

HUMAN VALIDATION

Although sentiment analysis is useful, it is based on mathematical models to determine alignment. Therefore, it's also sensible to explore the outputs of a model manually, through human validation. This might be through using prompts saved in the inference data set and evaluating responses, or by testing out different responses by generating new prompts to see how the model reacts. To get the same level of scope and coverage as with the inference testing would be too expensive for a team, but it can provide a more human perspective that can spot discrepancies and/or hallucinations that inference wouldn't.

Depending on what we learn from both, the automated processes of inference and our experimentation will inform our next decisions. Perhaps the fine-tuning resulted in a model that is acceptable, and we can release it for wider use. However, we will often likely conclude that the resulting tuned model isn't right for us. This would trigger further analysis to determine what our next steps are. Perhaps our data set needs changing, or we want to modify our prompt further, or perhaps the tokenizer could be replaced. Regardless of the choice—again, a decision-making process that is beyond the scope of this chapter—this highlights that fine-tuning projects require to experiment many times over to discover an optimal result. This is why teams that have a mature process around fine-tuning (or training in general) will run multiple fine-tuning experiments at once, tuning multiple models at once, with slightly different parameters to compare the results.

TESTING OUT OUR FINE-TUNING SESSION

Returning to our fine-tuned model, although we don't have enough data to run an inference testing session, we can launch our model to test it out manually. To do this, we run the following command:

```
accelerate launch -m axolotl.cli.inference examples/llama-2/lora.yml \
    --lora_model_dir="./lora-out" –gradio
```

With this command, we are loading up the Llama-2 model and loading in the LORA adapter we have created as part of our tuning. The command `--gradio` allows us to host a user interface for our model using the gradio library (https://www.gradio.app/) so that we can start to test out our model via a web browser.

With our model running, we can begin to check the results of our fine-tuning session. First, we can check the tuning by selecting an instruction and output set from our data set such as:

 Instruction:

How does the method `initialiseMocks` work for `BrandingServiceTest`?

Output:

```
@BeforeEach public void initialiseMocks() {
MockitoAnnotations.openMocks(this); }
```

Using the prompt from the tuning session, we can send the following request to our tuned model:

 Below is an instruction that describes a task. Write a response that appropriately completes the request.

Instruction:

How does the method `initialiseMocks` work for `BrandingServiceTest`?

Response:

Upon sending this, we would receive a response such as:

 Below is an instruction that describes a task. Write a response that appropriately completes the request.

Instruction:

How does the method `initialiseMocks` work for `BrandingServiceTest`?

Response:

```
@BeforeEach public void initialiseMocks()
{
    MockitoAnnotations.openMocks(this);
}
```

As we can see, the model has been tuned to the point that it is returning a strongly aligned response based on the instructions we've sent. Now we can turn our attention to how the model copes with new untested prompts, such as this basic, example prompt:

 What are the annotations found in the `BrandingResult` java class?

Sending this to an example tuned model returns a response like this:

 What are the annotations found in the `BrandingResult` java class?

```
public class BrandingResult {
    private HttpStatus brandingHttpStatus;
    private Branding branding;

    public HttpStatus getBrandingHttpStatus()
    {
        return brandingHttpStatus;
    }

    public void setBrandingHttpStatus(HttpStatus brandingHttpStatus)
    {
        this.brandingHttpStatus = brandingHttpStatus;
    }

    public Branding getBranding()
    {
        return branding;
    }

    public void setBranding(Branding branding)
    {
        this.branding = branding;
    }
}
```

Comparing this response to the original code on which the model was tuned (which can be found at https://mng.bz/aVlz), we can see that the model has demonstrated some success in listing aspects of the `BrandingResult` class such as the variables used and the getter/setter methods. However, it is also missing details such as the class constructor, and it got the names of variables wrong (although it is at least consistent across the code). It could also be argued that the prompt wasn't answered correctly as we were requesting details on annotations and not on the class as a whole.

So, in conclusion, we have seen some success with this tuning session, but more work is required. The tuning process has rebalanced the parameters within the model in a way that our context has become more dominant within it. However, the missing items and incorrect details mean that further tweaking is required for the tuning process. Perhaps we could look to improve the quality of the instructions in the data set or reconsider the prompt we use for tuning. Equally, we could look at more technical aspects of the tuning, such as choosing a model with a larger parameter count, or tweak hyper-parameters such as the amount of epochs we use for training or the learning rate.

12.2.6   *Lessons learned with fine-tuning*

This chapter gave us a taste of how the fine-tuning process works. At first, it may seem like an overwhelming activity. But although there is specific tooling and terminology to understand, by taking the fine-tuning process step by step, we can tackle each challenge as it comes. Ultimately, fine-tuning is very much about experimentation. What data we use, models we tune, tooling we employ, and hyper-parameters we set, they all affect the result.

At the time of writing, the cost of experimentation is not something that can be dismissed. Teams that want to carry out fine-tuning sessions require substantial financial backing for resources and experience. But as both private companies and the open source community grow, fine-tuning will become more accessible, and the price of hardware will likely decrease, making this a growing space in organizations and a challenge for teams to deliver high-quality models that can assist us and our organizations.

Summary

- Fine-tuning is the process of training a pre-existing model further, which is sometimes known as a foundational model.
- The fine-tuning process involves multiple steps such as goal setting, data preparation, processing, tuning, and testing.
- Setting clear goals around what we want a fine-tuned LLM to do informs how we approach the fine-tuning process.
- Fine-tuned models require specifying and preparation of data.
- Data sets massively influence the results of a fine-tuned model. This means finding data relevant to our goals and formatting it in a way that helps maximize the output of a model after fine-tuning.

- Fine-tuning relies on repeatedly sending prompts embedded with training data to get a response that we want to bias toward aligning with an expected output.
- Models need prompts to be converted into a machine-readable language. This is achieved through the tokenization process.
- Tokenization is the process in which data is sliced into smaller tokens.
- Models have a context length, which is the maximum number of tokens it can process at once. Send too many tokens at once, and some will be discarded, affecting the fine-tuning process.
- When fine-tuning, we can either build our frameworks, which require experience, or utilize existing frameworks, which are opinionated and/or cost money to use.
- Axolotl is a great framework for fine-tuning that is accessible to those with limited experience and looking to get started.
- Testing of fine-tuned models can be done in an automated fashion, using inference, or manually.
- Fine-tuning is becoming increasingly accessible to teams for use in the AI assistant tooling.

appendix A
Setting up and using ChatGPT

The process of getting set up with ChatGPT is relatively simple. First, we create an account with OpenAI, which can be done via the login and registration page, available at https://chat.openai.com/auth/login. From there, we create our account, focusing on registering for a free account for now.

Knowing whether to buy ChatGPT Plus

It's likely that ChatGPT Plus will be upsold during the registration process. At the time of writing, ChatGPT Plus costs $20 a month and grants you access to the latest version of ChatGPT (as opposed to the free version that uses gpt-3.5-turbo) along with a collection of plugins and other new features that extend the core prompting features of ChatGPT. We don't use Plus in this book, but the activities and examples can be used both on Plus and the free account. However, how ChatGPT responds will likely differ when using Plus.

Once we are registered, we can log in via https://chat.openai.com/ to be presented with the ChatGPT home page, where we can begin to send prompts.

To use ChatGPT, we need to provide it with instructions, or prompts, that we enter into the form at the bottom of the page titled Send a Message, as shown in figure A.1.

Figure A.1   The ChatGPT message form

Once a prompt is submitted, it will appear at the top of the page, a new chat will be added to the history bar on the left, and ChatGPT will respond as in the example shown in figure A.2.

Figure A.2   A prompt and a response

We can then add additional prompts, and the previous prompts and responses will be considered. For example, in figure A.3, we can see how ChatGPT takes the first prompt about the capital of the United Kingdom into account when responding to the second prompt that asks about city size.

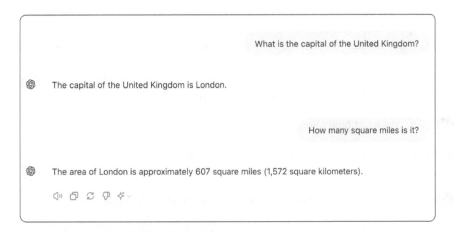

Figure A.3   Additional prompts and responses

We can also edit prompts after they have been sent to generate new responses from ChatGPT. To do so, we hover over the prompt and click the edit icon on the left, as shown in figure A.4.

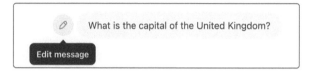

Figure A.4   A prompt with the edit icon

We can also click the Regenerate button to trigger ChatGPT to return an alternative response, as shown in figure A.5.

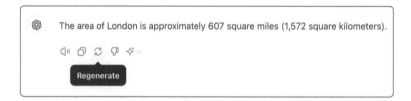

Figure A.5   The Regenerate button

A more advanced feature that is available for Free and Plus licenses is the use of custom instructions. These can be used to customize how ChatGPT responds to prompts by adding our instructions to each prompt we send. To access the instructions, we click our avatar in the top-right corner and select Customize ChatGPT to be presented with a pop-up like the one captured in figure A.6.

To demonstrate how instructions work, we could add an instruction to ensure that when ChatGPT is prompted to respond with code examples, it does so in Java rather than in Python, which it tends to default to. To do this, we add the following instruction to the section "How would you like ChatGPT to respond?":

MW   All code examples should be returned in a Java format

and save the instruction. We can then test the instructions by creating a new chat and sending the prompt:

MW   Create me a function that calculates the square root of a number

ChatGPT should respond with a code example that is written in Java. We can also test it again with the instruction removed to likely receive a new response written in Python.

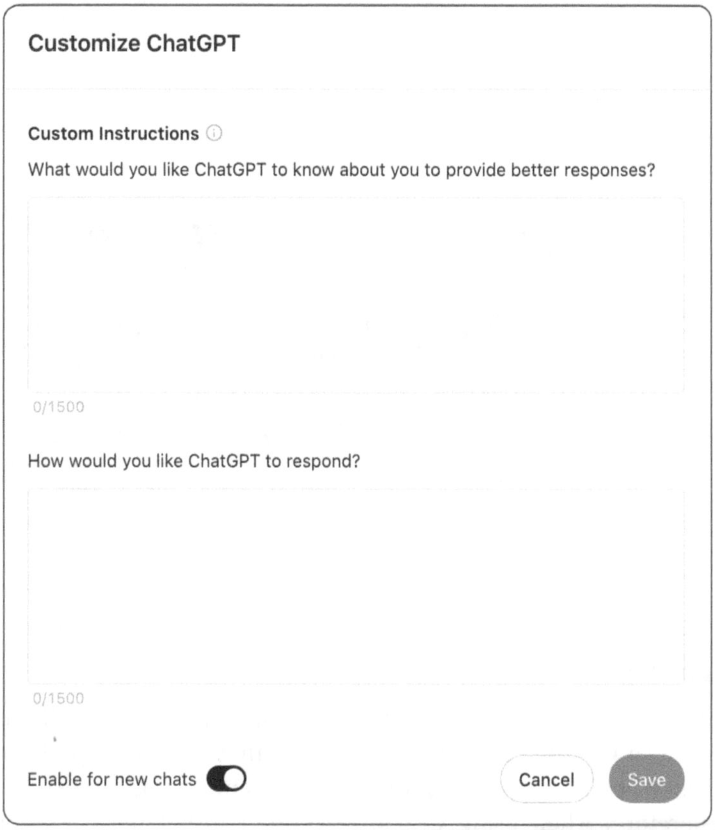

Customize ChatGPT

Custom Instructions ⓘ

What would you like ChatGPT to know about you to provide better responses?

0/1500

How would you like ChatGPT to respond?

0/1500

Enable for new chats 🔘   Cancel   Save

Figure A.6   The custom instructions pop-up window

appendix B
Setting up and using GitHub Copilot

B.1 Setting up Copilot

To better understand the process of setting up Copilot, let's briefly discuss how the tool works. Since Copilot relies on GPT models that need to rapidly analyze our work and suggest code snippets, it requires a large amount of resources to respond quickly. Therefore, when using Copilot, we don't install the AI system on our machines; instead, we install plugins that grant us the ability to send our snippets of work to Copilot for processing and to receive recommended code, as demonstrated in figure B.1.

As the diagram demonstrates, we install a plugin into our IDE and grant it access so that the plugin can monitor what we're typing, send it to Copilot, and then process and display Copilot's recommendations. Because of this structure, Copilot works with a range of IDEs, including JetBrains products, Visual Studio, VS Code, and more. For our example, we'll use IntelliJ Community Edition, but the process in which we set up an IDE for Copilot is largely the same regardless of the chosen IDE.

> **Finding GitHub support**
>
> If you require more specific details to set up Copilot on your machine, more info is available at https://mng.bz/gAll.

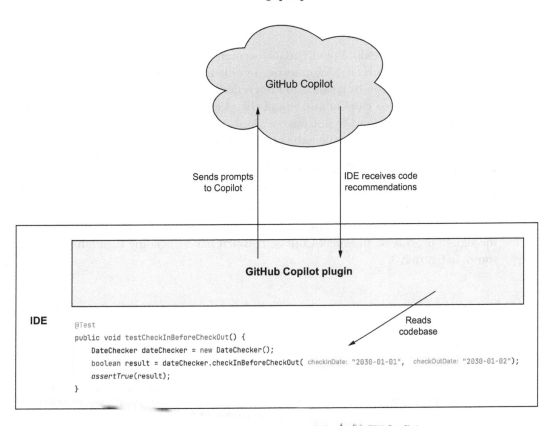

Figure B.1   A flowchart demonstrating the connection between IDE, plugin, and Copilot

B.1.1   Setting up a Copilot account

The first step is to set up an account with Copilot. At the time this chapter was written, Copilot offered two plans:

- $10 per month for individuals
- $19 per month for businesses

Although a Copilot account is paid for, GitHub offers a 30-day free trial. Payment details are required, but the account can be canceled via the billing page (https://github.com/settings/billing).

Copilot also requires that we have a GitHub account, so before setting up Copilot, we need to ensure that we have created a free GitHub account. Once that is done, or if you already have an account, head to https://github.com/features/copilot to complete the process of setting up a Copilot trial.

B.1.2   *Installing the Copilot plugin*

Once we've added Copilot to our GitHub account, we can set up our IDE to access it. For IntelliJ, we do this via its plugin service by either selecting Plugins via the Welcome to IntelliJ IDEA window or heading to Preferences > Plugins. Once the Plugin window is opened, search for Copilot and install the plugin. If for any reason more search results are returned for Copilot plugins, look for the plugin authored by GitHub. Finally, restart IntelliJ to complete the plugin installation.

B.1.3   *Granting access to your Copilot account*

With the plugin installed, upon reopening IntelliJ, we are presented with a small pop-up in the lower right corner that looks like the one shown in figure B.2.

Alternatively, if no pop-up appears (or if it is accidentally dismissed), we can access the sign-in process via the small Copilot icon that has a thick line through its face, as shown in figure B.3.

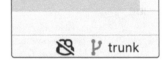

Figure B.3   **The location of the Copilot plugin in IntelliJ**

Figure B.2   **This popup asks you to sign in to GitHub.**

Upon clicking the pop-up, we are presented with a window that describes the process of signing in to GitHub and granting access to our IDE to Copilot, as shown in figure B.4.

Figure B.4   **This dialog box details how to sign in to GitHub via our IDE.**

To complete the sign-up process, we take the device code and head to the web page https://github.com/login/device. To enter the device code from the IDE, we can type or paste into the form and submit it. GitHub will then request us to grant access permission to Copilot, which, once confirmed, will complete the sign-in process. We can confirm that we are signed in when we return to our IDE and see a new pop-up informing us that we are connected, as shown in figure B.5.

Figure B.5 This popup confirms that we are connected to Copilot.

We also see a confirmation that the Copilot plugin is installed when we start editing our code and see a pop-up that shares details on how it works within our IDE, as shown in figure B.6.

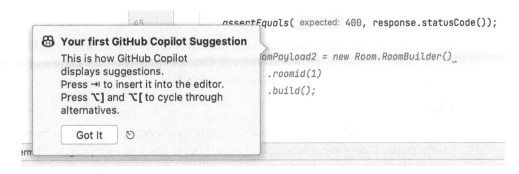

Figure B.6 This pop-up describes how Copilot works in the IDE and specifies shortcuts to use.

With our plugin now installed and set up, we can begin developing with Copilot as our assistant.

B.2 *Working with Copilot*

Once Copilot is set up, it will start to react and offer suggestions when we begin to write code into an IDE. For example, we could create an empty class called `TaxCalculator`, enter the keyword `public`, and after a few seconds receive a suggestion like the one shown in figure B.7.

```
public class TaxCalculator {

    public static double calculateTax(double salary) {
        double tax = 0;
        if (salary > 0 && salary <= 18200) {
            tax = 0;
        } else if (salary > 18200 && salary <= 37000) {
            tax = (salary - 18200) * 0.19;
        } else if (salary > 37000 && salary <= 90000) {
            tax = 3572 + (salary - 37000) * 0.325;
        } else if (salary > 90000 && salary <= 180000) {
            tax = 20797 + (salary - 90000) * 0.37;
        } else if (salary > 180000) {
            tax = 54097 + (salary - 180000) * 0.45;
        }
        return tax;
    }

}
```

Figure B.7   A suggested code coming from GitHub Copilot

Notice how the suggested code is grayed out. To confirm that we want to add the code to our class, we do so by hitting the Tab key. This will then insert the code and bring the cursor to the end of the code that has been added.

B.2.1   Exploring suggestions

If the suggested code is unsatisfactory, we can review other suggestions from Copilot to determine if they are a better fit. To do this, we need to open the GitHub Copilot window that is found on the right side of the IDE, as shown in figure B.8.

Figure B.8   The GitHub Copilot menu item, found on the right side of the IDE

Selecting that will then open a new window that presents a list of other suggested code that could be added to our class. The panel may ask you to click Refresh to request suggested code from Copilot, but once it's complete, you will see something similar to figure B.9.

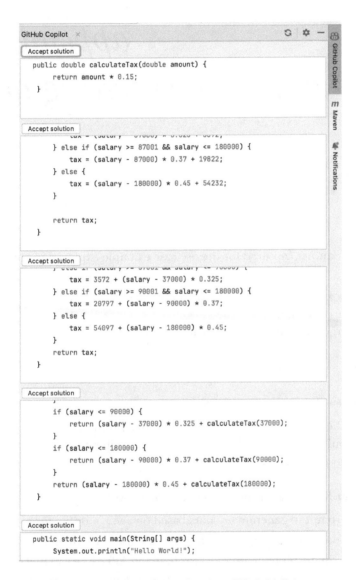

Figure B.9 The alternative suggestions from Github Copilot

To complete the process, we click the Accept solution button above the code snippet we want to see inserted into our class, which then closes the suggestion box.

appendix C
Exploratory testing notes

These are the raw notes captured for the use case example explored in chapter 8:

Charter

Explore how bookings are rendered in the report view
With a very large collection of bookings
To discover if large amounts of bookings are easy to read

Session notes

Session setup:

How can I create test data for the report page?

Analyzing how the code in the API and JS works with a prompt, it appears the report data is built by pulling data from the room API and then iterating over each room to retrieve bookings from the booking API.

How can I create SQL data for the room and booking APIs

1 Create a prompt to generate test data based on `seed.sql` file for room API.
2 Add the data into `seed.sql` and rebuild the room API with seeded data.
3 Create a script to generate test data for booking API using ChatGPT.
4 Unable to rebuild the booking API with the data in it as it broke tests, so loaded up booking API in IDE.

Investigation

What happens when I load the page?

- Bug: Page is very slow to load data when lots of bookings are in place.
- Once the page is loaded I can see two bookings in the calendar view and then the option to view more for a specific day.

What happens when I work with navigation controls?

- Bug: Calendar is also slow to load when navigating from a busy month to a quiet month.
- I'm able to navigate though despite the slowness in the page.

What if I want to view more bookings?

- Bug: The pop-up that shows booking for the day flows off the top of the page meaning certain bookings cannot be read.
- Bug: Slow to load the pop-up for days with considerable bookings.

What if I wanted to create a new booking?

- Days can still be clicked and dragged to open the admin booking pop-up.
- Bug: Clicking Cancel means a long wait for the calendar component to render again.

Keyboard accessibility?

- Able to tab through the calendar successfully.
- Hitting Enter on a View more opens up the pop-up with additional bookings.
- Bug: Tabbing into a pop-up with additional bookings isn't user-friendly. Either I have to click and then I can tab through, or cycle through all the calendar elements before I am brought to the first booking in the pop-up.
- Bug: Tabbing through pop-up with bookings doesn't bring into focus bookings that have overflowed off the top of the page.

Using PAOLO mnemonic for investigation

Prompt idea: How the report calendar displays in portrait mode across different screen sizes and resolutions.

What if I zoom in and out of the calendar?

- Bug: Resizing is slow to load.
- Bug: Zooming in hides the Show more buttons and eventually the entire contents of each day.
- The calendar renders ok when zoomed out.

Prompt idea: Test if the calendar responds quickly to changes in device orientation without lagging or delays.

What if I try out different screen sizes?

- Bug: Screen resizing is slow so initial layout is messy before it finally corrects itself.
- Does ultimately render correctly.
- Handles orientation changes nicely.

Prompt idea: Ensure that text and labels within the calendar remain clear and legible when the device is switched to portrait orientation.

- Bug: On mobile screen sizes text is tiny and hard to read.
- Text is easier to read on mobile devices that have larger resolution, such as tablets.

Prompt idea: Ensure that all features and functionalities available in portrait mode are also accessible and functional in landscape mode.

- Bug: Unable to click and drag on calendar to call up admin booking when in mobile device view.
- Can still use navigation controls in both portrait and landscape mode.
- Tabbing still works.

index